AMERICA IN LITERATURE

The Small Town

AMERICA IN LITERATURE

General Editor, Max Bogart

The Northeast, James Lape, editor
The South, Sara Marshall, editor
The West, Peter Monahan, editor
The Midwest, Ronald Szymanski, editor
The Small Town, Flory Jones Schultheiss, editor
The City, Adele Stern, editor

AMERICA IN LITERATURE

The Small Town

EDITED BY

Flory Jones Schultheiss

Beverly Hills High School
Beverly Hills, California

80998

CHARLES SCRIBNER'S SONS · NEW YORK

I am grateful to
John, for assistance and patience,
Sally and Rod, for understanding beyond their years,
Newark and Granville, Ohio, my own small towns.

Library of Congress Cataloging in Publication Data
Main entry under title:
America in literature: the small town
   Includes index
     1. Cities and towns—Literary collections.
     2. American literature—19th century.   3. American
     literature—20th century.   I. Schultheiss, Flory.
PS509.C57S6   810'.9'32   79-4209
ISBN 0-684-16138-9

1 3 5 7 9 11 13 15 17 19 V/P 20 18 16 14 12 10 8 6 4 2

Printed in the United States of America

Cover Illustration: *Stone City, Iowa* by Grant Wood. Courtesy of the Joslyn Art Museum, Omaha, Nebraska.

Picture Research: Yvonne Freund

ACKNOWLEDGMENTS
DOROTHY CANFIELD FISHER, "Sex Education." Copyright, 1945, by Dorothy Canfield Fisher; copyright, 1973, by Sarah Fisher Scott. Reprinted from *A Harvest of Stories* by Dorothy Canfield by permission of Harcourt Brace Jovanovich, Inc.

Acknowledgments continue on page 293, an extension of the copyright page.

CONTENTS

Contents

AMERICA IN LITERATURE

The Small Town

To my father,
Roderic Miller Jones, a "small town boy,"
who has always loved his home.

Introduction

. . . the history of a nation is only the history of its villages written large. —WOODROW WILSON

The small town has assumed a special place in American life and literature. It has been romanticized and idealized, satirized and ridiculed, extolled as the preserver of morality and virtue and condemned as the seat of backwardness and provincialism. Writers have used it as material for the most probing of insights into the individual mind and heart, as well as for more sweeping observations about the collective life of individuals in a community.

What is it about the small town that has made it such appealing literary material? Perhaps it affords something that other environments do not: a particular ordering of human relationships, a "microcosm"—a compressed universe in which the full spectrum of human behavior can be observed.

Mark Twain, master storyteller, was anything but blind to the rich literary possibilities of the small town setting; nor was he unaware of the raw materials, the sociological underpinnings that formed and shaped small town life.

> In the small town of Hannibal, Missouri, when I was a boy everybody was poor but didn't know it; and everybody was comfortable and did know it. And there were grades of society—people of good family, people of unclassified family, people of no family. Everybody knew everybody and was affable to everybody and nobody put on any visible airs; yet the class lines were quite clearly drawn and the familiar social life of each class was restricted to that class. It was a little democracy which was full of liberty, equality and the Fourth of July, and sincerely so, too; yet you perceived that the aristocratic taint was there. It was there and nobody found fault with the fact or ever stopped to reflect that its presence was an inconsistency.

1

New England Village,
American School, Early Nineteenth Century

This sense of community is in large part a function of size. Smallness breeds a kind of intimacy, a familiarity. Eric Sevareid writes of his youth in Velva, North Dakota: "I loved its memory always; it was, simply, *home,* and *all* of it home, not just the house but all the town." That is why childhood in the small town is different from childhood in the city. Everything is home." Many writers, William Allen White, Vachel Lindsay, and James Agee among them, have used the small town, both as setting and as motif. It has come to be associated with the comforts and joys of communal life, of belonging.

Familiarity, however, has been known to breed contempt; at least that is how the saying goes. And in this case it is true. Each writer has his own voice, his own story to tell—and it often turns out that what one writer perceives as warmth and security another perceives as a stifling sort of sameness and isolation. Whereas early American writers like Nathaniel Hawthorne, Harriet Beecher Stowe, and Henry Wadsworth Longfellow extolled the particular virtues of small-town community life, other, later writers took a very different tack—and for many reasons. In the 1920s there began a literary movement which came to be called the "Revolt from the Village," after the title of a famous essay by literary critic Carl Van Doren. He explained the changing attitudes toward the small town, and the ambivalence that characterized the revolt:

> The village seemed too cosy a microcosm to be disturbed. There it lay in the mind's eye, neat, compact, organized, traditional; the white church with tapering spire; the sober schoolhouse, the smithy of the ringing anvil, the corner grocery, the cluster of friendly houses, the venerable parson, the wise physician. . . . These were not elements to be discarded lightly even by those who perceived that time was discarding many of them as the industrial revolution went on planting droves of aliens who used unfamiliar tongues and customs, and fouling the atmosphere with smoke and gasoline. Mr. Howe in "The Story of a Country Town" had long ago made it cynically clear . . . that villages which prided themselves upon their pioneer energy might in fact be stagnant backwaters or dusty centers of futility, where existence went round and round while elsewhere the broad current moved away from them.

Writers such as Sherwood Anderson, Edgar Lee Masters, Sinclair Lewis, and H. L. Mencken were at the forefront of this revolt, and they used the genres of satire, tragedy, and comedy to dramatize their ideas.

However, because many of these writers were themselves small-towners, they displayed an ambivalent attitude toward the towns they attacked, and their scorn was often mingled with affection. Sherwood Anderson, for example, was critical of the small town in his novel *Winesburg, Ohio*, although elsewhere he was to refer to his own Ohio town of Clyde in warm and nostalgic tones. The range of attitudes about small town life is vast indeed.

During its three-hundred-year history, America has experienced great changes: industrialization, urbanization, civil war, world war, social upheaval. Many of these occurred, and continue to occur, in the name of progress—although their impact on small towns throughout the country is difficult to assess.

One of the most striking developments of the past fifty years is not so much the process of urbanization, but rather, suburbanization. Current census reports reveal that more Americans are now moving *out* of the cities than are moving *into* them—how will this affect small towns? Will they flourish as a result of this gradual influx, or remain unchanged while suburbia absorbs the transplanted populace? Do suburban towns have an advantage that other small towns do not—namely, their easy access to cities? Will today's suburban towns become the small towns of the future? These are difficult questions to answer. Writers like William Saroyan and Joyce Carol Oates examine these and other effects of the modern world on the small town; their insights are both amusing and chilling.

To all of these contributing factors we must add still another: the effect of regionalism. America is a land of striking diversity, both geographically and demographically. To reflect this great variety, this volume is divided into four sections: New England and the East, the Midwest, the South, and California and the West. Small towns abound in all four areas, but they are unique regionally as well as individually, each with its own relationship to the present and claim on the past. Literary scholar Ward Miner wrote of the summer he spent in two small towns—one in William Faulkner's Oxford, Mississippi, and the other in Miner's own Mount Pleasant, Iowa. Both towns were founded in the 1830s, both were county seats, both had 100-year old colleges in or near the town, and both had reached their peaks of prosperity immediately preceding the Civil War. In his words, they were "much alike, yet the spirit brooding over the two places is very much different. . . . Why should two rural communities of somewhat similar frontier experiences and histories be so fundamentally different? An answer is to say

4

that one is in Mississippi and the other in Iowa. The South and the Midwest are not the same, and that difference is basic."

Can we say anything about small towns that applies universally to all of them, with equal truth? Perhaps not—perhaps the quintessential American small town is a myth. What can be said, however, is that the writers represented in this volume, taken together, give us a remarkably varied set of impressions of small-town life. It is a subject that richly deserves our attention for the simple reason that it so intriguingly and successfully held theirs.

A unique New England landscape: village and sea

New England

"Where we love is home, Home that our feet may leave, but not our hearts," wrote Oliver Wendell Holmes from Cambridge, Massachusetts. And, indeed, home in early America was usually a small town and it was almost always fondly remembered and recorded. In Cambridge, in addition to the writing of Holmes, were the essays and letters of James Russell Lowell, Thomas Wentworth Higginson and the poetry of Henry Wadsworth Longfellow. Not far away lay Concord, a village also rich in American and literary history. Writers Ralph Waldo Emerson and Henry David Thoreau are most clearly associated with the village writing of Concord.

With the nineteenth century, however, came great changes, both technological and industrial—and with them came literary realism, a movement that vividly underscored the darker side of human life in an effort to offset the romanticism of earlier American writers. Realism proved an effective backlash, and produced a vast number of literary works written to strip away illusions and force men and women to confront the reality of their own lives. Sara Orne Jewett and Mary E. Wilkins Freeman were two writers who began to expose the tensions of industrial small-town life. Freeman evokes the harshness of the New England landscape in all its physical and social dimensions, as well as its more private psychological ones. In "Callah-Lillies and Hannah," the cruel, quick, and in this case misguided judgments of the townspeople provide a bleak background for Hannah's struggle to eke out a decent existence for herself and her aging relative. It is a story about the individual's defiance of frailty and defeat.

It wasn't until the publication of Edwin Arlington Robinson's

Children of the Night in 1897 that the unrelentingly bitter side of village life was portrayed. Robinson characterizes the malcontents of the village: the hopeless drunkards, the hard working poor, the lonely rich, the dreamer who cannot face the real world. His poem "Richard Cory" points out the despair and insularity of life in the small town; and in "Flammonde" he explores the curious role of the individual and of the stranger in small town life. In "Sex Education" Dorothy Canfield Fisher examines the effects of such an environment on the human psyche. She does so, interestingly, by focusing on an aging woman's attempts to come to terms with her own upbringing and adolescence, and the disturbing memories they harbor.

All is not harshness and despair, however, in the small town. Contemporary writers realistically deal with both sides of town life —Shirley Jackson writes with wit and humor, and not a little mockery, of the "small-mindedness" of small town life: its consuming curiosity about those who do not "fit in," and its own inflated sense of propriety. These same themes of curiosity and propriety are amusingly presented against the background of a small town supermarket in "A&P," by John Updike. And in "Kicking the Leaves," Donald Hall nostalgically recalls the autumns of his youth in New England.

Sex Education

DOROTHY CANFIELD FISHER

It was three times—but at intervals of many years—that I heard my Aunt Minnie tell about an experience of her girlhood that had made a never-to-be-forgotten impression on her. The first time she was in her thirties, still young. But she had then been married for ten years, so that to my group of friends, all in the early teens, she seemed quite of another generation.

The day she told us the story, we had been idling on one end of her porch as we made casual plans for a picnic supper in the woods. Darning stockings at the other end, she paid no attention to us until one of the girls said, "Let's take blankets and sleep out there. It'd be fun."

"No," Aunt Minnie broke in sharply, "you mustn't do that."

"Oh, for goodness' sakes, why not!" said one of the younger girls, rebelliously, "the boys are always doing it. Why can't we, just once?"

Aunt Minnie laid down her sewing. "Come here, girls," she said, "I want you should hear something that happened to me when I was your age."

Her voice had a special quality which, perhaps, young people of today would not recognize. But we did. We knew from experience that it was the dark voice grownups used when they were going to say something about sex.

Yet at first what she had to say was like any dull family ancedote; she had been ill when she was fifteen; and afterwards she was run down, thin, with no appetite. Her folks thought a change of air would do her good, and sent her from Vermont out to Ohio—or was it Illinois? I don't remember. Anyway, one of those places where the corn grows high. Her mother's Cousin Ella lived there, keeping house for her son-in-law.

The son-in-law was the minister of the village church. His wife had died some years before, leaving him a young widower with two little girls and a baby boy. He had been a normally personable man then, but the next summer, on the Fourth of July when he was trying to set off some fireworks to amuse his children, an imperfectly manufactured rocket had burst in his face. The explosion had left one side of his face badly scarred. Aunt Minnie made us see it, as she still saw it, in horrid detail: the stiffened, scarlet scar tissue distorting one cheek, the lower lip turned so far out at one corner that the moist red mucous-membrane lining always showed, one lower eyelid hanging loose, and watering.

After the accident, his face had been a long time healing. It was then that his wife's elderly mother had gone to keep house and take care of the children. When he was well enough to be about again, he found his position as pastor of the little church waiting for him. The farmers and village people in his congregation, moved by his misfortune, by his faithful service and by his unblemished character, said they would rather have Mr. Fairchild, even with his scarred face, than any other minister. He was a good preacher, Aunt Minnie told us, "and the way he prayed was kind of exciting. I'd never known a preacher, not to live in the same house with him, before. And when he was in the pulpit, with everybody looking up at him, I felt the way his children did, kind of proud to think we had just eaten breakfast at the same table. I liked to call him 'Cousin Malcolm' before folks. One side of his face was all right, anyhow. You could see from that that he *had* been a good-looking man. In fact, probably one of those ministers that all the women—" Aunt Minnie paused, drew her lips together, and looked at us uncertainly.

Then she went back to the story as it happened—as it happened that first time I heard her tell it. "I thought he was a saint. Everybody out there did. That was all *they* knew. Of course, it made a person sick to look at that awful scar—the drooling corner of his mouth was the worst. He tried to keep that side of his face turned away from folks. But you always knew it was there. That was what kept him from marrying again, so Cousin Ella said. I heard her say lots of times that he knew no woman would touch any man who looked the way he did, not with a ten-foot pole.

"Well, the change of air did do me good. I got my appetite back, and ate a lot and played outdoors a lot with my cousins. They were younger than I (I had my sixteenth birthday there) but I still liked to play games. I got taller and laid on some weight. Cousin Ella used to say I grew as fast as the corn did. Their house stood at the edge of the village. Beyond it was one of those big cornfields they have out west. At the time when I first got there, the stalks were only up to a person's knee. You could see over their tops.

But it grew like lightning, and before long, it was the way thick woods are here, way over your head, the stalks growing so close together it was dark under them.

"Cousin Ella told us youngsters that it was lots worse for getting lost in than woods, because there weren't any landmarks in it. One spot in a cornfield looked just like any other. 'You children keep out of it,' she used to tell us almost every day, *especially you girls.* It's no place for a decent girl. You could easy get so far from the house nobody could hear you if you hollered. There are plenty of men in this town that wouldn't like anything better than—' She never said what.

"In spite of what she said, my little cousins and I had figured out that if we went across one corner of the field, it would be a short cut to the village, and sometimes, without letting on to Cousin Ella, we'd go that way. After the corn got really tall, the farmer stopped cultivating, and we soon beat down a path in the loose dirt. The minute you were inside the field it was dark. You felt as if you were miles from anywhere. It sort of scared you. But in no time the path turned and brought you out on the far end of Main Street. Your breath was coming fast, maybe, but that was what made you like to do it.

"One day I missed the turn. Maybe I didn't keep my mind on it. Maybe it had rained and blurred the tramped-down look of the path. I don't know what. All of a sudden, I knew I was lost. And the minute I knew that, I began to run, just as hard as I could run. I couldn't help it, any more than you can help snatching your hand off a hot stove. I didn't know what I was scared of, I didn't even know I *was* running, till my heart was pounding so hard I had to stop.

"The minute I stood still, I could hear Cousin Ella saying 'There are plenty of men in this town that wouldn't like anything better than—' I didn't know, not really, what she meant. But I knew she meant something horrible. I opened my mouth to scream. But I put both hands over my mouth to keep the scream in. If I made any noise, one of those men would hear me. I thought I heard one just behind me, and whirled around. And then I thought another one had tiptoed up behind me, the other way, and I spun around so fast I almost fell over. I stuffed my hands hard up against my mouth. And then—I couldn't help it—I ran again—but my legs were shaking so I soon had to stop. There I stood, scared to move for fear of rustling

11

the corn and letting the men know where I was. My hair had come down, all over my face. I kept pushing it back and looking around, quick, to make sure one of the men hadn't found out where I was. Then I thought I saw a man coming towards me, and I ran away from him—and fell down, and burst some of the buttons off my dress, and was sick to my stomach—and thought I heard a man close to me and got up and staggered around, knocking into the corn because I couldn't even see where I was going.

"And then, off to one side, I saw Cousin Malcolm. Not a man. The minister. He was standing still, one hand up to his face, thinking. He hadn't heard me.

"I was so *terrible* glad to see him, instead of one of those men, I ran as fast as I could and just flung myself on him, to make myself feel how safe I was."

Aunt Minnie had become strangely agitated. Her hands were shaking, her face was crimson. She frightened us. We could not look away from her. As we waited for her to go on, I felt little spasms twitch at the muscles inside my body. "And what do you think that *saint*, that holy minister of the Gospel, did to an innocent child who clung to him for safety? The most terrible look came into his eyes—you girls are too young to know what he looked like. But once you're married, you'll find out. He grabbed hold of me—that dreadful face of his was *right on mine*—and began clawing the clothes off my back."

She stopped for a moment, panting. We were too frightened to speak. She went on, "He had torn my dress right down to the waist before I—then I *did* scream—all I could—and pulled away from him so hard I almost fell down, and ran and all of a sudden I came out of the corn, right in the back yard of the Fairchild house. The children were staring at the corn, and Cousin Ella ran out of the kitchen door. They had heard me screaming. Cousin Ella shrieked out, 'What is it? What happened? Did a man scare you?' And I said, 'Yes, yes, yes, a man—I ran—!' And then I fainted away. I must have. The next thing I knew I was on the sofa in the living room and Cousin Ella was slapping my face with a wet towel."

She had to wet her lips with her tongue before she could go on. Her face was gray now. "There! that's the kind of thing girls' folks ought to tell them about—so they'll know what men are like."

She finished her story as if she were dismissing us. We wanted to go away, but we were too horrified to stir. Finally one of the youngest girls asked in a low trembling voice, "Aunt Minnie, did you tell on him?"

"No, I was ashamed to," she said briefly. "They sent me home the next day anyhow. Nobody ever said a word to me about it. And I never did either. Till now."

By what gets printed in some of the modern child-psychology books, you would think that girls to whom such a story had been told would never develop normally. Yet, as far as I can remember what happened to the girls in that group, we all grew up about like anybody. Most of us married, some happily, some not so well. We kept house. We learned—more or less—how to live with our husbands, we had children and struggled to bring them up right—we went forward into life, just as if we had never been warned not to.

Perhaps, young as we were that day, we had already had enough experience of life so that we were not quite blank paper for Aunt Minnie's frightening story. Whether we thought of it then or not, we couldn't have failed to see that at this very time, Aunt Minnie had been married for ten years or more, comfortably and well married, too. Against what she tried by that story to brand into our minds stood the cheerful home life in that house, the good-natured, kind, hard-working husband, and the children—the three rough-and-tumble, nice little boys, so adored by their parents, and the sweet girl baby who died, of whom they could never speak without tears. It was such actual contact with adult life that probably kept generation after generation of girls from being scared by tales like Aunt Minnie's into a neurotic horror of living.

Of course, since Aunt Minnie was so much older than we, her boys grew up to be adolescents and young men while our children were still little enough so that our worries over them were nothing more serious than whooping cough and trying to get them to make their own beds. Two of our aunt's three boys followed, without losing their footing, the narrow path which leads across adolescence into normal adult life. But the middle one, Jake, repeatedly fell off into the morass. "Girl trouble," as the succinct family phrase put it. He was one of those boys who have "charm," whatever we mean by that, and was always being snatched at by girls who would be "all wrong" for him to marry. And once, at nineteen, he ran away from home, whether with one of these girls or not we never heard, for through all her ups and downs with this son, Aunt Minnie tried fiercely to protect him from scandal that might cloud his later life.

Her husband had to stay on his job to earn the family living. She was the one who went to find Jake. When it was gossiped around that Jake was in "bad company" his mother drew some money from the family savings-bank account, and silent, white-cheeked, took the train to the city where rumor said he had gone.

Some weeks later he came back with her. With no girl. She had cleared him of that entanglement. As of others, which followed, later. Her troubles seemed over when, at a "suitable" age, he fell in love with a "suitable" girl, married her and took her to live in our shire town, sixteen miles away, where he had a good position. Jake was always bright enough.

Sometimes, idly, people speculated as to what Aunt Minnie had seen that time she went after her runaway son, wondering where her search for him had taken her—very queer places for Aunt Minnie to be in, we imagined. And how could such an ignorant, homekeeping woman ever have known what to say to an errant willful boy to set him straight?

Well, of course, we reflected, watching her later struggles with Jake's erratic ways, she certainly could not have remained ignorant, after seeing over and over what she probably had; after talking with Jake about the things which, a good many times, must have come up with desperate openness between them.

She kept her own counsel. We never knew anything definite about the facts of those experiences of hers. But one day she told a group of us—all then married women—something which gave us a notion about what she had learned from them.

We were hastily making a layette for a not especially welcome baby in a poor family. In those days, our town had no such thing as a district-nursing service. Aunt Minnie, a vigorous woman of fifty-five, had come in to help. As we sewed, we talked, of course; and because our daughters were near or in their teens, we were comparing notes about the bewildering responsibility of bringing up girls.

After a while, Aunt Minnie remarked, "Well, I hope you teach your girls some *sense*. From what I read, I know you're great on telling them 'the facts,' facts we never heard of when we were girls. Like as not, some facts I don't know, now. But knowing the facts isn't going to do them any more good than *not* knowing the facts ever did, unless they have some sense taught them, too."

"What do you mean, Aunt Minnie?" one of us asked her uncertainly.

She reflected, threading a needle, "Well, I don't know but what the best way to tell you what I mean is to tell you about something that happened to me, forty years ago. I've never said anything about it before. But I've thought about it a good deal. Maybe—"

She had hardly begun when I recognized the story—her visit to her Cousin Ella's Midwestern home, the widower with his scarred face and saintly reputation and, very vividly, her getting lost in the great cornfield. I knew every word she was going to say—to the very end, I thought.

But no, I did not. Not at all.

She broke off, suddenly, to exclaim with impatience, "Wasn't I the big ninny? But not so big a ninny as that old cousin of mine. I could wring her neck for getting me in such a state. Only she didn't know any better, herself. That was the way they brought young people up in those days, scaring them out of their wits about the awfulness of getting lost, but not telling them a thing about how *not* to get lost. Or how to act, if they did.

"If I had had the sense I was born with, I'd have known that running my legs off in a zigzag was the worst thing I could do. I couldn't have been more than a few feet from the path when I noticed I wasn't on it. My tracks in the loose plow dirt must have been perfectly plain. If I'd h' stood still, and collected my wits, I could have looked down to see which way my footsteps went and just walked back over them to the path and gone on about my business.

"Now I ask you, if I'd been told how to do that, wouldn't it have been a lot better protection for me—if protection was what my aunt thought she wanted to give me—than to scare me so at the idea of being lost that I turned deef-dumb-and-blind when I thought I was?

"And anyhow that patch of corn wasn't as big as she let on. And she knew it wasn't. It was no more than a big field in a farming country. I was a well-grown girl of sixteen, as tall as I am now. If I couldn't have found the path, I could have just walked along one line of cornstalks—*straight*—and I'd have come out somewhere in ten minutes. Fifteen at the most. Maybe not just where I wanted to go. But all right, safe, where decent folks were living."

She paused, as if she had finished. But at the inquiring blankness in our faces, she went on, "Well, now, why isn't teaching girls—and boys, too, for the Lord's sake don't forget they need it as much as the girls—about this man-and-woman business, something like that? If you give them the idea— no matter whether it's *as* you tell them the facts, or as you *don't* tell them the facts, that it is such a terribly scary thing that if they take a step into it, something's likely to happen to them so awful that you're ashamed to tell them what—well, they'll lose their heads and run around like crazy things, first time they take one step away from the path.

"For they'll be trying out the paths, all right. You can't keep them from it. And a good thing too. How else are they going to find out what it's like? Boys' and girls' going together is a path across one corner of growing up. And when they go together, they're likely to get off the path some. Seems to me, it's up to their folks to bring them up so when they do, they don't start screaming and running in circles, but stand still, right where they are, and get their breath and figure out how to get back.

"And anyhow, you don't tell 'em the truth about sex" (I was astonished to hear her use the actual word, taboo to women of her generation) "if they get the idea from you that it's all there is to living. It's not. If you don't get to where you want to go in it, well, there's a lot of landscape all around it a person can have a good time in.

"D'you know, I believe one thing that gives girls and boys the wrong idea is the way folks *look!* My old cousin's face, I can see her now, it was as red as a rooster's comb when she was telling me about men in that corn-field. I believe now she kind of *liked* to talk about it."

(Oh, Aunt Minnie—and yours! I thought.)

Someone asked, "But how *did* you get out, Aunt Minnie?"

She shook her head, laid down her sewing. "More foolishness. That minister my mother's cousin was keeping house for—her son-in-law—I caught sight of him, down along one of the aisles of cornstalks, looking down at the ground, thinking, the way he often did. And I was so glad to see him I rushed right up to him, and flung my arms around his neck and hugged him. He hadn't heard me coming. He gave a great start, put one arm around me and turned his face full towards me—I suppose for just a second he had forgotten how awful one side of it was. His expression, his eyes— well, you're all married women, you know how he looked, the way any able-bodied man thirty-six or -seven, who'd been married and begotten children, would look—for a minute anyhow, if a full-blooded girl of sixteen, who

16

ought to have known better, flung herself at him without any warning, her hair tumbling down, her dress half unbottoned, and hugged him with all her might.

"I was what they called innocent in those days. That is, I knew just as little about what men are like as my folks could manage I should. But I was old enough to know all right what that look meant. And it gave me a start. But of course the real thing of it was that dreadful scar of his, so close to my face—that wet corner of his mouth, his eye drawn down with the red inside of the lower eyelid showing—

"It turned me so sick, I pulled away with all my might, so fast that I ripped one sleeve nearly loose, and let out a screech like a wildcat. And ran. Did I run? And in a minute, I was through the corn and had come out in the back yard of the house. I hadn't been more than a few feet from it, probably, any of the time. And then I fainted away. Girls were always fainting away; it was the way our corset strings were pulled tight, I suppose, and then—oh, a lot of fuss.

"But anyhow," she finished, picking up her work and going on, setting neat, firm stitches with steady hands, "there's one thing, I never told anybody it was Cousin Malcolm I had met in the cornfield. I told my old cousin that 'a man had scared me.' And nobody said anything more about it to me, not ever. That was the way they did in those days. They thought if they didn't let on about something, maybe it wouldn't have happened. I was sent back to Vermont right away and Cousin Malcolm went on being minister of the church. I've always been," said Aunt Minnie moderately, "kind of proud that I didn't go and ruin a man's life for just one second's slip-up. If you could have called it that. For it *would* have ruined him. You know how hard as stone people are about other folks' letdowns. If I'd have told, not one person in that town would have had any charity. Not one would have tried to understand. One slip, *once*, and they'd have pushed him down in the mud. If I had told, I'd have felt pretty bad about it, later—when I came to have more sense. But I declare, I can't see how I came to have the decency, dumb as I was then, to know that it wouldn't be fair."

It was not long after this talk that Aunt Minnie's elderly husband died, mourned by her, by all of us. She lived alone then. It was peaceful October weather for her, in which she kept a firm roundness of face and

figure, as quiet-living country-women often do, on into her late sixties.

But then Jake, the boy who had had girl trouble, had wife trouble. We heard he had taken to running after a young girl, or was it that she was running after him? It was something serious. For his nice wife left him and came back with the children to live with her mother in our town. Poor Aunt Minnie used to go to see her for long talks which made them both cry. And she went to keep house for Jake, for months at a time.

She grew old, during those years. When finally she (or something) managed to get the marriage mended so that Jake's wife relented and went back to live with him, there was no trace left of her pleasant brisk freshness. She was stooped and slow-footed and shrunken. We, her kins-people, although we would have given our lives for any one of our own children, wondered whether Jake was worth what it had cost his mother to—well, steady him, or reform him. Or perhaps just understand him. Whatever it took.

She came of a long-lived family and was able to go on keeping house for herself well into her eighties. Of course we and the other neighbors stepped in often to make sure she was all right. Mostly, during those brief calls, the talk turned on nothing more vital than her geraniums. But one midwinter afternoon, sitting with her in front of her cozy stove, I chanced to speak in rather hasty blame of someone who had, I thought, acted badly. To my surprise this brought from her the story about the cornfield which she had evidently quite forgotten telling me twice before.

This time she told it almost dreamily, swaying to and fro in her rocking chair, her eyes fixed on the long slope of snow outside her window. When she came to the encounter with the minister she said, looking away from the distance and back into my eyes, "I know now that I had been, all along, kind of *interested* in him, the way any girl as old as I was would be in any youngish man living in the same house with her. And a minister, too. They have to have the gift of gab so much more than most men, women get to thinking they are more alive than men who can't talk so well. I *thought* the reason I threw my arms around him was because I had been so scared. And I certainly had been scared, by my old cousin's horrible talk about the cornfield being full of men waiting to grab girls. But that wasn't all the reason I flung myself at Malcolm Fairchild and hugged him. I know that now. Why in the world shouldn't I have been taught *some* notion of it then? 'Twould do girls good to know that they are just like everybody else—human nature *and* sex, all mixed up together. I didn't have to hug him. I wouldn't have, if he'd been dirty or fat and old, or chewed tobacco."

19

I stirred in my chair, ready to say, "But it's not so simple as all that to tell girls—" and she hastily answered my unspoken protest. "I know, I know, most of it can't be put into words. There just aren't any words to say something that's so both-ways-at-once all the time as this man-and-woman business. But look here, you know as well as I do that there are lots more ways than in words to teach young folks what you want 'em to know."

The old woman stopped her swaying rocker to peer far back into the past with honest eyes. "What was in my mind back there in the cornfield—partly anyhow—was what had been there all the time I was living in the same house with Cousin Malcolm—that he had long straight legs, and broad shoulders, and lots of curly brown hair, and was nice and flat in front, and that one side of his face was goodlooking. But most of all, that he and I were really alone, for the first time, without anybody to see us.

"I suppose, if it hadn't been for that dreadful scar, he'd have drawn me up, tight, and—most any man would—kissed me. I know how I must have looked, all red and hot and my hair down and my dress torn open. And, used as he was to big cornfields, he probably never dreamed that the reason I looked that way was because I was scared to be by myself in one. He may have thought—you know what he may have thought.

"Well—if his face had been like anybody's—when he looked at me the way he did, the way a man does look at a woman he wants to have, it would have scared me—some. But I'd have cried, maybe. And probably he'd have kissed me again. You know how such things go. I might have come out of the cornfield halfway engaged to marry him. Why not? I was old enough, as people thought then. That would have been nature. That was probably what he thought of, in that first instant.

"But what did I do? I had one look at his poor, horrible face, and started back as though I'd stepped on a snake. And screamed and ran.

"What do you suppose *he* felt, left there in the corn? He must have been sure that I would tell everybody he had attacked me. He probably thought that when he came out and went back to the village he'd already be in disgrace and put out of the pulpit.

"But the worst must have been to find out, so rough, so plain from the way I acted—as if somebody had hit him with an ax—the way he would look to any woman he might try to get close to. That must have been—" she drew a long breath, "well, pretty hard on him."

After a silence, she murmured pityingly, "Poor man!"

20

Calla-Lilies and Hannah

MARY E. WILKINS FREEMAN

"Mis' Newhall!"

The tall, thin figure on the other side of the street pushed vigorously past. It held its black-bonneted head back stiffly, and strained its green-and-black woollen shawl tighter across its slim shoulders.

"Mis' *New*hall!"

The figure stopped with a jerk. "Oh, it's you, Marthy. Pleasant afternoon, ain't it?"

"Ain't you comin' in?"

"Well, I don't jest see how I can this afternoon. I was goin' up to Ellen's."

"Can't you jest come over a minute and see my calla-lilies?"

"Well, I don't see how I can. I can see 'em up to the window. Beautiful, ain't they?"

"You can't see nuthin' of 'em out there. Why can't you come in jest a minute? There ain't a soul been in to see 'em this week, and 'taint't often they blow out this way."

"Who's in there?—anybody?"

"No; there ain't a soul but me to home. Hannah's gone over to Wayne. Can't you come in?"

"Well, I dunno but I'll come over jest a minute; but I can't stay. I hadn't ought to stop at all."

Martha Wing waited for her in the door; she was quivering with impatience to show her the lilies. "Come right in," she cried, when the visitor came up the walk.

When she turned to follow her in she limped painfully; one whole side seemed to succumb so nearly that it was barely rescued by a quick spring from the other.

"How's your lameness?" asked Mrs. Newhall.

Martha's soft withered face flushed. "Here air the lilies," she said, shortly.

"My! ain't they beautiful!"

" 'Tain't often you see seven lilies and two buds together."

"Well, 'tain't, that's a fact. Ellen thought hers was pretty handsome, but it can't shake a stick at this. Hers ain't got but three on it. I'd like to know what you do to it, Marthy?"

"I don't do nuthin'. Flowers'll grow for some folks, and that's all there is about it. I allers had jest sech luck." Martha stood staring at the lilies. A self-gratulation that had something noble about it was in her smiling old face.

"I tell Hannah," she went on, "if I be miser'ble in health, an' poor, flowers'll blow for me, and that's more than they'll do for some folks, no matter how hard they try. Look at Mis' Walker over there. I can't help thinkin' of it sometimes when I see her go nippin' past with her ruffles and gimcracks. She's young an' good-lookin', but she's had her calla-lily five year, an' she ain't had but one bud, and that blasted."

"Well, flowers is a good deal of company."

"I guess they air. They're most as good as folks. Mis' Newhall, why don't Jennie come in an' see Hannah sometimes?"

All the lines in Mrs. Newhall's face lengthened. She looked harder at the callas. "Well, I dunno, Marthy; Jenny don't go much of anywhere. Those lilies are beautiful. You'd ought to have 'em carried into the meetin'-house next Sunday, an' set in front of the pulpit."

Martha turned white. Her voice quavered up shrilly. 'There's one lily I could mention's been took out of that meetin'-house, Maria Newhall, an' there ain't no more of mine goin' to be took in, not if I know it."

"Now, Marthy, you know I didn't mean a thing. I no more dreamed of hurtin' your feelin's than the dead."

"No, I don't s'pose you did; an' I don't s'pose your Jenny an' the other girls mean anything by stayin' away an' never comin' near Hannah. They act as if they was afraid of her; but I guess she wouldn't hurt 'em none. She's as good as any of 'em, an' they'll find it out some day."

"Now, Marthy—"

"You needn't talk. I know all about it. I've heerd a good deal of palaver, but I kin see through it. I—"

"Well, I guess I'll have to be goin', Marthy. Good-afternoon."

Martha suddenly recovered her dignity. "Good-afternoon, Mis' Newhall," said she, and relapsed into silence.

After the door had closed behind her guest, she sat down at the window with her knitting. She had an old shawl over her shoulders; the room was very chilly. She pursed up her lips and knitted very fast, a lean, homey figure in the clean, bare room, with its bulging old satin-papered walls. A square of pale sunlight lay on the thin, dull carpet, and the pot of calla-lilies stood in the window.

Before long Hannah came. She entered without a word, and stood silently taking off her wraps.

"Did you git your pay, Hannah?"

"Yes."

When Hannah laid aside her thick, faded shawl, she showed a tall young figure in a clinging old woollen gown of a drab color. She stooped a little, although the stoop did not seem anything but the natural result of her tallness, and was thus graceful rather than awkward. It was as if her whole slender body bent from her feet, lily fashion. She got a brush out of a little chimney cupboard and began smoothing her light hair, which her hood had rumpled a little. She had a full, small face; there was a lovely delicate pink on her cheeks. People said of Hannah, "She is delicate-looking." They said "delicate" in the place of pretty; it suited her better.

"Why don't you say somethin'?" Martha asked, querulously.

"What do you want me to say?"

"Where's your bundle of boots?"

"I haven't got any."

"Ain't got no boots?"

"No."

"Didn't Mr. Allen give you any?"

"No."

"Ain't he going to?"

"No."

"Why not?"

Hannah went on brushing her hair, and made no answer.

"Has—he heard of—that?"

"I suppose so."

"What did he say?"

"Said he couldn't trust me to take any more boots home." One soft flush spread over Hannah's face as she said that, then it receded. She knelt down by the air-tight stove and began poking the fire.

"Course he'd heerd, then. What air you goin' to do, Hannah?"

"I don't know."

"You take it easy 'nough, I hope. Ef you don't hev work, I don't see what's goin' to keep a roof over us."

Hannah, going out into the kitchen, half turned in the doorway. "Don't worry, I'll get some work somewhere, I guess," she said.

But Martha kept on calling out her complaint in a shriller voice, so Hannah could hear as she stepped about in the other room. "I don't see what you're goin' to do; I'm 'bout discouraged. Mis' Newhall, she's been in here, pretended she wanted to see my caller, but she give me no end of digs, the way she allers does. This kind of work is killin' me. Here's this calla-lily's been blowed out the way it has lately, an' not a soul comin' in to see it. Hannah Redman, I don't see what possessed you to do such a thing."

No answering voice came from the kitchen.

"You did do it, didn't you, Hannah? You wouldn't let folks go on in this way if you hadn't."

Hannah said nothing. Martha broke into a fit of loud weeping. She held her hands over her face, and rocked herself back and forth in her chair. "Oh me! Oh me!" she wailed, shrilly.

Hannah paid no attention. She went about getting tea ready. It was a frugal meal, bread and butter and weak tea, but she fried a bit of ham and put it on Martha's plate. The old woman liked something hearty for supper.

"Come," she said at length—"come, Martha, tea's ready."

"I don't want nothin'," wailed the old woman. But she sat sniffing down at the table, and ate heartily.

After tea Hannah got her hood and shawl and went out again. It was a chilly March night; the clouds were flying wildly, there was an uncertain moon, the ground was covered with melting snow. Hannah held up her skirts and stepped along through the slush. The snow-water penetrated her old shoes; she had no rubbers.

Presently she stopped and rang a door-bell. The woman who answered it stood eying her amazedly a minute before she spoke. "Good-evenin', Hannah," she said, stiffly, at length.

"Good-evening, Mrs. Ward. Are your boarders in?"

"Y-e-s."

24

"Can I see them?"

"Well—I guess so. Mis' Mellen, she's been pretty busy all day. Come in, won't you?"

Hannah followed her into the lighted sitting-room. A young, smooth-faced man and a woman who looked older and stronger were in there. Mrs. Ward introduced them in an embarrassed way to Hannah. "Mis' Mellen, this is Miss Redman," said she, "an' Mr. Mellen."

Hannah opened at once upon the subject of her errand. She had heard that the Mellens wished to begin housekeeping, and were anxious to hire a tenement. She proposed that they should hire her house; she and Martha would reserve only two rooms for themselves. The rent which she suggested was very low. The husband and wife looked at each other.

"We might—go and look at it—to-morrow," he said, hesitatingly, with his eyes on his wife.

"We'll come in some time to-morrow and see how it suits," said she, in a crisp voice. "Perhaps—" She stopped suddenly. Mrs. Ward had given her a violent nudge. But she looked wonderingly at her and kept on. "We should want—" said she.

"It ain't anything you want, Mis' Mellen," spoke up Mrs. Ward.

"Why, what's the trouble?"

"You don't want it; 'twon't suit you." Mrs. Ward nodded significantly.

Hannah looked at one and the other. The delicate color in her cheeks deepened a little, but she spoke softly. "There are locks and keys on the doors," said she.

Mrs. Ward colored furiously. "I didn't mean—" she began. Then she stopped.

Hannah arose. "If you want to come and look at the rooms, I'll be glad to show them," said she. She stood waiting with a dignity which had something appealing about it.

"Well, I'll see," said Mrs. Mellen.

After Hannah had gone she turned eagerly to Mrs. Ward. "What is the matter?" said she.

" 'Tain't safe for you to go there, unless—you want all your things—*stole*."

"Why, does she—"

"She stole some money from John Arnold up here a year ago. That's a fact."

"You don't mean it!"

"Yes. She was sewin' up there. He left it on the sittin'-room table a minute, an' when he came back it was gone. There hadn't been anybody but her in the room, so of course she took it."

"Did he get the money back?"

"That was the queer part of it. Nobody could ever find out what she did with the money."

"Didn't they take her up?"

"No; they made a good deal of fuss about it at first, but Mr. Arnold didn't prosecute her. I s'pose he thought they couldn't really prove anything, not findin' the money. And then he's a deacon of the church; he'd hate to do such a thing, anyway. But everybody in town thinks she took it, fast enough. Nobody has anything to do with her. She used to go out sewin' for folks, but they say she stole lots of pieces. I heard she took enough black silk here and there to make a dress. Nobody has her now, that I know of. You don't want anybody in your house that you can't trust."

"Of course you don't."

"She was a church member, an' it came up before the church, an' they dismissed her. They asked her if it was so, an' she wouldn't answer one word, yes or no. They couldn't get a thing out of her."

"Well, of course if she hadn't taken it she'd said so."

"It's likely she would."

"I'm real glad you told me. I'd hated awfully to have gone in there with anybody like that."

"I thought you would. I felt as if I ought to tell you, seein' as you was strangers here. I kind of pity her. I s'pose she thought she could raise a little money that way. I guess she's havin' a pretty hard time. She can't get no work anywhere. She's been sewin' boots for Allen over in Wayne, but I heard the other day he was goin' to shut down on her. She's gettin' some of her punishment in this world. Folks said Arnold's son George had a notion of goin' with her once, but I guess it put a stop to that pretty quick. He's down East somewhere."

Hannah, plodding along out in the windy, moonlit night, knew as well what they were saying as if she had been at their elbows. The wind sung in her ears, the light clouds drove overhead; those nearest the moon had yellow edges. Hannah kept looking up at them.

26

She had five dollars and fifty cents in her pocket, and no prospect of more. She had herself and a helpless old relative to support. All the village, every friend and acquaintance she had ever had, were crying out against her. That was the case of Hannah Redman when she entered her silent house that night; but she followed her old relative to bed, and went to sleep like a child.

The next morning she got out an old blue cashmere of hers and began ripping it.

"What are you goin' to do?" asked Martha, who had been eying her furtively all the morning.

"I'm going to make over this dress. I haven't got a thing fit to wear."

"I shouldn't think you'd feel much like fixin' over dresses. I don't see what's goin' to become of us. I don't s'pose a soul will be in to see my calla-lily to-day. It's killin' me."

Hannah said nothing, but she worked steadily on the dress all day. She turned it, and it looked like new.

The next day was Sunday. Hannah, going to church in her remodelled dress, heard distinctly some one behind her say, "See, Hannah Redman's got a new dress, I do believe. I shouldn't think she'd feel much like it, should you?"

Hannah sat alone in the pew, where her father and mother had sat before her. They had all been churchgoing people. Hannah herself had been a member ever since her childhood. Not one Sunday had she missed of stepping modestly up the aisle in her humble Sunday best, and seating herself with gentle gravity. The pew was a conspicuous one beside the pulpit, at right angles with the others. Hannah was in full view of the whole congregation. She sat erect and composed in her pretty dress. The delicate color in her cheeks was the same as ever; her soft eyes were as steady. She found the hymns and sang; she listened to the preaching.

Women looked at her, then at one another. Hannah knew it. Still it had never been as bad since that first Sunday after her dismissal from the church.

There had been a tangible breeze then that had whistled in her ears. Nobody had dreamed that she would come to meeting, but she came.

There was no question but that Hannah's unshaken demeanor brought somewhat harder judgment upon herself. A smile in an object of pity is a grievance. The one claim which Hannah now had upon her friends she did not extort, consequently she got nothing. She showed no need of pity, and was, if anything, more condemned for that than for her actual fault.

"If she wasn't so dreadful bold," they said. "If she acted as if she felt bad about it."

In one of the foremost body-pews sat John Arnold, a large, fair-faced old man, who wore his white hair like a tonsure. He never looked at Hannah. He had a gold-headed cane. He clasped both hands around it, and leaned heavily forward upon it as he listened. It was a habit of his. He settled himself solemnly into this attitude at his entrance. People watched him respectfully. John Arnold was the one wealthy man in this poor country church. Over across the aisle a shattered, threadbare old grandfather leaned impressively upon his poor pine stick in the same way that John Arnold did. He stole frequent, studious glances at him. He was an artist who made himself into a caricature.

There was a communion-service to-day. After the sermon Hannah arose quietly and went down the aisle with the non-communicants. She felt people looking at her, but when she turned, their eyes were somewhere else. No one spoke to her.

"Did anybody speak to you?" old Martha asked when she got home.

"No," said Hannah.

"I don't see how you stand it. I should think it would kill you, an' you don't look as if it wore on you a bit. Hannah, what made you do sech a thing?"

Hannah said nothing.

"I should think, after the way your father an' mother brought you up— Well, it's killin' me. I've been most crazy the whole forenoon thinkin' on't. What air you goin' to do if you can't git no work, Hannah?"

"I guess I can get some, perhaps."

"I don't see where."

The next morning Hannah went over to East Wayne, a town about four miles away. There was a new boot-and-shoe manufactory there, and she thought she might get some employment. The overseer was a pleasant young fellow, who treated her courteously. They had no work just then, but trade was improving. He told her to come again in a month.

"I rather guess I can get some work over at the new shop in East Wayne," she said to Martha when she got home.

28

"They'll hear on't, an' then you'll lose it, jest the way you've done before," was Martha's reply.

But Hannah lived on the hope of it for a month. She literally lived on little else. They had some potatoes and a few apples in the cellar. Hannah ate them. With her little stock of money she bought food for Martha.

At the end of the month she walked over to East Wayne again. The overseer remembered her. He greeted her very pleasantly, but his honest young face flushed.

"I'm real sorry," he stammered, "but—I'm afraid we can't give you any work."

Hannah turned white. He had heard.

"As far as I am concerned," he went on, "I would; but it don't depend on me, you know." He stood staring irresolutely at Hannah.

"See here, wait a minute," said he, "I'll speak to the boss."

Pretty soon he returned with a troubled look. "It's no use," said he; "he says he hasn't got any work."

"Will he have any by-and-by?" asked Hannah, feebly.

"I'm afraid not," replied the young man, pitifully. He opened the door for her. "Good-by," he said; "don't get down-hearted."

Hannah looked at him, then the tears sprang to her eyes. "Thank you," she said.

When she got past the shop she sat down on a stone beside the road and cried. "I wish he hadn't spoken kind to me," she whispered, sobbingly, to herself—"I wish he hadn't."

The road was bordered with willow bushes; they were just beginning to bud. The new grass was springing, and there was a smell of it in the air. Presently Hannah rose and walked on. She had ten cents in her pocket. She stopped at a store on her way home and bought with it a herring and a couple of fresh biscuit for Martha's supper. She ate nothing herself. She said she was not hungry.

"I knew they'd hear on't," Martha said, when she told her of her disappointment.

The next day Hannah tried to raise some money on her house. It was a large cottage, somewhat out of repair; it was worth some twenty-five hundred dollars.

Hannah could not obtain a loan of a cent upon it. There was no bank in the village, and only one wealthy man, John Arnold. She would not apply to him, and the others, close-fisted, narrow-minded farmers, were afraid of some trap, they knew not what, in the transaction.

"How do I know you'll pay me the interest regular?" asked one man.

"If I don't, you can take the house," said Hannah.

"How do I know I can?" The man looked after her with an air of dull triumph as she went away, drooping more than ever. She was faint from want of food. Still, the look of delicate resolution had not gone from her face. She went home, got out a heavy gold watch-chain which had belonged to her father, took it over to Wayne, and offered it to a jeweller. He looked at her and it curiously. The chain was an old one, but heavy and solid.

"What's your name!" asked the jeweller.

"Hannah Redman."

He pushed it towards her. "No, I guess I can't take it. We have to be pretty careful about these things, you know. If any question should come up—"

Hannah put the chain in her pocket and went home. Old Martha greeted her fretfully.

"I've been dretful lonesome," said she. "There's another lily blowed out, an' there ain't a soul been in to see it."

Hannah sat looking at her moodily. If it were not for this old woman she would lock her house and leave the village this very night. It must be that she would find toleration somewhere in the great world. Some of her kind would be willing to let her live. But here was Martha, whom she would not leave; Martha and her calla-lily, which to a fanciful mind might well seem a very part of her; maybe the grace and beauty which her querulous old age lacked came to her in this form. At all events it recompensed her for them in a measure. Martha plus her calla-lily might equal something almost beautiful—who knew?

Looking at this helpless old creature, something stronger than love took possession of Hannah—a spirit of fierce protection and faithfulness.

"Why don't you take your things off?" Martha groaned.

"I'm going out again."

When Hannah gathered herself up and went out she had a fixed purpose; she was going to get some supper for Martha. There was not a morsel in the house. Martha must have something to eat. There was nothing desperate in her mind, only that fixed intention—the food she would have, she did not know how, but she would have it.

She was so weak from fasting that she could scarcely step herself, but she did not think of that. "It's awful for an old woman to go hungry," she muttered, going down the street.

There was some kindly women in the village; they would give her food if they knew of her terrible need, she was sure of it; she had only to ask. She paused at several gates; once she laid her hand on a latch, then she moved on. She could not beg with this stigma upon her. Suddenly in her weakness a half delirious fancy took possession of her. She seemed to be thinking other people's thoughts of herself instead of her own. "There's that Hannah Redman," she thought; "the girl that stole. Now she's gone to begging. Who wants to give to a girl like that? What's the sense of her begging? She's down as low as she can be; if she wants anything, why doesn't she steal? It's all over with her. People can't think any worse of her than they do now."

Hannah came to the post-office, and entered mechanically. The post-office merely occupied a corner of the large country store. The postmaster dealt out postage-stamps or cheeses to demand. When Hannah entered there was no one in the great rank room. The proprietor had gone to tea; the two clerks were out in the back yard unloading a team. It was not the hour for customers.

Hannah glanced about. A great heap of fresh loaves was on the counter near the door. She leaned over and smelled of them hungrily, then—she snatched one, hid it under her shawl, and went out.

"Hannah Redman has been stealing again," she thought, with those thoughts of others, as she went down the street.

She made the bread into some toast for Martha, and the old woman ate it complainingly. "I'd ha' relished a leetle bit of bacon," she muttered.

"Hannah Redman might just as well have stolen some bacon while she was about it," she thought. She could not touch the bread herself. She looked badly to-night; her soft eyes glittered, the delicate fineness of her color had deepened. Even Martha noticed it.

"What makes you look so queer, Hannah?" she asked.

"Nothing."

"Don't you feel well? You ain't eatin' a thing. I guess you'd relished a leetle bit of meat."

"I'm all right," said Hannah.

After the supper was cleared away, and old Martha had gone to bed, Hannah sat down by one of the front windows. It was dusk; she could just

31

discern the dark figures passing in the street, but could not identify them. Presently one paused at her gate, unfastened it, and entered. Hannah heard steps on the gravel walk. Then there was a knock on the door.

"They've missed it," Hannah thought. She wondered that she did not care more. "Martha's had her supper, anyhow," she chuckled, fiercely.

She opened the door. "Hannah," said a man's voice.

"Oh!" she gasped. "George Arnold! Go away! go away!"

"Hannah, what's the matter? Oh, you poor girl, have I frightened you to death, after all the rest? Hannah—there; lean against me, dear. You feel better now, don't you? Don't shake so. Come, let's go in and light a lamp, and I'll get you some water."

"Oh, go away!"

"I guess I sha'n't go away till— O Lord! Hannah, I never knew what you'd been through till five minutes ago. I've just heard. Hannah, I'd lie down and die at your feet if it would do any good. Oh, you poor girl!"

The man's voice was all rough and husky. Hannah leaned against the door, gasping faintly, while he struck a match and lit a lamp. She never offered to help him. He went out in the kitchen and brought her a glass of water. She pushed it away.

"No," she motioned with silent lips.

"Do take it, dear; you look dreadfully. You frighten me. Take it just to please me."

She took it then, and drank.

"There, that's a good girl. Now sit down here while I talk to you."

She sat down in the chair he placed for her, and he drew another beside her. He sat for a minute looking at her, then suddenly he reached forward and seized her hands. He held them tightly while he talked. "Hannah, look here; you knew I took that money, didn't you?"

She nodded.

"And you let everybody think you did it; you never said a word to clear yourself. Hannah Redman, there never was a woman like you in the whole world! To think of everybody's being down on you, and—your being turned out of the church! Oh, Lord! Hannah, I can't bear it."

The poor fellow fairly sobbed for a minute. Hannah sat still, looking straight ahead.

"See here," he went on, "I want to tell you the whole story, how I came

32

to do it. It wasn't quite so bad as it looked. It was my money, really; it came from the sale of some woodland that one of my uncles gave me when I was a child, before my mother died. Father sold the land when I was about ten, and put the money in the bank. I knew about it, and I'd ask father a good many times to let me have it, but he never would. You know what father is about money matters. He'd put it in under his name. Well, I wanted a little money dreadfully. There was a good chance—I've made it pay since, too— but father wouldn't give me any. Hannah, father never gave me a dollar to help me in business, and he's a rich man too. Well, I don't know what possessed him, but the day I was going away he drew that money out of the bank; he wanted to invest it somewhere. I saw it; he was counting it over, and he had the bank-book. I asked him for it again, but he wouldn't let me have a dollar of it. Then—I never knew him to be so careless before; I don't see how it happened—but he laid that money in a roll on the sitting-room table. I saw it when I came in to say good-by to you, and I took it, and crammed it into my pocket. All of a sudden I thought to myself, 'It's my own money, and I'll *have* it.' You were looking right at me when I took it, but I knew you'd think it was mine, I was so cool about it. You did, didn't you?"

"Yes."

"I went down to the depot, expecting every minute I'd hear father behind me, but I got off. I wrote to father after a while and owned up, though I thought he'd know I took it anyway. I never dreamed of his making any fuss about it. I didn't think he'd mention it to a soul; and as for suspecting you—

"Father wrote me an awful letter, but he didn't say a word about that. He told me I needn't come home again. I ain't stopping there now. He must have known after they accused you, but he never said a word. He knew I liked you, too. Well, I'll clear you, I'll clear you, dear. Every soul in town shall know just what you are, and just what you've done, and then I'm going to take you away from the whole of them, out of the reach of their tongues. I'll do all I can to make it up to you, Hannah."

"Oh, go away, George, please go!"

"Hannah, what do you mean?"

"It's all over."

"Hannah!"

"I wish you'd go away; I can't bear any more."

His face turned pale and rigid as he sat watching her. "Look here," he said, slowly, "I ought to have thought—Of course I'll go right away and never come near you again. I might have known you wouldn't want a fellow that stole. I'll go, Hannah, and I won't say another word."

He rose, and was half-way to the door when he turned. "Good-by," he said.

"Don't, don't! oh, don't! George, you don't know! It's dreadful! I've got to tell you!"

Hannah was beside him, clinging to his arm. All her composure was gone. Her voice rose into a shrill clamor.

"George, George! Oh, what shall I do! what shall I do!"

"Hannah, you'll kill yourself! You mustn't!"

"I can't help it! It isn't you! it isn't you! It was right for you to take it. But it's me! it's me! Oh, what shall I do?"

"Hannah, are you crazy?"

"No; but it's all over. It wasn't true before, but it is now."

"What do you mean?"

"I stole. I did, George, I did!"

"When? You didn't either. You've been dwelling on this till you don't know what you have done."

"Yes, I do. I stole. I did!"

"What did you steal?"

"A loaf of bread."

"Hannah!"

"Martha didn't have anything for supper. Oh, what shall I do?"

"Hannah Redman, you don't mean it's come to this?"

"They wouldn't give me any work; they couldn't trust me, you know, because I'd stole. I never have given up, but now I've got to."

"When—did you have anything to—eat?"

"Yesterday. I didn't eat any of that—bread."

The young man looked at her a moment, then he led her back to her seat.

"See here, Hannah, you sit here a minute till I come back. I won't be gone long."

She sat down weakly. She suddenly felt to exhausted to speak, and

34

leaned her head back and closed her eyes. She hardly knew when George returned.

Presently he came to her with a glass of milk. "Here, drink this, dear," he said.

He held the glass while she drank. In the midst of it she stopped and looked at him piteously.

"What is it, dear?"

"Have you been down to the store?"

"Yes."

"Do they know? Have they found it out yet?"

His tender face grew stern. "No, they hadn't. Don't you think of that again. I've paid them for the bread."

"But they ought to know I—stole it."

"No, you didn't. Hannah, never think of this again. They're paid."

"Did you tell them—I took it?"

"Yes, I told them—all that was necessary. Hannah, dear, don't ever speak of this again, or think of it. Finish your milk now; then I want you to eat some cakes I've got for you. Oh, you poor girl; it seems to me I can't live through this myself. Here I've had plenty to eat, and you—"

A week from the next Sunday Hannah wore a white dress to the meeting. It was an old muslin, but she had washed and ironed it nicely, and sewed some lace in the neck and sleeves. She had trimmed her straw bonnet with white ribbons. Everybody stared when she came up the aisle. George Arnold entered at the same time and seated himself beside her in her pew. The women rustled and whispered. John Arnold was not present to-day. The old grandfather looked across at his empty pew uneasily.

After the service, the minister, an itinerant one—this poor parish had no settled preacher—in a solemn voice requested the congregation to be seated. Then he added—he was an old man, with a certain dull impressiveness of manner—"You are requested to remain a moment. One of your number, a young man whom I this morning joined in the bands of holy wedlock, has something which he wishes to communicate to you."

There was a deathly calm. George Arnold arose. He was a tall, fair man, like his father. His yellow, curled head towered up bravely; the light from the pulpit window settled on it. He was very pale. "I wish to make a statement in the presence of this congregation," he said, in a loud, clear voice.

35

"The lady beside me, who is now my wife, has been accused of theft from my father. The accusation was a false one. I stole the money myself. She has borne what she has had to bear from you all to shield me."

Before he had quite finished Hannah rose; she caught hold of his arm and leaned her cheek against it before them all. They sat down side by side, and waited while the congregation went out. A carriage stood before the church. The bridal couple were to leave town that day. A few stood staring at a distance as George Arnold assisted his bride into the carriage after the crowd had dispersed.

They drove straight to Hannah's house. There was an old figure waiting at the gate. Beside her stood a great pot of calla-lilies.

"You jest lift in them lilies first, afore I git in," said she, "an' be real keerful you don't break 'em. The stalks is tender."

Richard Cory

EDWARD ARLINGTON ROBINSON

Whenever Richard Cory went down town,
We people on the pavement looked at him:
He was a gentleman from sole to crown,
Clean favored, and imperially slim.

And he was always quietly arrayed,
And he was always human when he talked;
But still he fluttered pulses when he said,
"Good-morning," and he glittered when he walked.

And he was rich—yes, richer than a king—
And admirably schooled in every grace:
In fine, we thought that he was everything
To make us wish that we were in his place.

So on we worked, and waited for the light,
And went without the meat, and cursed the bread;
And Richard Cory, one calm summer night,
Went home and put a bullet through his head.

Flammonde

EDWARD ARLINGTON ROBINSON

The man Flammonde, from God knows where,
With firm address and foreign air,
With news of nations in his talk
And something royal in his walk,
With glint of iron in his eyes,
But never doubt, nor yet surprise,
Appeared, and stayed, and held his head
As one by kings accredited.

Erect, with his alert repose
About him, and about his clothes,
He pictured all tradition hears
Of what we owe to fifty years.
His cleansing heritage of taste
Paraded neither want nor waste;
And what he needed for his fee
To live, he borrowed graciously.

He never told us what he was,
Or what mischance, or other cause,
Had banished him from better days
To play the Prince of Castaways.
Meanwhile he played surpassing well
A part, for most, unplayable;
In fine, one pauses, half afraid
To say for certain that he played.

For that, one may as well forego
Conviction as to yes or no;
Nor can I say just how intense
Would then have been the difference
To several, who, having striven
In vain to get what he was given,
Would see the stranger taken on
By friends not easy to be won.

Moreover, many a malcontent
He soothed and found munificent;
His courtesy beguiled and foiled
Suspicion that his years were soiled;
His mien distinguished any crowd,
His credit strengthened when he bowed;
And women, young and old, were fond
Of looking at the man Flammonde.

There was a woman in our town
On whom the fashion was to frown;
But while our talk renewed the tinge
Of a long-faded scarlet fringe,
The man Flammonde saw none of that,
And what he saw we wondered at—
That none of us, in her distress,
Could hide or find our littleness.

There was a boy that all agreed
Had shut within him the rare seed
Of learning. We could understand,
But none of us could lift a hand.
The man Flammonde appraised the youth,
And told a few of us the truth;
And thereby, for a little gold,
A flowered future was unrolled.

New England

There were two citizens who fought
For years and years, and over nought;
They made life awkward for their friends,
And shortened their own dividends.
The man Flammonde said what was wrong
Should be made right; nor was it long
Before they were again in line,
And had each other in to dine.

And these I mention are but four
Of many out of many more.
So much for them. But what of him—
So firm in every look and limb?
What small satanic sort of kink
Was in his brain? What broken link
Withheld him from the destinies
That came so near to being his?

What was he, when we came to sift
His meaning, and to note the drift
Of incommunicable ways
That make us ponder while we praise?
Why was it that his charm revealed
Somehow the surface of a shield?
What was it that we never caught?
What was he, and what was he not?

How much it was of him we met
We cannot ever know; nor yet
Shall all he gave us quite atone
For what was his, and his alone;
Nor need we now, since he knew best,
Nourish an ethical unrest:
Rarely at once will nature give
The power to be Flammonde and live.

We cannot know how much we learn
From those who never will return,
Until a flash of unforeseen
Rembrance falls on what has been.
We've each a darkening hill to climb;
And this is why, from time to time
In Tilbury Town, we look beyond
Horizons for the man Flammonde.

Strangers in Town

SHIRLEY JACKSON

I don't gossip. If there is anything in this world I loathe, it is gossip. A week or so ago in the store, Dora Powers started to tell me that nasty rumor about the Harris boy again, and I came right out and said to her if she repeated one more word of that story to me I wouldn't speak to her for the rest of my life, and I haven't. It's been a week and not one word have I said to Dora Powers, and that's what I think of gossip. Tom Harris has always been too easy on that boy anyway; the young fellow needs a good whipping and he'd stop all this ranting around, and I've said so to Tom Harris a hundred times and more.

If I didn't get so mad when I think about that house next door, I'd almost have to laugh, seeing people in town standing in the store and on corners and dropping their voices to talk about fairies and leprechauns, when every living one of them knows there isn't any such thing and never has been, and them just racking their brains to find new tales to tell. I don't hold with gossip, as I say, even if it's about leprechauns and fairies, and it's my held opinion that Jane Dollar is getting feeble in the mind. The Dollars weren't ever noted for keeping their senses right up to the end anyway, and Jane's no older than her mother was when she sent a cake to the bake sale and forgot to put the eggs in it. Some said she did it on purpose to get even with the ladies for not asking her to take a booth, but most just said the old lady had lost track of things, and I dare say she could have looked out and seen fairies in her garden if it ever came into her mind. When the Dollars get that age, they'll tell anything, and that's right where Jane Dollar is now, give or take six months.

My name is Addie Spinner, and I live down on Main Street, the last house but one. There's just one house after mine, and then Main Street kind of runs off into the woods—Spinner's Thicket, they call the woods, on account of my grandfather building the first house in the village. Before the crazy people moved in, the house past mine belonged to the Bartons, but they moved away because he got a job in the city, and high time, too, after them living off her sister and her husband for upward of a year.

Well, after the Bartons finally moved out—owing everyone in town, if you want my guess—it wasn't long before the crazy people moved in, and I knew they were crazy right off when I saw that furniture. I already knew they were young folks, and probably not married long because I saw them when they came to look at the house. Then when I saw the furniture go in I knew there was going to be trouble between me and her.

The moving van got to the house about eight in the morning. Of course, I always have my dishes done and my house swept up long before that, so I took my mending for the poor out on the side porch and really got caught up on a lot I'd been letting slide. It was a hot day, so I just fixed myself a salad for my lunch, and the side porch is a nice cool place to sit and eat on a hot day, so I never missed a thing going into that house.

First, there were the chairs, all modern, with no proper legs and seats, and I always say that a woman who buys herself that fly-away kind of furniture has no proper feeling for her house—for one thing, it's too easy to clean around those little thin legs; you can't get a floor well-swept without a lot of hard work. Then, she had a lot of low tables, and you can't fool me with them—when you see those little low tables, you can always tell there's going to be a lot of drinking liquor go on in that house; those little tables are made for people who give cocktail parties and need a lot of places to put glasses down. Hattie Martin, she has one of those low tables, and the way Martin drinks is a crime. Then when I saw the barrels going in next door, I was sure. No one just married has that many dishes without a lot of cocktail glasses, and you can't tell me any different.

When I went down to the store later, after they were all moved in, I met Jane Dollar, and I told her about the drinking that was going to go on next door, and she said she wasn't a bit surprised because the people had a maid. Not someone to come one day a week and do the heavy cleaning—a maid. Lived in the house and everything. I said I hadn't noticed any maid, and Jane said most things if I hadn't noticed them she wouldn't believe they existed in this world, but the Wests' maid was sure enough; she'd been in the store not ten minutes earlier buying a chicken. We didn't think she'd rightly have time enough to cook a chicken before supper-time, but then we decided that probably the chicken was for tomorrow, and tonight the Wests were planning on going over to the inn for dinner and the maid could fix herself an egg or something. Jane did say that one trouble with having a maid—Jane never had a maid in her life, and I wouldn't speak to her if she did—was that you never had anything left over. No matter what you planned, you had to get new meat every day.

I looked around for the maid on my way home. The quickest way to get to my house from the store is to take the path that cuts across the back garden of the house next door, and even though I don't use it generally—you don't meet neighbors to pass the time of day with, going along a back path—I thought I'd better be hurrying a little to fix my own supper, so I cut across the Wests' back garden. West, that was their name, and what the maid was called I didn't know, because Jane hadn't been able to find out. It was a good thing I did take the path, because there was the maid, right out there in the garden, down on her hands and knees, digging.

"Good evening," I said, just as polite as I could. "It's kind of damp to be down on the ground."

"I don't mind," she said. "I like things that grow."

I must say she was a pleasant-speaking woman, although too old, I'd think, for domestic work. The poor thing must have been in sad straits to hire out, and yet here she was just as jolly and round as an apple. I thought maybe she was an old aunt or something and they took this way of keeping her, so I said, still very polite, "I see you just moved in today?"

"Yes," she said, not really telling me much.

"The family's name is West?"

"Yes."

"You might be Mrs. West's mother?"

"No."

"An aunt, possibly?"

"No."

"Not related at all?"

"No."

"You're just the maid?" I thought afterward that she might not like it mentioned, but once it was out I couldn't take it back.

"Yes." She answered pleasant enough, I will say that for her.

"The work is hard, I expect?"

"No."

"Just the two of them to care for?"

"Yes."

44

"I'd say you wouldn't like it much,"

"It's not bad," she said. "I use magic a lot, of course."

"Magic?" I said. "Does that get your work done sooner?"

"Indeed it does," she said with not so much as a smile or a wink. "You wouldn't think, would you, that right now I'm down on my hands and knees making dinner for my family?"

"No," I said. "I wouldn't think that."

"See?" she said. "Here's our dinner." And she showed me an acorn, I swear she did, with a mushroom and a scrap of grass in it.

"It hardly looks like enough to go around," I said, kind of backing away.

She laughed at me, kneeling there on the ground with her acorn, and said, "If there's any left over, I'll bring you a dish; you'll find it wonderfully filling."

"But what about your chicken?" I said; I was well along the path away from her, and I did want to know why she got the chicken if she didn't think they were going to eat it.

"Oh, that," she said. "That's for my cat."

Well, who buys a whole chicken for a cat, that shouldn't have chicken bones anyway? Like I told Jane over the phone as soon as I got home, Mr. Honeywell down at the store ought to refuse to sell it to her or at least make her take something more fitting, like ground meat, even though neither of us believed for a minute that the cat was really going to get the chicken, or that she even had a cat, come to think of it; crazy people will say anything that comes into their heads.

I know for a fact that no one next door ate chicken that night, though; my kitchen window overlooks their dining room if I stand on a chair, and what they ate for dinner was something steaming in a big brown bowl. I had to laugh, thinking about that acorn, because that was just what the bowl looked like—a big acorn. Probably that was what put the notion in her head. And, sure enough, later she brought over a dish of it and left it on my back steps, me not wanting to open the door late at night with a crazy lady outside, and like I told Jane, I certainly wasn't going to eat any outlandish concoction made by a crazy lady. But I kind of stirred it around with the end of a spoon, and it smelled all right. It had mushrooms in it and beans, but I couldn't tell what else, and Jane and I decided that probably we were right in the first time and the chicken was for tomorrow.

New England

I had to promise Jane I'd try to get a look inside to see how they set out that fancy furniture, so next morning I brought back their bowl and marched right up to the front door—mostly around town we go in and out back doors but being as they were new and especially since I wasn't sure how you went about calling when people had a maid, I used the front—and gave a knock. I had gotten up early to make a batch of doughnuts, so I'd have something to put in the bowl when I took it back, so I knew that the people next door were up and about because I saw him leaving for work at seven-thirty. He must have worked in the city, to have to get off so early. Jane thinks he's in an office, because she saw him going toward the depot, and he wasn't running; people who work in offices don't have to get in on the dot, Jane said, although how she would know I couldn't tell you.

It was little Mrs. West who opened the door, and I must say she looked agreeable enough. I thought with the maid to bring her breakfast and all she might still be lying in bed, the way they do, but she was all dressed in a pink house dress and was wide awake. She didn't ask me in right away, so I kind of moved a little toward the door, and then she stepped back and said wouldn't I come in, and I must say, funny as that furniture is, she had it fixed up nice, with green curtains on the windows. I couldn't tell from my house what the pattern was on those curtains, but once I was inside I could see it was a pattern of green leaves kind of woven in, and the rug, which of course I had seen when they brought it in, was green too. Some of those big boxes that went in must have held books, because there were a lot of books all put away in bookcases, and before I had a chance to think I said, "My, you must have worked all night to get everything arranged so quick. I didn't see your lights on, though."

"Mallie did it," she said.

"Mallie being the maid?"

She kind of smiled, and then she said, "She's more like a godmother than a maid, really."

I do hate to seem curious, so I just said, "Mallie must keep herself pretty busy. Yesterday she was out digging your garden."

"Yes." It was hard to learn anything out of these people, with their short answers.

"I brought you some doughnuts," I said.

"Thank you." She put the bowl down on one of those little tables—Jane thinks they must hide the wine, because there wasn't a sight of any such

46

thing that I could see—and then she said, "We'll offer them to the cat."

Well, I can tell you I didn't much care for that. "You must have quite a hungry cat," I said to her.

"Yes," she said. "I don't know what we'd do without him. He's Mallie's cat, of course."

"I haven't seen him," I said. If we were going to talk about cats, I figured I could hold my own, having had one cat or another for a matter of sixty years, although it hardly seemed a sensible subject for two ladies to chat over. Like I told Jane, there was a lot she ought to be wanting to know about the village and the people in it and who to go to for hardware and what not—I know for a fact I've put a dozen people off Tom Harris' hardware store since he charged me seventeen cents for a pound of nails—and I was just the person to set her straight on the town. But she was going on about the cat. "—fond of children," she was saying.

"I expect he's company for Mallie," I said.

"Well, he helps her, you know," she said, and then I began to think maybe she was crazy too.

"And how does the cat help Mallie?"

"With her magic."

"I see," I said, and I started to say good-by fast, figuring to get home to the telephone, because people around the village certainly ought to be hearing about what was going on. But before I could get to the door the maid came out of the kitchen and said good morning to me, real polite, and then the maid said to Mrs. West that she was putting together the curtains for the front bedroom and would Mrs. West like to decide on the pattern? And while I just stood there with my jaw hanging, she held out a handful of cobwebs—and I never did see anyone before or since who was able to hold a cobweb pulled out neat, or anyone who would want to, for that matter—and she had a blue jay's feather and a curl of blue ribbon, and she asked me how I liked her curtains.

Well, that did for me, and I got out of there and ran all the way to Jane's house, and, of course, she never believed me. She walked me home just so she could get a look at the outside of the house, and I will be everlastingly shaken if they hadn't gone and put up curtains in that front bedroom, soft white net with a design of blue that Jane said looked like a blue jay's feather. Jane said they were the prettiest curtains she ever saw, but they gave me the shivers every time I looked at them.

It wasn't two days after that I began finding things. Little things, and even some inside my own house. Once there was a basket of grapes on my back steps and I swear those grapes were never grown around our village. For one thing, they shone like they were covered with silver dust, and smelled like some foreign perfume. I threw them in the garbage, but I kept a little embroidered handkerchief I found on the table in my front hall, and I've got it still in my dresser drawer.

Once I found a colored thimble on the fence post, and once my cat Samantha, that I've had for eleven years and more, came in wearing a little green collar and spat at me when I took it off. One day I found a leaf basket on my kitchen table filled with hazelnuts, and it make me downright shaking mad to think of someone's coming in and out of my house without so much as asking, and me never seeing them come or go.

Things like that never happened before the crazy people moved into the house next door, and I was telling Mrs. Acton so, down on the corner one morning, when young Mrs. O'Neil came by and told us that when she was in the store with her baby she met Mallie the maid. The baby was crying because he was having a time with his teething, and Mallie gave him a little green candy to bite on. We thought Mrs. O'Neil was crazy herself to let her baby have candy that came from that family and said so, and I told them about the drinking that went on and the furniture getting arranged in the dark and the digging in the garden, and Mrs. Acton said she certainly hoped they weren't going to think that just because they had a garden they had any claim to be in the Garden Club.

Mrs. Acton is president of the Garden Club. Jane says I ought to be president, if things were done right, on account of having the oldest garden in town, but Mrs. Acton's husband is the doctor, and I don't know what people thought he might do to them when they were sick if Mrs. Acton didn't get to be president. Anyway, you'd think Mrs. Acton had some say about who got into the Garden Club and who didn't, but I had to admit that in this case we'd all vote with her, even though Mrs. O'Neil did tell us the next day that she didn't think the people could be all crazy, because the baby's tooth came through that night with no more trouble.

Do you know, all this time that maid came into the store every day, and every day she bought one chicken. Nothing else. Jane took to dropping in the store when she saw the maid going along, and she says the maid never bought but one chicken a day. Once Jane got her nerve up and said to the maid that they must be fond of chicken, and the maid looked straight at her and told her right to her face that they were vegetarians.

"All but the cat, I suppose," Jane said, being pretty nervy when she gets her nerve up.

"Yes," the maid said, "all but the cat."

We finally decided that he must bring food home from the city, although why Mr. Honeywell's store wasn't good enough for them I couldn't tell you. After the baby's tooth was better, Tom O'Neil took them over a batch of fresh-picked sweet corn, and they must have liked that, because they sent the baby a furry blue blanket that was so soft that young Mrs. O'Neil said the baby never needed another, winter or summer, and after being so sickly, that baby began to grow and got so healthy you wouldn't know it was the same one, even though the O'Neils never should have accepted presents from strangers, not knowing whether the wool might be clean or not.

Then I found out they were dancing next door. Night after night after night, dancing. Sometimes I'd lie there awake until ten, eleven o'clock, listening to that heathen music and wishing I could get up the nerve to go over and give them a piece of my mind. It wasn't so much the noise keeping me from sleeping—I will say the music was soft and kind of like a lullaby—but people haven't got any right to live like that. Folks should go to bed at a sensible hour and get up at a sensible hour and spend their days doing good deeds and housework. A wife ought to cook dinner for her husband—and not out of cans from the city, either—and she ought to run over next door sometimes with a home-baked cake to pass the time of day and keep up with the news. And most of all a wife ought to go to the store herself where she can meet her neighbors and not just send the maid.

Every morning I'd go out and find fairy rings on the grass, and anyone around here will tell you that means an early winter, and here next door they hadn't even thought to get in coal. I watched every day for Adams and his truck because I knew for a fact that cellar was empty of coal, all I had to do was lean down a little when I was in my garden and I could see right into the cellar, just as swept and clear as though they planned to treat their guests in there. Jane thought they were the kind who went off on a trip somewhere in the winter, shirking responsibilities for facing the snow with their neighbors. The cellar was all you could see, though. They had those green curtains pulled so tight against the windows that even right up close there wasn't a chink to look through from outside, and them inside dancing away. I do wish I could have nerved myself to go right up to that front door and knock some night.

Now, Mary Corn thought I ought to. "You got a right, Addie," she told me one day in the store. "You got every right in the world to make them quiet down at night. You're the nearest neighbor they got, and it's the right thing to do. Tell them they're making a name for themselves around the village."

Well, I couldn't nerve myself, and that's the gracious truth. Every now and then I'd see little Mrs. West walking in the garden, or Mallie the maid coming out of the woods with a basket—gathering acorns, never a doubt of it—but I never so much as nodded my head at them. Down at the store I had to tell Mary Corn I couldn't do it. "They're foreigners, that's why," I said. "Foreigners of some kind. They don't rightly seem to understand what a person says—it's like they're always answering some other question you didn't ask."

"If they're foreigners," Dora Powers put in, being at the store to pick up some sugar to frost a cake, "it stands to reason there's something wrong to bring them here."

"Well, I won't call on foreigners," Mary said.

"You can't treat them the same as you'd treat regular people," I said. "I went inside the house, remember, although not as you might say to pay a call."

So then I had to tell them all over again about the furniture and the drinking—and it stands to reason that anyone who dances all night is going to be drinking too—and my good doughnuts from my grandmother's recipe going to the cat. And Dora, she thought they were up to no good in the village. Mary said she didn't know anyone who was going to call, not being sure they were proper, and then we had to stop talking because in came Mallie the maid for her chicken.

You would have thought I was the chairman of a committee or something, the way Dora and Mary kept nudging me and winking that I should go over and speak to her, but I wasn't going to make a fool of myself twice, I can tell you. Finally Dora saw there was no use pushing me, so she marched over and stood there until the maid turned around and said, "Good morning."

50

Dora came right out and said, "There's a lot of people around this village, miss, would like to know a few things."

"I imagine so," the maid said.

"We'd like to know what you're doing in our village," Dora said.

"We thought it would be a nice place to live," the maid said. You could see that Dora was caught up short on that, because who picks a place to live because it's nice? People live in our village because they were born here; they don't just come.

I guess Dora knew we were all waiting for her, because she took a big breath and asked, "And how long do you plan on staying?"

"Oh," the maid said, "I don't think we'll stay very long, after all."

"Even if they don't stay," Mary said later, "they can do a lot of harm while they're here, setting a bad example for our young folk. Just for instance, I heard that the Harris boy got picked up again by the state police for driving without a license."

"Tom Harris is too gentle on that boy," I said. "A boy like that needs whipping and not people living in a house right in town showing him how to drink and dance all night."

Jane came in right then, and she had heard that all the children in town had taken to dropping by the house next door to bring dandelions and berries from the woods—and from their own father's gardens, too, I'll be bound—and the children were telling around that the cat next door could talk. They said he told them stories.

Well, that just about did for me, you can imagine. Chilren have too much freedom nowadays anyway, without getting nonsense like that into their heads. We asked Annie Lee when she came into the store, and she thought somebody ought to call the police on them, so it could all be stopped before somebody got hurt. She said, suppose one of those kids got a step too far inside that house—how did we know he'd ever get out again? Well, it wasn't too pleasant a thought, I can tell you, but trust Annie Lee to be always looking on the black side. I don't have much dealing with the children as a rule once they learned they'd better keep away from my apple trees and my melons, and I can't say I know one from the next except for the Martin boy I had to call the police on once for stealing a piece of tin from my front yard, but I can't say I relished the notion that that cat had his eyes on them. It's not natural, somehow.

And don't you think it was the very next day that they stole the littlest

51

Quilting Contest

Acton boy? Not quite three years old, and Mrs. Acton so busy with her Garden Club she let him run along into the woods with his sister, and first thing anyone knew they got him. Jane phoned and told me. She heard from Dora, who had been right in the store when the Acton girl came running in to find her mother and tell her the baby had wandered away in the woods, and Mallie the maid had been digging around not ten feet from where they saw him last. Jane said Mrs. Acton and Dora and Mary Corn and half a dozen others were heading right over to the house next door, and I better get outside fast before I missed something, and if she got there late to let her know everything that happened. I barely got out my own front door when down the street they came, maybe ten or twelve mothers, marching along so mad they never had time to be scared.

"Come on, Addie," Dora said to me. "They've finally done it this time."

I knew Jane would never forgive me if I hung back, so out I went and up the front walk to the house next door. Mrs. Acton was ready to go right up and knock, because she was so mad, but before she had a chance the door opened and there was Mrs. West and the little boy, smiling all over as if nothing had happened.

"Mallie found him in the woods," Mrs. West said, and Mrs. Acton grabbed the boy away from her; you could tell they had been frightening him by the way he started to cry as soon as he got to his own mother. All he would say was "kitty," and that put a chill down our backs, you can imagine.

Mrs. Acton was so mad she could hardly talk, but she did manage to say, "You keep away from my children, you hear me?" And Mrs. West looked surprised.

"Mallie found him in the woods," she said. "We were going to bring him home."

"We can guess how you were going to bring him home," Dora shouted, and then Annie Lee piped up, from well in the back, "Why don't you get out of our town?"

"I guess we will," Mrs. West said. "It's not the way we thought it was going to be."

That was nice, wasn't it? Nothing riles me like people knocking this town, where my grandfather built the first house, and I just spoke up right then and there.

"Foreign ways!" I said. "You're heathen wicked people, with your dancing and your maid, and the sooner you leave this town, the better it's going to be for you. Because I might as well tell you"—and I shook my finger right at her—"that certain people in this town aren't going to put up with your fancy ways much longer, and you would be well advised—very well advised, I say—to pack up your furniture and your curtains and your maid and cat and get out of our town before we put you out."

Jane claims she doesn't think I really said it, but all the others were there and can testify I did—all but Mrs. Acton, who never had a good word to say for anybody.

Anyway, right then we found out they have given the little boy something, trying to buy his affection, because Mrs. Acton pried it out of his hand, and he was crying all the time. When she held it out, it was hard to believe, but of course with them there's nothing too low. It was a little gold-colored apple, all shiny and bright, and Mrs. Acton threw it right at the porch-floor, as hard as she could, and that little toy shattered into dust.

"We don't want anything from you," Mrs. Acton said, and as I told Jane afterward, it was terrible to see the look on Mrs. West's face. For a minute she just stood there looking at us. Then she turned and went back inside and shut the door.

Someone wanted to throw rocks through the windows, but, as I told them, destroying private property is a crime and we might better leave violence to the menfolks, so Mrs. Acton took her little boy home, and I went in and called Jane. Poor Jane; the whole thing had gone off so fast she hadn't had time to get her corset on.

I hadn't any more than gotten Jane on the phone when I saw through the hall window that a moving van was right there next door, and the men were starting to carry out that fancy furniture. Jane wasn't surprised when I told her over the phone. "Nobody can get moving that fast," she said. "They were probably planning to slip out with that little boy."

"Or maybe the maid did it with magic," I said, and Jane laughed.

"Listen," she said, "go and see what else is going on—I'll hang on the phone."

There wasn't anything to see, even from my front porch, except the moving van and the furniture coming out; not a sign of Mrs. West or the maid.

"He hasn't come home from the city yet," Jane said. "I can see the street from here. They'll have news for him tonight."

That was how they left. I take a lot of the credit for myself, even though

54

Jane tries to make me mad by saying Mrs. Acton did her share. By that night they were gone, bag and baggage, and Jane and I went over the house next door with a flashlight to see what damage they left behind. There wasn't a thing left in that house—not a chicken bone, not an acorn—except for one blue jay's wing upstairs, and that wasn't worth taking home. Jane put it in the incinerator when we came downstairs.

One more thing. My cat Samantha had kittens. That may not surprise you, but it sure as judgment surprised me and Samantha, her being over eleven years old and well past her kitten days, the old fool. But you would have laughed to see her dancing around like a young lady cat, just as light-footed and as pleased as if she thought she was doing something no cat ever did before; and those kittens troubled me.

Folks don't dare come right out and say anything to me about my kittens, of course, but they do keep on with that silly talk about fairies and leprechauns. And there's no denying that the kittens are bright yellow, with orange eyes, and much bigger than normal kittens have a right to be. Sometimes I see them all watching me when I go around the kitchen, and it gives me a cold finger down my back. Half the children in town are begging for those kittens—"fairy kittens," they're calling them—but there isn't a grownup in town would take one.

Jane says there's something downright uncanny about those kittens, but then Jane would even gossip about cats, and I may never speak to her again in all my life. She won't tell me what folks are saying about my kittens, and gossip is one thing I simply cannot endure.

A & P

JOHN UPDIKE

In walks these three girls in nothing but bathing suits. I'm in the third checkout slot, with my back to the door, so I don't see them until they're over by the bread. The one that caught my eye first was the one in the plaid green two-piece. She was a chunky kid, with a good tan and a sweet broad soft-looking can with those two crescents of white just under it, where the sun never seems to hit, at the top of the backs of her legs. I stood there with my hand on a box of HiHo crackers trying to remember if I rang it up or not. I ring it up again and the customer starts giving me hell. She's one of these cash-register-watchers, a witch about fifty with rouge on her cheekbones and no eyebrows, and I know it made her day to trip me up. She'd been watching cash registers for fifty years and probably never seen a mistake before.

By the time I got her feathers smoothed and her goodies into a bag—she gives me a little snort in passing, if she'd been born at the right time they would have burned her over in Salem—by the time I get her on her way the girls had circled around the bread and were coming back, without a pushcart, back my way along the counters, in the aisle between the check-outs and the Special bins. They didn't even have shoes on. There was this chunky one, with the two-piece—it was bright green and the seams on the bra were still sharp and her belly was still pretty pale so I guessed she just got it (the suit)—there was this one, with one of those chubby berryfaces, the lips all bunched together under her nose, this one, and a tall one, with black hair that hadn't quite frizzed right, and one of these sunburns right across under the eyes, and a chin that was too long—you know, the kind of girl other girls think is "striking" and "attractive" but never quite makes it, as they very well know, which is why they like her so much—and then the third one, that wasn't quite so tall. She was the queen. She kind of led them, the other two peeking around and making their shoulders round. She didn't look around, not this queen, she just walked straight on slowly, on these long white prima-donna legs. She came down a little hard on her heels, as if she didn't walk in her bare feet that much, putting down her heels and then letting the weight move along to her toes as if she was testing the floor with every step, putting a little deliberate extra action into it. You never know for sure how girls' minds work (do you really think it's a mind in there or just a little buzz like a bee in a glass jar?) but you got the idea she had talked the other two into coming in here with her, and now she was showing them how to do it, walk slow and hold yourself straight.

She had on a kind of dirty-pink—beige, maybe, I don't know—bathing suit with a little nubble all over it and, what got me, the straps were down. They were off her shoulders looped loose around the cool tops of her arms, and I guess as a result the suit had slipped a little on her, so all around the top of the cloth there was this shining rim. If it hadn't been there you wouldn't have known there could have been anything whiter than those shoulders. With the straps pushed off, there was nothing between the top of the suit and the top of her head except just *her*, this clear bare plane of the top of her chest down from the shoulder bones like a dented sheet of metal tilted in the light. I mean, it was more than pretty.

She had sort of oaky hair that the sun and salt had bleached, done up in a bun that was unravelling, and a kind of prim face. Walking into the A & P with your straps down, I suppose it's the only kind of face you *can* have. She held her head so high her neck, coming up out of those white shoulders, looked kind of stretched, but I didn't mind. The longer her neck was, the more of her there was.

She must have felt in the corner of her eye me and over my shoulder Stokesie in the second slot watching, but she didn't tip. Not this queen. She kept her eyes moving across the racks, and stopped, and turned so slow it made my stomach rub the inside of my apron, and buzzed to the other two, who kind of huddled against her for relief, and then they all three of them went up the cat-and-dog-food-breakfast-cereal-macaroni-rice-raisins-seasoning-spreads-spaghetti-soft-drinks-crackers-and-cookies aisle. From the third slot I look straight up this aisle to the meat counter, and I watched them all the way. The fat one with the tan sort of fumbled with the cookies, but on second thought she put the package back. The sheep pushing their carts down the aisle—the girls were walking against the usual traffic (not that we have one-way signs or anything)—were pretty hilarious. You could see them, when Queenie's white shoulders dawned on them, kind of jerk, or hop, or hiccup, but their eyes snapped back to their own baskets and on they pushed. I bet you could set off dynamite in an A & P and the people would by and large keep reaching and checking oatmeal off their lists and muttering "Let me see, there was a third thing, began with A, asparagus, no, ah, yes, applesauce!" or whatever it is they do mutter. But there was no doubt, this jiggled them. A few houseslaves in pin curlers even looked around after pushing their carts past to make sure what they had seen was correct.

You know, it's one thing to have a girl in a bathing suit down on the beach, where what with the glare nobody can look at each other much anyway, and another thing in the cool of the A & P, under the fluorescent lights, against all those stacked packages, with her feet paddling along naked over our checkerboard green-and-cream rubber-tile floor.

"Oh, Daddy," Stokesie said beside me. "I feel so faint."

"Darling," I said. "Hold me tight." Stokesie's married, with two babies chalked up on his fuselage already, but as far as I can tell that's the only difference. He's twenty-two, and I was nineteen this April.

"Is it done?" he asks, the responsible married man finding his voice. I forgot to say he thinks he's going to be manager some sunny day, maybe in 1990 when it's called the Great Alexandrov and Petrooshki Tea Company or something.

What he meant was, our town is five miles from a beach, with a big summer colony out on the Point, but we're right in the middle of town, and the women generally put on a shirt or shorts or something before they get out of the car into the street. And anyway these are usually women with six children and varicose veins mapping their legs and nobody, including them, could care less. As I say, we're right in the middle of town, and if you stand at our front doors you can see two banks and the Congregational church and the newspaper store and three real-estate offices and about twenty-seven old freeloaders tearing up Central Street because the sewer broke again. It's not as if we're on the Cape; we're north of Boston and there's people in this town haven't seen the ocean for twenty years.

The girls had reached the meat counter and were asking McMahon something. He pointed, they pointed, and they shuffled out of sight behind a pyramid of Diet Delight peaches. All that was left for us to see was old McMahon patting his mouth and looking after them sizing up their joints. Poor kids, I began to feel sorry for them, they couldn't help it.

Now here comes the sad part of the story, at least my family says it's sad, but I don't think it's so sad myself. The store's pretty empty, it being Thursday afternoon, so there was nothing much to do except lean on the register and wait for the girls to show up again. The whole store was like a pinball machine and I didn't know which tunnel they'd come out of. After a while they come around out of the far aisle, around the light bulbs, records at discount of the Caribbean Six or Tony Martin Sings or some such gunk you wonder they waste the wax on, sixpacks of candy bars, and plastic toys done up in cellophane that fall apart when a kid looks at them anyway. Around they come, Queenie still leading the way, and holding a little gray jar in her hand. Slots Three through Seven are unmanned and I could see her wondering between Stokes and me, but Stokesie with his usual luck draws an old party in baggy gray pants who stumbles up with four giant cans of pineapple juice (what do these bums *do* with all that pineapple juice? I've often asked myself) so the girls come to me. Queenie puts down the jar and I take it into my fingers icy cold. Kingfish Fancy Herring Snacks in Pure Sour Cream: 49¢. Now her hands are empty, not a ring or a bracelet, bare as God made them, and I wonder where the money's coming from. Still with her prim look she lifts a folded dollar bill out of the hollow at the center of her nubbled pink top. The jar went heavy in my hand. Really, I thought that was so cute.

Then everybody's luck begins to run out. Lengel comes in from haggling with a truck full of cabbages on the lot and is about to scuttle into the door marked MANAGER behind which he hides all day when the girls touch his eye. Lengel's pretty dreary, teaches Sunday school and the rest, but he doesn't miss that much. He comes over and says, "Girls, this isn't the beach."

Queenie blushes, though maybe it's just a brush of sunburn I was noticing for the first time, now that she was so close. "My mother asked me to pick up a jar of herring snacks." Her voice kind of startled me, the way voices do when you see the people first, coming out so flat and dumb yet kind of tony, too, the way it tickled over "pick up" and "snacks." All of a sudden I slid right down her voice into her living room. Her father and the other men were standing around in ice-cream coats and bow ties and the women were in sandals picking up herring snacks on toothpicks off a big glass plate and they were all holding drinks the color of water with olives and sprigs of mint in them. When my parents have somebody over they get lemonade and if it's a real racy affair Schlitz in tall glasses with "They'll Do It Every Time" cartoons stencilled on.

"That's all right," Lengel said. "But this isn't the beach." His repeating this struck me as funny, as if it had just occurred to him, and he had been thinking all these years the A & P was a great big dune and he was the head lifeguard. He didn't like my smiling—as I say he doesn't miss much—but he concentrates on giving the girls that sad Sunday-school-superintendent stare.

Queenie's blush is no sunburn now, and the plump one in plaid, that I liked better from the back—a really sweet can—pipes up, "We weren't doing any shopping. We just came in for the one thing."

"That makes no difference." Lengel tells her, and I could see from the way his eyes went that he hadn't noticed she was wearing a two-piece before. "We want you decently dressed when you come in here."

"We *are* decent," Queenie says suddenly, her lower lip pushing, getting sore now that she remembers her place, a place from which the crowd that runs the A & P must look pretty crummy. Fancy Herring Snacks flashed in her very blue eyes.

"Girls, I don't want to argue with you. After this come in here with your shoulders covered. It's our policy." He turns his back. That's policy for you. Policy is what the kingpins want. What the others want is juvenile delinquency.

All this while, the customers had been showing up with their carts but, you know, sheep, seeing a scene, they had all bunched up on Stokesie, who shook open a paper bag as gently as peeling a peach, not wanting to miss a word. I could feel in the silence everybody getting nervous, most of all Lengel, who asks me, "Sammy, have you rung up their purchase?"

I thought and said "No" but it wasn't about that I was thinking. I go through the punches, 4, 9, GROC. TOT—it's more complicated than you think, and after you do it often enough, it begins to make a little song, that you hear words to, in my case "Hello (*bing*) there, you (*gung*) hap-py *pee*-pul (*splat*)!"—the *splat* being the drawer flying out. I uncrease the bill, tenderly as you may imagine, it just having come from between the two smoothest scoops of vanilla I have ever known were there, and pass a half and a penny into her narrow pink palm, and nestle the herrings in a bag and twist its neck and hand it over, all the time thinking.

The girls, and who'd blame them, are in a hurry to get out, so I say "I quit" to Lengel quick enough for them to hear, hoping they'll stop and watch me, their unsuspected hero. They keep right on going, into the electric eye; the door flies open they flicker across the lot to their car. Queenie and Plaid and Big Tall Goony-Goony (not that as raw material she was so bad), leaving me with Lengel and a kink in his eyebrow.

"Did you say something, Sammy?"

"I said I quit."

"I thought you did."

"You didn't have to embarrass them."

"It was they who were embarrassing us."

I started to say something that came out "Fiddle-de-doo." It's a saying of my grandmother's, and I know she would have been pleased.

"I don't think you know what you're saying," Lengel said.

"I know you don't," I said, "But I do." I pull the bow at the back of my apron and start shrugging it off my shoulders. A couple customers that had been heading for my slot begin to knock against each other, like scared pigs in a chute.

Lengel sighs and begins to look very patient and old and gray. He's been a friend of my parents for years. "Sammy, you don't want to do this to your Mom and Dad," he tells me. It's true, I don't. But it seems to me that once you begin a gesture it's fatal not to go through with it. I fold the apron, "Sammy" stitched in red on the pocket, and put it on the counter, and drop the bow tie on top of it. The bow tie is theirs, if you've ever wondered. "You'll feel this for the rest of your life," Lengel says, and I know that's true, too, but remembering how he made that pretty girl blush makes me so scrunchy inside I punch the No Sale tab and the machine whirs "peepul" and the drawer splats out. One advantage of this scene taking place in summer, I can follow this up with a clean exit, there's no fumbling around getting your coat and galoshes, I just saunter into the electric eye in my white shirt that my mother ironed the night before, and the door heaves itself open, and outside the sunshine is skating around on the asphalt.

I look around for my girls, but they're gone, of course. There wasn't anybody but some young married screaming with her children about some candy they didn't get by the door of a powder-blue Falcon station wagon. Looking back in the big windows, over the bags of peat moss and aluminum lawn furniture stacked on the pavement, I could see Lengel in my place in the slot, checking the sheep through. His face was dark gray and his back stiff, as if he'd just had an injection of iron, and my stomach kind of fell as I felt how hard the world was going to be to me hereafter.

Kicking the Leaves

DONALD HALL

I

Kicking the leaves, October, as we walk home together
from the game, in Ann Arbor,
on a day the color of soot, rain in the air;
I kick at the leaves of maples,
reds of seventy different shades, yellow
like old paper; and poplar leaves, fragile and pale;
and elm leaves, flags of a doomed race.
I kick at the leaves, making a sound I remember
as the leaves swirl upward from my boot,
and flutter; and I remember
Octobers walking to school in Connecticut,
wearing corduroy knickers that swished
with a sound like leaves; and a Sunday buying
a cup of cider at a roadside stand
on a dirt road in New Hampshire; and kicking the leaves,
autumn 1955 in Massachusetts, knowing
my father would die when the leaves were gone.

II

Each fall in New Hampshire, on the farm
where my mother grew up, a girl in the country,
my grandfather and grandmother
finished the autumn work, taking the last vegetables in
from the cold fields, canning, storing roots and apples
in the cellar under the kitchen. Then my grandfather

raked leaves against the house
as the final chore of autumn.
One November I drove up from college to see them.
We pulled big rakes, as we did when we hayed in summer,
pulling leaves against the granite foundation
around the house, on every side of the house,
and then, to keep them in place, we cut pine boughs
and laid them across the leaves
green on red, until the house
was tucked up, ready for snow
that would freeze the leaves in tight, like a stiff skirt.
Then we puffed through the shed door,
taking off boots and overcoats, slapping our hands,
and sat in the kitchen, rocking, and drank
black coffee my grandmother made,
three of us sitting together, silent, in gray November.

III

One Saturday when I was little, before the war,
my father came home at noon, from his half day at the office,
and wore his Bates sweater, black on red,
with the crossed hockey sticks on it, and raked beside me
in the back yard, and tumbled in the leaves with me,
laughing, and carried me, laughing, my hair full of leaves,
to he kitchen window
where my mother could see us, and smile, and motion
to set me down, afraid I would fall and be hurt.

IV

Kicking the leaves today, as we walk home together
from the game, among crowds of people
with their bright pennants, as many and bright as leaves,
my daughter's hair is the red-yellow color
of birch leaves, and she is tall like a birch,
growing up, fifteen, growing older; and my son

New England

flamboyant as maple, twenty,
visits from college, and walks ahead of us, his step
springing, impatient to travel
the woods of the earth. Now I watch them
from a pile of leaves beside this clapboard house
in Ann Arbor, across from the school
where they learned to read,
as their shapes grow small with distance, waving,
and I know that I
diminish them, not them, as I go first
into the leaves, taking
the step they will follow, Octobers and years from now.

V

This year the poems came back, when the leaves fell.
Kicking the leaves, I heard the leaves tell stories,
remembering, and therefore looking ahead, and building
the house of dying. I looked up into the maples
and found them, the vowels of bright desire.
I thought they had gone forever
while the bird sang I love you, I love you,
and shook its black head
from side to side, and its red eye with no lid,
through years of winter, cold
as the taste of chicken wire, the music of cinder block.

VI

Kicking the leaves, I uncover the lids of graves.
My grandfather died at seventy-seven, in March
when the sap was running, and waits in a northern grave
where elms still drop their leaves;
and I think of my father again, dead twenty years,
coughing himself to death, at fifty-two, in the house
in the suburbs. Oh, how we flung

64

leaves in the air! How they tumbled and fluttered around us,
like slowly cascading water, when we walked together
in Hamden, before the war, when Johnson's Pond
had not surrendered to houses, the two of us
hand in hand, and in the wet air the smell of leaves
burning;
and in six years I will be fifty-two.

VII

Now I fall, now I leap and fall
to feel the leaves crush under my body, to feel my body
buoyant in the ocean of leaves, rocking like the ocean.
Oh, this delicious falling into the arms of leaves,
into the soft laps of leaves!
Face down, I swim into the leaves, feathery,
breathing the acrid odor of maple, swooping
in long glides to the bottom of October,
where the farm lies curled against winter, and soup steams
its breath of onion and carrot
onto damp curtains and windows; and past the windows
the tall bare maple trunks and branches, the oak
with its few brown weathery remnant leaves,
and the pine trees, holding their green.
Now I leap and fall, exultant, recovering
from death, on account of death, in accord with the dead,
the smell and taste of leaves again,
and the pleasure, the only long pleasure, of taking a place
in the story of leaves.

The Midwest

The midwestern small town has been called the archetypal small town—its virtues and vices are those of small towns everywhere. Perhaps that is why so many writers have focused on this region in particular; here, they reasoned, one could identify a prototypical small town that would become a universal statement of small-town life in America. One could easily dispute this position, but the fact remains that during the twentieth century, writers have criticized the provincialism and intellectual sterility of small-town life—and it was the midwestern small town that bore the brunt of their attacks.

Edgar Lee Masters gives us *Spoon River Anthology*, a collection of "auto-epitaphs" in which the ghosts of a small midwestern village recount the events and feelings that shaped their lives. Masters' satiric, realistic portraits are sharp insights into the frustrations and failures which are reflected, at least in part, by the drab surroundings of the small-town environment.

Similarly, H. L. Mencken's essay "The Libido for the Ugly," is a stinging indictment of the small town landscape. He establishes a relationship between the architecture of a decaying Pittsburgh suburb and the "architecture" of the human minds and hearts that gave rise to it.

Willa Cather's "The Sculptor's Funeral" is also about the "aesthetics" of small-town life, and the confrontation of small-town midwestern attitudes and urban eastern ones. More damning, perhaps, is Sinclair Lewis' *Main Street*, in which the pettiness and monotony of small-town life are vividly, and often painfully, evoked. "I tell you it's dull," protagonist Carol Kennicott complains to a sympathetic

visitor from the outside world. "Dull!" Gopher Prairie, the fictional town based on Lewis' hometown of Sauk Center, Minnesota, became for literary America a symbol of the sterility and rigidity of small towns throughout the country.

Sherwood Anderson takes a gentler view of small-town life in the selections from "The American Small Town" which follow; and in a piece called "The Age" from his *Memoirs,* Anderson speaks of his own hometown of Clyde, Ohio, as a "fair and sweet town." William Allen White's memorial to his daughter, "Mary White," is at the same time a moving tribute to the fairness and sweetness of all those who mourned her, the entire population of Emporia, Kansas. Poet Vachel Lindsay praises the beauty and serenity of village life in his poem, "The Illinois Village"; it is a paean to the joys of the simple life.

Joyce Carol Oates' story "Normal Love" presents a disturbing picture of contemporary small-town life seen through the eyes of a midwestern housewife, who reveals the controlled anguish of her own existence against the backdrop of her alienation—from husband, family, and community. The story is unsettling because in it we witness the faltering both of personal as well as community relationships.

FROM *Spoon River Anthology*

EDGAR LEE MASTERS

MINERVA JONES

I am Minerva, the village poetess,
Hooted at, jeered at by the Yahoos of the street
For my heavy body, cock-eye, and rolling walk,
And all the more when "Butch" Weldy
Captured me after a brutal hunt.
He left me to my fate with Doctor Meyers;
And I sank into death, growing numb from the feet up,
Like one stepping deeper and deeper into a stream of ice.
Will some one go to the village newspaper,
And gather into a book the verses I wrote?—
I thirsted so for love!
I hungered so for life!

"INDIGNATION" JONES

You would not believe, would you,
That I came from good Welsh stock?
That I was purer blooded than the white trash here?
And of more direct lineage than the New Englanders
And Virginians of Spoon River?
You would not believe that I had been to school
And read some books.
You saw me only as a run-down man,
With matted hair and beard
And ragged clothes.
Sometimes a man's life turns into a cancer
From being bruised and continually bruised,
And swells into a purplish mass,
Like growths on stalks of corn.
Here was I, a carpenter, mired in a bog of life
Into which I walked, thinking it was a meadow,
With a slattern for a wife, and poor Minerva, my daughter,
Whom you tormented and drove to death.
So I crept, crept, like a snail through the days
Of my life.
No more you hear my footsteps in the morning,
Resounding on the hollow sidewalk,
Going to the grocery store for a little corn meal
And a nickel's worth of bacon.

DOCTOR MEYERS

No other man, unless it was Doc Hill,
Did more for people in this town than I.
And all the weak, the halt, the improvident
And those who could not pay flocked to me.
I was good-hearted, easy Doctor Meyers.
I was healthy, happy, in comfortable fortune,
Blest with a congenial mate, my children raised,
All wedded, doing well in the world.
And then one night, Minerva, the poetess,
Came to me in her trouble, crying.
I tried to help her out—she died—
They indicted me, the newspapers disgraced me,
My wife perished of a broken heart.
And pneumonia finished me.

MRS. MEYERS

He protested all his life long
The newspapers lied about him villainously;
That he was not at fault for Minerva's fall,
But only tried to help her.
Poor soul so sunk in sin he could not see
That even trying to help her, as he called it,
He had broken the law human and divine.
Passers by, an ancient admonition to you:
If your ways would be ways of pleasantness,
And all your pathways peace,
Love God and keep his commandments.

"BUTCH" WELDY

After I got religion and steadied down
They gave me a job in the canning works,
And every morning I had to fill
The tank in the yard with gasoline,
That fed the blow-fires in the sheds
To heat the soldering irons.
And I mounted a rickety ladder to do it,
Carrying buckets full of the stuff.
One morning, as I stood there pouring,
The air grew still and seemed to heave,
And I shot up as the tank exploded,
And down I came with both legs broken,
And my eyes burned crisp as a couple of eggs.
For someone left a blow-fire going,
And something sucked the flame in the tank.
The Circuit Judge said whoever did it
Was a fellow-servant of mine, and so
Old Rhodes' son didn't have to pay me.
And I sat on the witness stand as blind
As Jack the Fiddler, saying over and over,
"I didn't know him at all."

CHAPTER THREE OF *Main Street* *

SINCLAIR LEWIS

Under the rolling clouds of the prairie a moving mass of steel. An irritable clank and rattle beneath a prolonged roar. The sharp scent of oranges cutting the soggy smell of unbathed people and ancient baggage.

Towns as planless as a scattering of pasteboard boxes on an attic floor. The stretch of faded gold stubble broken only by clumps of willows encircling white houses and red barns.

No. 7, the way train, grumbling through Minnesota, imperceptibly climbing the giant tableland that slopes in a thousand-mile rise from hot Mississippi bottoms to the Rockies.

It is September, hot, very dusty.

There is no smug Pullman attached to the train, and the day coaches of the East are replaced by free chair cars, with each seat cut into two adjustable plush chairs, the head-rests covered with doubtful linen towels. Halfway down the car is a semi-partition of carved oak columns, but the aisle is of bare, splintery, grease-blackened wood. There is no porter, no pillows, no provision for beds, but all today and all tonight they will ride in this long steel box—farmers with perpetually tired wives and children who seem all to be of the same age; workmen going to new jobs; traveling salesmen with derbies and freshly shined shoes.

They are parched and cramped, the lines of their hands filled with grime; they go to sleep curled in distorted attitudes, heads against the window-panes or propped on rolled coats on seat-arms, and legs thrust into the aisle. They do not read; apparently they do not think. They wait. An early-wrinkled, young-old mother, moving as though her joints were dry, opens a suit-case in which are seen creased blouses, a pair of slippers worn through at the toes, a bottle of patent medicine, a tin cup, a paper-covered book about dreams which the news-butcher has coaxed her into buying. She

*Parts I-III.

brings out a graham cracker which she feeds to a baby lying flat on a seat and wailing hopelessly. Most of the crumbs drop on the red plush of the seat, and the woman sighs and tries to brush them away, but they leap up impishly and fall back on the plush.

A soiled man and woman munch sandwiches and throw the crusts on the floor. A large brick-colored Norwegian takes off his shoes, grunts in relief, and props his feet in their thick gray socks against the seat in front of him.

An old woman whose toothless mouth shuts like a mud-turtle's, and whose hair is not so much white as yellow like moldy linen, with bands of pink skull apparent between the tresses, anxiously lifts her bag, opens it, peers in, closes it, puts it under the seat, and hastily picks it up and opens it and hides it all over again. The bag is full of treasures and of memories: a leather buckle, an ancient band-concert program, scraps of ribbon, lace, satin. In the aisle beside her is an extremely indignant parrakeet in a cage.

Two facing seats, overflowing with a Slovene iron-miner's family, are littered with shoes, dolls, whisky bottles, bundles wrapped in newspapers, a sewing bag. The oldest boy takes a mouth-organ out of his coat pocket, wipes the tobacco crumbs off, and plays "Marching through Georgia" till every head in the car begins to ache.

The news-butcher comes through selling chocolate bars and lemon drops. A girl-child ceaselessly trots down to the water-cooler and back to her seat. The stiff paper envelope which she uses for cup drips in the aisle as she goes, and on each trip she stumbles over the feet of a carpenter, who grunts, "Ouch! Look out!"

The dust-caked doors are open, and from the smoking-car drifts back a visible blue line of stinging tobacco smoke, and with it a crackle of laughter over the story which the young man in the bright blue suit and lavender tie and light yellow shoes has just told to the squat man in garage overalls.

The smell grows constantly thicker, more stale.

II

To each of the passengers his seat was his temporary home, and most of the passengers were slatternly housekeepers. But one seat looked clean and deceptively cool. In it were an obviously prosperous man and a black-haired, fine-skinned girl whose pumps rested on an immaculate horsehide bag.

They were Dr. Will Kennicott and his bride, Carol.

They had been married at the end of a year of conversational courtship, and they were on their way to Gopher Prairie after a wedding journey in the Colorado mountains.

The hordes of the way-train were not altogether new to Carol. She had seen them on trips from St. Paul to Chicago. But now that they had become her own people, to bathe and encourage and adorn, she had an acute and uncomfortable interest in them. They distressed her. They were so stolid. She had always maintained that there is no American peasantry, and she sought now to defend her faith by seeing imagination and enterprise in the young Swedish farmers, and in a traveling man working over his order-blanks. But the older people, Yankees as well as Norwegians, Germans, Finns, Canucks, had settled into submission to poverty. They were peasants, she groaned.

"Isn't there any way of waking them up? What would happen if they understood scientific agriculture?" she begged of Kennicott, her hand groping for his.

It had been a transforming honeymoon. She had been frightened to discover how tumultuous a feeling could be roused in her. Will had been lordly—stalwart, jolly, impressively competent in making camp, tender and understanding through the hours when they had lain side by side in a tent pitched among pines high up a lonely mountain spur.

His hand swallowed hers as he started from thoughts of the practise to which he was returning. "These people? Wake 'em up? What for? They're happy."

"But they're so provincial. No, that isn't what I mean. They're—oh, so sunk in the mud."

"Look here, Carrie. You want to get over your city idea that because a man's pants aren't pressed, he's a fool. These farmers are mighty keen and up-and-coming."

"I know! That's what hurts. Life seems so hard for them—these lonely farms and this gritty train."

"Oh, they don't mind it. Besides, things are changing. The auto, the telephone, rural free delivery; they're bringing the farmers in closer touch with the town. Takes time, you know, to change a wilderness like this was fifty years ago. But already, why, they can hop into the Ford or the Overland and get in to the movies on Saturday evening quicker than you could get down to 'em by trolley in St. Paul."

"But if it's these towns we've been passing that the farmers run to for relief from their bleakness—— Can't you understand? Just *look* at them!"

Kennicott was amazed. Ever since childhood he had seen these towns from trains on this same line. He grumbled, "Why, what's the matter with 'em? Good hustling burgs. It would astonish you to know how much wheat and rye and corn and potatoes they ship in a year."

"But they're so ugly."

"I'll admit they aren't comfy like Gopher Prairie. But give 'em time."

"What's the use of giving them time unless some one has desire and training enough to plan them? Hundreds of factories trying to make attractive motor cars, but these towns—left to chance. No! That can't be true. It must have take genius to make them so scrawny!"

"Oh, they're not so bad," was all he answered. He pretended that his hand was the cat and hers the mouse. For the first time she tolerated him rather than encouraged him. She was staring out at Schoenstrom, a hamlet of perhaps a hundred and fifty inhabitants, at which the train was stopping.

A bearded German and his pucker-mouthed wife tugged their enormous imitation-leather satchel from under a seat and waddled out. The station agent hoisted a dead calf aboard the baggage-car. There were no other visible activities in Schoenstrom. In the quiet of the halt, Carol could hear a horse kicking his stall, a carpenter shingling a roof.

The business-center of Schoenstrom took up one side of one block, facing the railroad. It was a row of one-story shops covered with galvanized iron, or with clapboards painted red and bilious yellow. The buildings were as ill-assorted, as temporary-looking, as a mining-camp street in the motion-pictures. The railroad station was a one-room frame box, a mirey cattle-pen on one side and a crimson wheat-elevator on the other. The elevator, with its cupola on the ridge of a shingled roof, resembled a broad-shouldered man with a small, vicious, pointed head. The only habitable structures to be seen were the florid red-brick Catholic church and rectory at the end of Main Street.

Carol picked at Kennicott's sleeve. "You wouldn't call this a not-so-bad town, would you?"

"These Dutch burgs *are* kind of slow. Still, at that—— See that fellow coming out of the general store there, getting into the big car? I met him once. He owns about half the town, besides the store. Rauskukle, his name is. He owns a lot of mortgages, and he gambles in farm-lands. Good nut on him, that fellow. Why, they say he's worth three or four hundred thousand dollars! Got a dandy great big yellow brick house with tiled walks and a garden and everything, other end of town—can't see it from here—I've gone past it when I've driven through here. Yes sir!"

"Then, if he has all that, there's no excuse whatever for this place! If his three hundred thousand went back into the town, where it belongs, they could burn up these shacks, and build a dream-village, a jewel! Why do the farmers and the town-people let the Baron keep it?"

"I must say I don't quite get you sometimes, Carrie. Let him? They can't help themselves! He's a dumm old Dutchman, and probably the priest can twist him around his finger, but when it comes to picking good farming land, he's a regular wiz!"

"I see. He's their symbol of beauty. The town erects him, instead of erecting buildings."

"Honestly, don't know what you're driving at. You're kind of played out, after this long trip. You'll feel better when you get home and have a good bath, and put on the blue negligée. That's some vampire costume, you witch!"

He squeezed her arm, looked at her knowingly.

They moved on from the desert stillness of the Schoenstrom station. The train creaked, banged, swayed. The air was nauseatingly thick. Kennicott turned her face from the window, rested her head on his shoulder. She was coaxed from her unhappy mood. But she came out of it unwillingly and when Kennicott was satisfied that he had corrected all her worries and had opened a magazine of saffron detective stories, she sat upright.

Here—she meditated—is the newest empire of the world; the Northern Middlewest; a land of dairy herds and exquisite lakes, of new automobiles and tar-paper shanties and silos like red towers, of clumsy speech and a hope that is boundless. An empire which feeds a quarter of the world—yet its work is merely begun. They are pioneers, these sweaty wayfarers, for all their telephones and bank-accounts and automatic pianos and co-operative leagues. And for all its fat richness, theirs is a pioneer land. What is its future? she wondered. A future of cities and factory smut where now are loping empty fields? Homes universal and secure? Or placid châteaux ringed with sullen huts? Youth free to find knowledge and laughter? Willingness to sift the sanctified lies? Or creamy-skinned fat women, smeared with grease and chalk, gorgeous in the skins of beasts and the bloody feathers of slain

81

birds, playing bridge with puffy pink-nailed jeweled fingers, women who after much expenditure of labor and bad temper still grotesquely resemble their own flatulent lap-dogs? The ancient stale inequalities, or something different in history, unlike the tedious maturity of other empires? What future and what hope?

Carol's head ached with the riddle.

She saw the prairie, flat in giant patches or rolling in long hummocks. The width and bigness of it, which had expanded her spirit an hour ago, began to frighten her. It spread out so; it went on so uncontrollably; she could never know it. Kennicott was closeted in his detective story. With the loneliness which comes most depressingly in the midst of many people she tried to forget problems, to look at the prairie objectively.

The grass beside the railroad had been burnt over; it was a smudge prickly with charred stalks of weeds. Beyond the undeviating barbed-wire fences were clumps of golden rod. Only this thin hedge shut them off from the plains—shorn wheat-lands of autumn, a hundred acres to a field, prickly and gray near-by but in the blurred distance like tawny velvet stretched over dipping hillocks. The long rows of wheatshocks marched like soldiers in worn yellow tabards. The newly plowed fields were black banners fallen on the distant slope. It was a martial immensity, vigorous, a little harsh, unsoftened by kindly gardens.

The expanse was relieved by clumps of oaks with patches of short wild grass; and every mile or two was a chain of cobalt slews, with the flicker of blackbirds' wings across them.

All this working land was turned into exuberance by the light. The sunshine was dizzy on open stubble; shadows from immense cumulus clouds were forever sliding across low mounds; and the sky was wider and loftier and more resolutely blue than the sky of cities . . . she declared.

"It's a glorious country; a land to be big in," she crooned.

Then Kennicott startled her by chuckling, "D' you realize the town after the next is Gopher Prairie? Home!"

III

That one word—home—it terrified her. Had she really bound herself to live, inescapably, in this town called Gopher Prairie? And this thick man beside her, who dared to define her future, he was a stranger! She turned in her seat, stared at him. Who was he? Why was he sitting with her? He wasn't of her kind! His neck was heavy; his speech was heavy; he was twelve or thirteen years older than she; and about him was none of the magic of shared adventures and eagerness. She could not believe that she had ever slept in his arms. That was one of the dreams which you had but did not officially admit.

She told herself how good he was, how dependable and understanding. She touched his ear, smoothed the plane of his solid jaw, and, turning away again, concentrated upon liking his town. It wouldn't be like these barren settlements. It couldn't be! Why, it had three thousand population. That was a great many people. There would be six hundred houses or more. And—— The lakes near it would be so lovely. She'd seen them in the photographs. They had looked charming . . . hadn't they?

As the train left Wahkeenyan she began nervously to watch for the lakes—the entrance to all her future life. But when she discovered them, to the left of the track, her only impression of them was that they resembled the photographs.

A mile from Gopher Prairie the track mounts a curving low ridge, and she could see the town as a whole. With a passionate jerk she pushed up the window, looked out, the arched fingers of her left hand trembling on the sill, her right hand at her breast.

And she saw that Gopher Prairie was merely an enlargement of all the hamlets which they had been passing. Only to the eyes of a Kennicott was it exceptional. The huddled low wooden houses broke the plains scarcely more than would a hazel thicket. The fields swept up to it, past it. It was unprotected and unprotecting; there was no dignity in it nor any hope of greatness. Only the tall red grain-elevator and a few tinny church-steeples rose from the mass. It was a frontier camp. It was not a place to live in, not possibly, not conceivably.

The people—they'd be as drab as their houses, as flat as their fields. She couldn't stay here. She would have to wrench loose from this man, and flee.

She peeped at him. She was at once helpless before his mature fixity, and touched by his excitement as he sent his magazine skittering along the aisle, stooped for their bags, came up with flushed face, and gloated, "Here we are!"

She smiled loyally, and looked away. The train was entering town. The houses on the outskirts were dusky old red mansions with wooden frills, or gaunt frame shelters like grocery boxes, or new bungalows with concrete foundations imitating stone.

Now the train was passing the elevator, the grim storage-tanks for oil, a creamery, a lumber-yard, a stock-yard muddy and trampled and stinking. Now they were stopping at a squat red frame station, the platform crowded with unshaven farmers and with loafers—unadventurous people with dead eyes. She was here. She could not go on. It was the end—the end of the world. She sat with closed eyes, longing to push past Kennicott, hide somewhere in the train, flee on toward the Pacific.

Something large arose in her soul and commanded, "Stop it! Stop being a whining baby!" She stood up quickly; she said, "Isn't it wonderful to be here at last!"

He trusted her so. She would make herself like the place. And she was going to do tremendous things——

She followed Kennicott and the bobbing ends of the two bags which he carried. They were held back by the slow line of disembarking passengers. She reminded herself that she was actually at the dramatic moment of the bride's homecoming. She ought to feel exalted. She felt nothing at all except irritation at their slow progress toward the door.

Kennicott stooped to peer through the windows. He shyly exulted:

"Look! Look! There's a bunch come down to welcome us! Sam Clark and the missus and Dave Dyer and Jack Elder, and, yes sir, Harry Haydock and Juanita, and a whole crowd! I guess they see us now. Yuh, yuh sure, they see us! See 'em waving!"

She obediently bent her head to look out at them. She had hold of herself. She was ready to love them. But she was embarrassed by the heartiness of the cheering group. From the vestibule she waved to them, but she clung a second to the sleeve of the brakeman who helped her down before she had the courage to dive into the cataract of hand-shaking people, people whom she could not tell apart. She had the impression that all the men had coarse voices, large damp hands, toothbrush mustaches, bald spots, and Masonic watch-charms.

She knew that they were welcoming her. Their hands, their smiles, their shouts, their affectionate eyes overcame her. She stammered, "Thank you, oh, thank you!"

One of the men was clamoring at Kennicott, "I brought my machine down to take you home, doc."

"Fine business, Sam!" cried Kennicott; and, to Carol, "Let's jump in. That big Paige over there. Some boat, too, believe me! Sam can show speed to any of these Marmons from Minneapolis!"

Only when she was in the motor car did she distinguish the three people who were to accompany them. The owner, now at the wheel, was the essence of decent self-satisfaction; a baldish, largish, level-eyed man, rugged of neck but sleek and round of face—face like the back of a spoon bowl. He was chuckling at her, "Have you got us all straight yet?"

"Course she has! Trust Carrie to get things straight and get 'em darn quick! I bet she could tell you every date in history!" boasted her husband.

But the man looked at her reassuringly and with a certainty that he was a person whom she could trust she confessed, "As a matter of fact I haven't got anybody straight."

"Course you haven't, child. Well, I'm Sam Clark, dealer in hardware, sporting goods, cream separators, and almost any kind of heavy junk you can think of. You can call me Sam—anyway, I'm going to call you Carrie, seein' 's you've been and gone and married this poor fish of a bum medic that we keep round here." Carol smiled lavishly, and wished that she called people by their given names more easily. "The fat cranky lady back there beside you, who is pretending that she can't hear me giving her away, is Mrs. Sam'l Clark; and this hungry-looking squirt up here beside me is Dave Dyer, who keeps his drug store running by not filling your hubby's prescriptions right—fact you might say he's the guy that put the 'shun' in 'prescription.' So! Well, leave us take the bonny bride home. Say, doc, I'll sell you the Candersen place for three thousand plunks. Better be thinking about building a new home for Carrie. Prettiest *Frau* in G. P., if you asks me!"

Contentedly Sam Clark drove off, in the heavy traffic of three Fords and the Minniemashie House Free 'Bus.

"I shall like Mr. Clark . . . I *can't* call him 'Sam'! They're all so friendly." She glanced at the houses; tried not to see what she saw; gave way in: "Why do these stories lie so? They always make the bride's homecoming a bower of roses. Complete trust in noble spouse. Lies about marriage. I'm *not* changed. And this town—O my God! I can't go through with it. This junk-heap!"

Her husband bent over her. "You look like you were in a brown study. Scared? I don't expect you to think Gopher Prairie is a paradise, after St. Paul. I don't expect you to be crazy about it, at first. But you'll come to like it so much—life's so free here and best people on earth."

She whispered to him (while Mrs. Clark considerately turned away), "I love you for understanding. I'm just—I'm beastly over-sensitive. Too many books. It's my lack of shoulder-muscles and sense. Give me time, dear."

"You bet! All the time you want!"

She laid the back of his hand against her cheek, snuggled near him. She was ready for her new home.

Kennicott had told her that, with his widowed mother as housekeeper, he had occupied an old house, "but nice and roomy, and well-heated, best furnace I could find on the market." His mother had left Carol her love, and gone back to Lac-qui-Meurt.

It would be wonderful, she exulted, not to have to live in Other People's Houses, but to make her own shrine. She held his hand tightly and stared ahead as the car swung round a corner and stopped in the street before a prosaic frame house in a small parched lawn.

The Libido for the Ugly

H. L. MENCKEN

On a Winter day some years ago, coming out of Pittsburgh on one of the expresses of the Pennsylvania Railroad, I rolled eastward for an hour through the coal and steel towns of Westmoreland county. It was familiar ground; boy and man, I had been through it often before. But somehow I had never quite sensed its appalling desolation. Here was the very heart of industrial America, the center of its most lucrative and characteristic activity, the boast and pride of the richest and grandest nation ever seen on earth—and here was a scene so dreadfully hideous, so intolerably bleak and forlorn that it reduced the whole aspiration of man to a macabre and depressing joke. Here was wealth beyond computation, almost beyond imagination—and here were human habitations so abominable that they would have disgraced a race of alley cats.

I am not speaking of mere filth. One expects steel towns to be dirty. What I allude to is the unbroken and agonizing ugliness, the sheer revolting monstrousness, of every house in sight. From East Liberty to Greensburg, a distance of twenty-five miles, there was not one in sight from the train that did not insult and lacerate the eye. Some were so bad, and they were among the most pretentious—churches, stores, warehouses, and the like— that they were downright startling; one blinked before them as one blinks before a man with his face shot away. A few linger in memory, horrible even there: a crazy little church just west of Jeannette, set like a dormer-window on the side of a bare leprous hill; the headquarters of the Veterans of Foreign Wars at another forlorn town, a steel stadium like a huge rat-trap somewhere further down the line. But most of all I recall the general effect—of hideousness without a break. There was not a single decent house within eye-range from the Pittsburgh suburbs to the Greensburg yards. There was not one that was not misshapen, and there was not one that was not shabby.

The country itself is not uncomely despite the grime of the endless mills. It is, in form, a narrow river valley, with deep gullies running up into the hills. It is thickly settled, but not noticeably overcrowded. There is still plenty of room for building, even in the larger towns, and there are very few solid blocks. Nearly every house, big and little, has space on all four sides. Obviously, if there were architects of any professional sense or dignity in the region, they would have perfected a chalet to hug the hillsides—a chalet with a high-pitched roof, to throw off the heavy Winter snows, but still essentially a low and clinging building, wider than it was tall. But what have they done? They have taken as their model a brick set on end. This they have converted into a thing of dingy clapboards, with a narrow, low-pitched roof. And the whole they have set upon thin, preposterous brick piers. By the hundreds and thousands these abominable houses cover the bare hillsides like gravestones in some gigantic and decaying cemetery. On their deep sides they are three, four and even five stories high; on their low sides they bury themselves swinishly in the sand. Not a fifth of them are perpendicular. They lean this way and that, hanging on to their bases percariously. And one and all they are streaked in grime, with dead and eczematous patches of paint peeping through the streaks.

Now and then there is a house of brick. But what brick! When it is new it is the color of a fried egg. When it has taken on the patina of the mills it is the color of an egg long past all hope or caring. Was it necesary to adopt that shocking color? No more than it was necessary to set all the houses on end. Red brick, even in a steel town, ages with some dignity. Let it become downright black, and it is still sightly, especially if its trimmings are of white stone, with soot in the depths of the high spots washed by the rain. But in Westmoreland they prefer that uremic yellow, and so they have the most loathsome towns and villages ever seen by mortal eye.

I award this championship only after laborious research and incessant prayer. I have seen, I believe, all of the most unlovely towns of the world; they are all to be found in the United States. I have seen the mill towns of decomposing New England and the desert towns of Utah, Arizona and Texas. I am familiar with the back streets of Newark, Brooklyn and Chicago, and have made scientific explorations to Camden, N. J., and Newport News, Va. Safe in a Pullman, I have whirled through the gloomy, God-forsaken villages of Iowa and Kansas, and the malarious tide-water hamlets of Georgia. I have been to Bridgeport, Conn., and to Los Angeles. But nowhere on this earth, at home or abroad, have I seen anything to compare to the villages that huddle along the line of the Pensylvania from the Pittsburgh yards to Greensburg. They are incomparable in color, and they are incomparable in design. It is as if some titanic and aberrant genius, uncompromisingly inimical to man, had devoted all the ingenuity of Hell to the making of them. They show grotesqueries of ugliness that, in retrospect, become almost diabolical. One cannot imagine mere human beings concocting such dreadful things, and one can scarcely imagine human beings bearing life in them.

Are they so frightful because the valley is full of foreigners—dull, insensate brutes, with no love of beauty in them? Then why didn't these foreigners set up similar abominations in the countries that they came from? You will, in fact, find nothing of the sort in Europe—save perhaps in the more putrid parts of England. There is scarcely an ugly village on the whole Continent. The peasants, however poor, somehow manage to make themselves graceful and charming habitations, even in Spain. But in the American village and small town the pull is always toward ugliness, and in that Westmoreland valley it has ben yielded to with an eagerness bordering upon passion. It is incredible that mere ignorance should have achieved such masterpieces of horror.

On certain levels of the American race, indeed, there seems to be a positive libido for the ugly, as on other and less Christian levels there is a libido for the beautiful. It is impossible to put down the wallpaper that defaces the average American home of the lower middle class to mere inadvertence, or to the obscene humor of the manufacturers. Such ghastly designs, it must be obvious, give a genuine delight to a certain type of mind. They meet, in some unfathomable way, its obscure and unintelligible demands. They caress it as "The Palms" caress it, or the art of the movie, or jazz. The taste of them is as enigmatical and yet as common as the taste of dogmatic theology and the poetry of Edgar A. Guest.

Thus I suspect (though confessedly without knowing) that the vast majority of the honest folk of Westmoreland county, and especially the 100% Americans among them, actually admire the houses they live in, and are proud of them. For the same money they could get vastly better ones, but they prefer what they have got. Certainly there was no pressure upon the Veterans of Foreign Wars to choose the dreadful edifice that bears their banner, for there are plenty of vacant buildings along the track-side, and some of them are appreciably better. They might, indeed, have built a better one of their own. But they chose that clapboarded horror with their eyes open, and having chosen it, they let it mellow into its present shocking depravity. They like it as it is: beside it, the Parthenon would no doubt offend them. In precisely the same way the authors of the rat-trap stadium that I have mentioned made a deliberate choice. After painfully designing and erecting it, they made it perfect in their own sight by putting a completely impossible pent-house, painted a staring yellow, on top of it. The effect is that of a fat woman with a black eye. It is that of a Presbyterian grinning. But they like it.

Here is something that the psychologists have so far neglected: the love of ugliness for its own sake, the lust to make the world intolerable. Its habitat is the United States. Out of the melting pot emerges a race which hates beauty as it hates truth. The etiology of this madness deserves a great deal more study than it has got. There must be causes behind it; it arises and flourishes in obedience to biological laws, and not as a mere act of God. What, precisely, are the terms of those laws? And why do they run stronger in America than elsewhere? Let some honest *Privat Dozent* in pathological sociology apply himself to the problem.

The Sculptor's Funeral

WILLA CATHER

A group of the townspeople stood on the station siding of a little
Kansas town, awaiting the coming of the night train, which was already
twenty minutes overdue. The snow had fallen thick over everything; in the
pale starlight the line of bluffs across the wide, white meadows south of the
town made soft, smoke-colored curves against the clear sky. The men on the
siding stood first on one foot and then on the other, their hands thrust deep
into their trousers pockets, their overcoats open, their shoulders screwed
up with the cold; and they glanced from time to time toward the southwest,
where the railroad track wound along the river shore. They conversed in
low tones and moved about restlessly, seeming uncertain as to what was expected of them. There was but one of the company who looked as though he
knew exactly why he was there, and he kept conspicuously apart, walking to
the far end of the platform, returning to the station door, then pacing up the
track again, his chin sunk in the high collar of his overcoat, his burly
shoulders drooping forward, his gait heavy and dogged. Presently he was
approached by a tall, spare grizzled man clad in a faded Grand Army suit,
who shuffled out from the group and advanced with a certain deference,
craning his neck forward until his back made the angle of a jack-knife three-
quarters open.

"I reckon she's a-goin' to be pretty late again to-night, Jim," he remarked in a squeaky falsetto. "S'pose it's the snow?"

"I don't know," responded the other man with a shade of annoyance,
speaking from out an astonishing cataract of red beard that grew fiercely and
thickly in all directions.

The spare man shifted the quill toothpick he was chewing to the other
side of his mouth. "It ain't likely that anybody from the East will come with
the corpse, I'spose," he went on reflectively.

"I don't know," responded the other, more curtly than before.

"It's too bad he didn't belong to some lodge or other. I like an order funeral myself. They seem more appropriate for people of some repytation," the spare man continued, with an ingratiating concession in his shrill voice, as he carefully placed his toothpick in his vest pocket. He always carried the flag at the G. A. R. funerals in the town.

The heavy man turned on his heel without replying, and walked up the siding. The spare man shuffled back to the uneasy group. "Jim's ez full ez a tick, ez ushel," he commented commiseratingly.

Just then a distant whistle sounded, and there was a shuffling of feet on the platform. A number of lanky boys of all ages appeared as suddenly and slimily as eels wakened by the crack of thunder; some came from the waiting-room, where they had been warming themselves by the red stove, or half asleep on the slat benches; others uncoiled themselves from baggage trucks or slid out of express wagons. Two clambered down from the driver's seat of a hearse that stood backed up against the siding. They straightened their stooping shoulders and lifted their heads, and a flash of momentary animation kindled their dull eyes at that cold, vibrant scream, the world-wide call for men. It stirred them like the note of a trumpet, just as it had often stirred in his boyhood the man who was coming home to-night.

The night express shot, red as a rocket, from out the eastward marsh lands and wound along the river shore under the long lines of shivering poplars that sentinelled the meadows, the escaping steam hanging in grey masses against the pale sky and blotting out the Milky Way. In a moment the red glare from the headlight streamed up the snow-covered track before the siding and glittered on the wet, black rails. The burly man with the dishevelled red beard walked swiftly up the platform toward the approaching train, uncovering his head as he went. The group of men behind him hesitated, glanced questioningly at one another, and awkwardly followed his example. The train stopped, and the crowd shuffled up to the express car just as the door was thrown open, the spare man in the G. A. R. suit thrusting his head forward with curiosity. The express messenger appeared in the doorway, accompanied by a young man in a long ulster and traveling-cap.

"Are Mr. Merrick's friends here?" inquired the young man.

The group on the platform swayed and shuffled uneasily. Philip Phelps, the banker, responded with dignity: "We have come to take charge of the body. Mr. Merrick's father is very feeble and can't be about."

"Send the agent out here," growled the express messenger, "and tell the operator to lend a hand."

The coffin was got out of its rough box and down on the snowy platform. The townspeople drew back enough to make room for it and then formed a close semicircle about it, looking curiously at the palm-leaf which lay across the black cover. No one said anything. The baggage man stood by his truck, waiting to get at the trunks. The engine panted heavily, and the fireman dodged in and out among the wheels with his yellow torch and long oil-can, snapping the spindle boxes. The young Bostonian, one of the dead sculptor's pupils who had come with the body, looked about him helplessly. He turned to the banker, the only one of that black, uneasy, stoop-shouldered group who seemed enough of an individual to be addressed.

"None of Mr. Merrick's brothers are here?" he asked uncertainly.

The man with the red beard for the first time stepped up and joined the group. "No, they have not come yet; the family is scattered. The body will be taken directly to the house." He stooped and took hold of one of the handles of the coffin.

"Take the long hill road up, Thompson, it will be easier on the horses," called the liveryman as the undertaker snapped the door of the hearse and prepared to mount to the driver's seat.

Laird, the red-bearded lawyer, turned again to the stranger: "We didn't know whether there would be any one with him or not," he explained. "It's a long walk, so you'd better go up in the hack." He pointed to a single battered conveyance, but the young man replied stiffly: "Thank you, but I think I will go up with the hearse. If you don't object," turning to the undertaker, "I'll ride with you."

They clambered up over the wheels and drove off in the starlight up the long, white hill toward the town. The lamps in the still village were shining from under the low, snow-burdened roofs; and beyond, on every side, the plains reached out into emptiness, peaceful and wide as the soft sky itself, and wrapped in a tangible, white silence.

When the hearse backed up to a wooden sidewalk before a naked, weather-beaten frame house, the same composite, ill-defined group that had stood upon the station siding was huddled about the gate. The front yard was an icy swamp, and a couple of warped planks, extending from the sidewalk to the door, made a sort of rickety footbridge. The gate hung on one hinge, and was opened wide with difficulty. Steavens, the young stranger, noticed that something black was tied to the knob of the front door.

The grating sound made by the casket, as it was drawn from the hearse, was answered by a scream from the house; the front door was wrenched open, and a tall, corpulent woman rushed out bareheaded into the snow and flung herself upon the coffin, shrieking: "My boy, my boy! And this is how you've come home to me!"

As Steavens turned away and closed his eyes with a shudder of unutterable repulsion, another woman, also tall, but flat and angular, dressed entirely in black, darted out of the house and caught Mrs. Merrick by the shoulders, crying sharply: "Come, come, mother; you mustn't go on like this!" Her tone changed to one of obsequious solemnity as she turned to the banker: "The parlor is ready, Mr. Phelps."

The bearers carried the coffin along the narrow boards, while the undertaker ran ahead with the coffin-rests. They bore it into a large, unheated room that smelled dampness and disuse and furniture polish, and set it down under a hanging lamp ornamented with jingling glass prisms and before a "Rogers group" of John Alden and Priscilla, wreathed with smilax. Henry Steavens stared about him with the sickening conviction that there had been some horrible mistake, and that he had somehow arrived at the wrong destination. He looked painfully about over the clover-green Brussels, the fat plush upholstery; among the hand-painted china plaques and panels, and vases, for some mark of identification, for something that might once conceivably have belonged to Harvey Merrick. It was not until he recognized his friend in the crayon portrait of a little boy in kilts and curls hanging above the piano, that he felt willing to let any of these people approach the coffin.

"Take the lid off, Mr. Thompson; let me see my boy's face," wailed the elder women between her sobs. This time Steavens looked fearfully, almost beseechingly into her face, red and swollen under its masses of strong, black, shiny hair. He flushed, dropped his eyes, and then, almost incredulously, looked again. There was a kind of power about her face—a kind of brutal handsomeness, even; but it was scarred and furrowed by violence, and so colored and coarsened by fiercer passions that grief seemed never to have laid a gentle finger there. The long nose was distended and knobbed at the end, and there were deep lines on either side of it; her heavy, black brows almost met across her forehead, her teeth were large and square, and set far apart—teeth that could tear. She filled the room; the men were obliterated, seemed tossed about like twigs in an angry water, and even Steavens felt himself being drawn into the whirlpool.

The daughter—the tall, raw-boned woman in crêpe, with a mourning comb in her hair which curiously lengthened her long face—sat stiffly upon the sofa, her hands, conspicuous for their large knuckles, folded in her lap, her mouth and eyes drawn down, solemnly awaiting the opening of the coffin. Near the door stood a mulatto woman, evidently a servant in the house, with a timid bearing and an emaciated face pitifully sad and gentle. She was weeping silently, the corner of her calico apron lifted to her eyes, occasionally suppressing a long, quivering sob. Steavens walked over and stood beside her.

Feeble steps were heard on the stairs, and an old man, tall and frail, odorous of pipe smoke, with shaggy, unkept grey hair and a dingy beard, tobacco-stained about the mouth, entered uncertainly. He went slowly up to the coffin and stood rolling a blue cotton handkerchief between his hands, seeming so pained and embarrassed by his wife's orgy of grief that he had no consciousness of anything else.

"There, there, Annie, dear, don't take on so," he quavered timidly, putting out a shaking hand and awkwardly patting her elbow. She turned with a cry, and sank upon his shoulder with such violence that he tottered a little. He did not even glance toward the coffin, but continued to look at her with a dull, frightened, appealing expression, as a spaniel looks at the whip. His sunken cheeks slowly reddened and burned with miserable shame. When his wife rushed from the room, her daughter strode after her with set lips. The servant stole up to the coffin, bent over it for a moment, and then slipped away to the kitchen, leaving Steavens, the lawyer and the father to themselves. The old man stood trembling and looking down at his dead son's face. The sculptor's splendid head seemed even more noble in its rigid stillness than in life. The dark hair had crept upon the wide forehead; the face seemed strangely long, but in it there was not that beautiful and chaste repose which we expect to find in the faces of the dead. The brows were so drawn that there were two deep lines above the beaked nose, and the chin was thrust forward defiantly. It was as though the strain of life had been so sharp and bitter that death could not at once wholly relax the tension and smooth the countenance into perfect peace—as though he were still guarding something precious and holy which might even yet be wrested from him.

The old man's lips were working under his stained beard. He turned to the lawyer with timid deference: "Phelps and the rest are comin' back to set up with Harve, ain't they?" he asked. "Thank 'ee, Jim, thank 'ee." He brushed the hair back gently from his son's forehead. "He was a good boy, Jim; always a good boy. He was ez gentle ez a child and the kindest of 'em all—only we didn't none of us ever onderstand him." The tears trickled slowly down his beard and dropped upon the sculptor's coat.

"Martin, Martin—Oh, Martin! come here," his wife wailed from the top of the stairs. The old man started timorously: "Yes, Annie, I'm coming." He turned away, hesitated, stood for a moment in miserable indecision; then reached back and patted the dead man's hair softly, and stumbled from the room.

"Poor old man, I didn't think he had any tears left. Seems as if his eyes would have gone dry long ago. At his age nothing cuts very deep," remarked the lawyer.

Something in his tone made Steavens glance up. While the mother had been in the room, the young man had scarcely seen any one else; but now, from the moment he first glanced into Jim Laird's florid face and bloodshot eyes, he knew that he had found what he had been heart-sick at not finding before—the feeling, the understanding, that must exist in some one, even here.

The man was red as his beard, with features swollen and blurred by dissipation, and a hot, blazing blue eye. His face was strained—that of a man who is controlling himself with difficulty—and he kept plucking at his beard with a sort of fierce resentment. Steavens, sitting by the window, watched him turn down the glaring lamp, still its jangling pendants with an angry gesture, and then stand with his hands locked behind him, staring down into the master's face. He could not help wondering what link there could have been between the porcelain vessel and so sooty a lump of potter's clay.

From the kitchen an uproar was sounding; when the dining-room door opened, the import of it was clear. The mother was abusing the maid for having forgotten to make the dressing for the chicken salad which had been prepared for the watchers. Steavens had never heard anything in the least like it; it was injured, emotional, dramatic abuse, unique and masterly in its excruciating cruelty, as violent and unrestrained as had been her grief of twenty minutes before. With a shudder of disgust the lawyer went into the dining-room and closed the door into the kitchen.

"Poor Roxy's getting it now," he remarked when he came back. "The Merricks took her out of the poor-house years ago; and if her loyalty would let her, I guess the poor old thing could tell tales that would curdle your blood. She's the mulatto woman who was standing in here a while ago, with her apron to her eyes. The old woman is a fury; there never was anybody like her for demonstrative piety and ingenious cruelty. She made Harvey's life a hell for him when he lived at home; he was so sick ashamed of it. I never could see how he kept himself so sweet."

"He was wonderful," said Steavens slowly, "wonderful; but until tonight I have never known how wonderful."

"That is the true and eternal wonder of it, anyway; that it can come even from such a dung-heap as this," the lawyer cried, with a sweeping gesture which seemed to indicate much more than the four walls within which they stood.

"I think I'll see whether I can get a little air. The room is so close I am beginning to feel rather faint," murmured Steavens, struggling with one of the windows. The sash was stuck, however, and would not yield, so he sat down dejectedly and began pulling at his collar. The lawyer came over, loosened the sash with one blow of his red fist and sent the window up a few inches. Steavens thanked him, but the nausea which had been gradually climbing into his throat for the last half hour left him with but one desire—a desperate feeling that he must get away from this place with what was left of Harvey Merrick. Oh, he comprehended well enough now the quiet bitterness of the smile that he had seen so often on his master's lips!

He remembered that once, when Merrick returned from a visit home, he brought with him a singularly feeling and suggestive bas-relief of a thin, faded old woman, sitting and sewing something pinned to her knee; while a full-lipped, full-blooded little urchin, his trousers held up by a single gallows, stood beside her, impatiently twitching her gown to call her attention to a butterfly he had caught. Steavens, impressed by the tender and delicate modeling of the thin, tired face, had asked him if it were his mother. He remembered the dull flush that had burned up in the sculptor's face.

The lawyer was sitting in a rocking-chair beside the coffin, his head thrown back and his eyes closed. Steavens looked at him earnestly, puzzled at the line of the chin, and wondering why a man should conceal a feature of such distinction under that disfiguring shock of beard. Suddenly, as though he felt the young sculptor's keen glance, he opened his eyes.

"Was he always a good deal of an oyster?" he asked abruptly. "He was terribly shy as a boy."

97

"Yes, he was an oyster, since you put it so," rejoined Steavens. "Although he could be very fond of people, he always gave one the impression of being detached. He disliked violent emotion; he was reflective, and rather distrustful of himself—except, of course, as regarded his work. He was sure-footed enough there. He distrusted men pretty thoroughly and women even more, yet somehow without believing ill of them. He was determined, indeed, to believe the best, but he seemed afraid to investigate."

"A burnt dog dreads the fire," said the lawyer grimly, and closed his eyes.

Steavens went on and on, reconstructing that whole miserable boyhood. All this raw, biting ugliness had been the portion of the man whose tastes were refined beyond the limits of the reasonable—whose mind was an exhaustless gallery of beautiful impressions, and so sensitive that the mere shadow of a poplar leaf flickering against a sunny wall would be etched and held there forever. Surely, if ever a man had the magic word in his finger tips, it was Merrick. Whatever he touched, he revealed its holiest secret; liberated it from enchantment and restored it to its pristine loveliness, like the Arabian prince who fought the enchantress spell for spell. Upon whatever he had come in contact with, he had left a beautiful record of the experience—a sort of ethereal signature; a scent, a sound, a color that was his own.

Steavens understood now the real tragedy of his master's life; neither love nor wine, as many had conjectured, but a blow which had fallen earlier and cut deeper than these could have done—a shame not his, and yet so unescapably his, to hide in his heart from his very boyhood. And without, the frontier warfare; the yearning of a boy, cast ashore upon a desert of newness and ugliness and sordidness, for all that is chastened and old, and noble with traditions.

At eleven o'clock the tall, flat woman in black crêpe entered and announced that the watchers were arriving, and asked them "to step into the dining-room." As Steavens rose, the lawyer said dryly: "You go on—it'll be a good experience for you, doubtless; as for me, I'm not equal to that crowd to-night; I've had twenty years of them."

As Steavens closed the door after him he glanced back at the lawyer, sitting by the coffin in the dim light, with his chin resting on his hand.

The same misty group that had stood before the door of the express car shuffled into the dining room. In the light of the kerosene lamp they separated and became individuals. The minister, a pale, feeble-looking man with white hair and blond chin-whiskers, took his seat beside a small side table and placed his Bible upon it. The Grand Army man sat down behind the stove and tilted his chair back comfortably against the wall, fishing his quill toothpick from his waistcoat pocket. The two bankers, Phelps and Elder, sat off in a corner behind the dinner-table, where they could finish their discussion of the new usury law and its effect on chattel security loans. The real estate agent, an old man with a smiling, hypocritical face, soon joined them. The coal and lumber dealer and the cattle shipper sat on opposite sides of the hard coal-burner, their feet on the nickel-work. Steavens took a book from his pocket and began to read. The talk around him ranged through various topics of local interest while the house was quieting down. When it was clear that the members of the family were in bed, the Grand Army man hitched his shoulders and, untangling his long legs, caught his heels on the rounds of the chair.

"S'pose there'll be a will, Phelps?" he queried in his weak falsetto.

The banker laughed disagreeably, and began trimming his nails with a pearl-handled pocket-knife.

"There'll scarcely be any need for one, will there?" he queried in his turn.

The restless Grand Army man shifted his position again, getting his knees still nearer his chin. "Why, the ole man says Harve's done right well lately," he chirped.

The other banker spoke up. "I reckon he means by that Harve ain't asked him to mortgage any more farms lately so as he could go on with his education."

"Seems like my mind don't reach back to a time when Harve wasn't bein' edycated," tittered the Grand Army man.

There was a general chuckle. The minister took out his handkerchief and blew his nose sonorously. Banker Phelps closed his knife with a snap. "It's too bad the old man's sons didn't turn out better," he remarked with reflective authority. "They never hung together. He spent money enough on Harve to stock a dozen cattle-farms and he might as well have poured it into Sand Creek. If Harve had stayed at home and helped nurse what little they had, and gone into stock on the old man's bottom farm, they might all have been well fixed. But the old man had to trust everything to tenants and was cheated right and left."

"Harve never could have handled stock none," interposed the cattle-man. "He hadn't it in him to be sharp. Do you remember when he bought Sander's mules for eight-year olds, when everybody in town knew that Sander's father-in-law give 'em to his wife for a wedding present eighteen years before, an' they was full-grown mules then."

Every one chuckled, and the Grand Army man rubbed his knees with a spasm of childish delight.

"Harve never was much account for anything practical, and he shore was never fond of work," began the coal and lumber dealer. "I mind the last time he was home; the day he left, when the old man was out to the barn helpin' his hand hitch up to take Harve to the train, and Cal. Moots was patchin' up the fence, Harve, he come out on the step and sings out, in his lady-like voice: 'Cal. Moots, Cal. Moots! please come cord my trunk.'"

"That's Harve for you," approved the Grand Army man gleefully. "I kin hear him howlin' yet when he was a big feller in long pants, and his mother used to whale him with a rawhide in the barn for lettin' the cows git foundered in the cornfield when he was drivin' 'em home from pasture. He killed a cow of mine that-a-way onct—a pure Jersey and the best milker I had, an' the ole man had to put up for her. Harve, he was watchin' the sun set acrost the marshes when the anamile got away; he argued that sunset was oncommon fine."

"Where the old man made his mistake was in sending the boy East to schools," said Phelps, stroking his goatee and speaking in a deliberate, judicial tone. "There was where he got his head full of traipsing to Paris and all such folly. What Harve needed, of all people, was a course in some first-class Kansas City business college."

The letters were swimming before Steavens's eyes. Was it possible that these men did not understand, that the palm on the coffin meant nothing to them? The very name of their town would have remained forever buried in the postal guide had it not been now and again mentioned in the world in connection with Harvey Merrick's. He remembered what his master had said to him on the day of his death, after the congestion of both lungs had shut off any probability of recovery, and the sculptor had asked his pupil to send his body home. "It's not a pleasant place to be lying while the world is moving and doing and bettering," he had said with a feeble smile, "but it rather seems as though we ought to go back to the place we came from in the end. The townspeople will come in for a look at me; and after they have

100

had their say I shan't have much to fear from the judgment of God. The wings of the Victory, in there"—with a weak gesture toward his studio—"will not shelter me."

The cattleman took up the comment. "Forty's young for a Merrick to cash in; they usually hang on pretty well. Probably he helped it along with whisky."

"His mother's people were not long-lived, and Harvey never had a robust constitution," said the minister mildly. He would have liked to say more. He had been the boy's Sunday-school teacher, and had been fond of him; but felt that he was not in a position to speak. His own sons had turned out badly, and it was not a year since one of them had made his last trip home in the express car, shot in a gambling-house in the Black Hills.

"Nevertheless, there is no disputin' that Harve frequently looked upon the wine when it was red, also variegated, and it shore made an oncommon fool of him," moralized the cattleman.

Just then the door leading into the parlor rattled loudly and every one started involuntarily, looking relieved when only Jim Laird came out. His red face was convulsed with anger, and the Grand Army man ducked his head when he saw the spark in his blue, blood-shot eye. They were all afraid of Jim; he was a drunkard, but he could twist the law to suit his client's needs as no other man in all western Kansas could do; and there were many who tried. The lawyer closed the door gently behind him, leaned back against it and folded his arms, cocking his head a little to one side. When he assumed this attitude in the courtroom, ears were always pricked up, as it usually foretold a flood of withering sarcasm.

"I've been with you gentlemen before," he began in a dry, even tone, "when you've sat by the coffins of boys born and raised in this town; and, if I remember rightly, you were never any too well satisfied when you checked them up. What's the matter, anyhow? Why is it that reputable young men are as scarce as millionaires in Sand City? It might almost seem to a stranger that there was some way something the matter with your progressive town. Why did Ruben Sayer, the brightest young lawyer you ever turned out, after he had come home from the university as straight as a die, take to drinking and forge a check and shoot himself? Why did Bill Merrit's son die of the shakes in a saloon in Omaha? Why was Mr. Thomas's son, here, shot in a gambling-house? Why did young Adams burn his mill to beat the insurance companies and go to the pen?"

101

The lawyer paused and unfolded his arms, laying one clenched fist quietly on the table. "I'll tell you why. Because you drummed nothing but money and knavery into their ears from the time they wore knickerbockers; because you carped away at them as you've been carping here to-night, holding our friends Phelps and Elder up to them for their models, as our grandfathers held up George Washington and John Adams. But the boys, worse luck, were young, and raw at the business you put them to; and how could they match coppers with such artists as Phelps and Elder? You wanted them to be successful rascals; they were only unsuccessful ones— that's all the difference. There was only one boy ever raised in this bor- derland between ruffianism and civilization, who didn't come to grief, and you hated Harvey Merrick more for winning out than you hated all the other boys who got under the wheels. Lord, Lord, how you did hate him! Phelps, here, is fond of saying that he could buy and sell us all out any time he's a mind to; but he knew Harve wouldn't have given a tinker's damn for his bank and all his cattle-farms put together; and a lack of appreciation, that way, goes hard with Phelps.

"Old Nimrod, here, thinks Harve drank too much; and this from such as Nimrod and me!

"Brother Elder says Harve was too free with the old man's money—fell short in filial consideration, maybe. Well, we can all remember the very tone in which brother Elder swore his own father was a liar, in the county court; and we all know that the old man came out of that partnership with his son as bare as a sheared lamb. But maybe I'm getting personal, and I'd better be driving ahead at what I want to say."

The lawyer paused a moment, squared his heavy shoulders, and went on: "Harvey Merrick and I went to school together, back East. We were dead in earnest, and we wanted you all to be proud of us some day. We meant to be great men. Even I, and I haven't lost my sense of humor, gen- tlemen, I meant to be a great man. I came back here to practise, and I found you didn't in the least want me to be a great man. You wanted me to be a shrewd lawyer—oh, yes! Our veteran here wanted me to get him an increase of pension, because he had dyspepsia; Phelps wanted a new county survey that would put the widow Wilson's little bottom farm inside his south line; Elder wanted to lend money at 5 per cent a month and get it collected; Old Stark here wanted to wheedle old women up in Vermont into investing their annuities in real-estate mortgages that are not worth the paper they are written on. Oh, you needed me hard enough, and you'll go on needing me; and that's why I'm not afraid to plug the truth home to you this once.

"Well, I came back here and became the damned shyster you wanted me to be. You pretend you have some sort of respect for me; and yet you'll stand up and throw mud at Harvey Merrick, whose soul you couldn't dirty, and whose hands you couldn't tie. Oh, you're a discriminating lot of Christians! There have been times when the sight of Harvey's name in some Eastern paper has made me hang my head like a whipped dog; and, again, times when I liked to think of him off there in the world, away from all this hog-wallow, doing his great work and climbing the big, clean up-grade he'd set for himself.

"And we? Now that we've fought and lied and sweated and stolen, and hated as only the disappointed strugglers in a bitter, dead little Western town know how to do, what have we got to show for it? Harvey Merrick wouldn't have given one sunset over your marshes for all you've got put together, and you know it. It's not for me to say why, in the inscrutable wisdom of God, a genius should ever have been called from his place of hatred and bitter waters; but I want this Boston man to know that the drivel he's been hearing here to-night is the only tribute any truly great man could ever have from such a lot of sick, side-tracked, burnt-dog, land-poor sharks as the here-present financiers of Sand City—upon which town may God have mercy!"

The lawyer thrust out his hand to Steavens as he passed him, caught up his overcoat in the hall, and had left the house before the Grand Army man had had time to lift his ducked head and crane his long neck about at his fellows.

Next day Jim Laird was drunk and unable to attend the funeral services. Steavens called twice at his office, but was compelled to start East without seeing him. He had a presentiment that he would hear from him again, and left his address on the lawyer's table; but if Laird found it, he never acknowledged it. The thing in him that Harvey Merrick had loved must have gone under ground with Harvey Merrick's coffin; for it never spoke again, and Jim got the cold he died of driving-across the Colorado mountains to defend one of Phelps's sons who had got into trouble out there by cutting government timber.

The American Small Town*

SHERWOOD ANDERSON

I have just returned from another of my periods of wandering over America visiting many states, talking to farmers out on the wide plains of Texas and little Southern cotton-patch farmers, going to many cities, going in and out of many, many towns. Now here I am back in my own town and happy.

Familiar walks to be taken, roads to be driven over in the car, familiar faces to be seen on the street! Places to be visited, certain country roads that lead up into the hills, spots by the river bank . . .

The shapes of the hills about our town, the little bunches of trees on certain hills . . . I am a confirmed small-towner, and you know how all we small-towners feel about our town, our pride in it, our belief that it is the best town on earth, our hopes for its future. With me it's a case of love. You can see the beauty of many women and yet love only one. Perhaps I am in love with my own town of Marion and my Virginia country because I have been here for a long time now. I realize the same thing might have happened to me in Kansas, in Georgia, or Connecticut. Love of a town and a countryside, like love of a woman, may be a matter of proximity. Whatever the reason, my town and countryside seem especially beautiful to me.

Perhaps only a passionate traveler like myself can realize how lucky he is to be able to call a small town his home. My work is constantly calling me away from Marion, but I always hunger to get back. There is in the life of the small town a possibility of intimacy, a chance to know others—an intimacy oftentimes frightening, but which can be healing. Day after day, under all sorts of circumstances, in sickness and health, in good fortune and bad, we small-towners are close to one another and know each other in ways the city man can never experience. A man goes away and comes back. Cer-

*Selection from *Home Town*.

104

tain people have died. Babies have been born. Children of yesterday have suddenly become young men and women. Life has been going on. Still nothing has really changed. On the streets, day after day, mostly the same faces. There is this narrow but facinating panorama. In a way it is too intimate. Life can never be intimate enough.

I

There is a long letter on my desk from a young man. Something I have written and that has been published has upset him. He is one of the young men you meet everywhere now. He has a burning desire to remake life, the whole social scheme. He is a little fretful and angry at me because I like the Oak Hills, the smaller scenes, because I have doubts about the ends to be achieved by trying to be a big thinker, a mover of masses of men.

He scolds at me. I had somewhere said something about the necessity nowadays of staying put. In saying that, I had in mind staying closer home in our thoughts and feelings. The big world outside now is so filled with confusion. It seemed to me that our only hope, in the present muddle, was to try thinking small.

It must be that the young man who has written the letter to me feels that he has something great to give to the world. In his letter he speaks of the rapidity with which men now move from place to place. I had, in what I had written, spoken about the advisability of a man's wanting to live fully, at the beginning, in a small way; trying, for example, to get a little better understanding of the people in his own house, in the street on which his house stands; trying to get closer to the people of his own town.

It had seemed to me, as I wrote, that a man like Lincoln must have begun like that. With what strange sadness he left the then small town of Springfield, Illinois, to become President. There was a little speech made to the people of the town at the railroad station when he left, and it is one of the most moving things in literature. As you read, you feel Lincoln was a man who grew like a tree, beginning small, getting keen understanding of the little life about him, and emerging into the large.

The young man who has written to me says that he is going off to New York City. He feels that he must get among other intellectuals, bigger people than he finds in his home town, people who have bigger thoughts, vaster dreams. He declares that the day of the individual has passed, that now we must think of people only in the mass. A man must learn to love and work for the masses.

The proletariat, the middle class, the capitalist class! A man is no longer just a man going along, trying a little to cultivate his own senses, trying to see more, hear more. That day has passed now. The young man feels that Oak Hill is not big enough for the big life he says he feels in himself. It may be that I am being unfair to him. It seems to me that a man like Lincoln would still have been Lincoln had he never left Springfield, Illinois; that he grew naturally, as a tree grows, out of the soil of Springfield, Illinois, out of the people about him whom he knew so intimately.

It seems to me that he grew out of a house, a street, a shabby little country lawyer's office; out of his touch with the common men he met in the little country courtrooms; and that all this made him the man he became.

Such a man was not thinking, I am sure, of masses of men, the middle class, the proletariat, etc., but of other individuals about him everywhere. You will remember how angry he made some of the Civil War generals. There were country boys who went to sleep on picket duty, or grew afraid and ran away before a battle. The generals declared such boys must be shot, but Lincoln wouldn't agree. He kept pardoning them. They kept declaring he was bringing ruin to the big things, the army, the State; but he did not ruin the army or the State. In the end he saved the State.

He kept seeing the country boy as some country boy he had known. His mind and his heart functioned that way.

It may be that there is a bigness every man should seek, but the world is full now of false bigness, men speaking at meetings, trying to move masses of other men, getting a big feeling in that way; there's a trickiness in that approach to others—through applause, feeling a false power and importance.

The Oak Hills are too small for such men. Their own houses are too small. They must have a great field, millions of men as listeners to their voices.

The young man who wrote is half-angry with me because I said to him, 'Why not Oak Hill? What's the matter with Oak Hill?'

He can't wait for the slow growth of understanding of others in such a small place. That is what he says.

He says that he is going to New York and that in the great city he will learn to give himself to others.

106

He declares he can't do it in Oak Hill, that he isn't understood there. He feels cramped.

But as I read his letter, I kept asking myself over and over the same question:

'What's the matter with Oak Hill?'

I kept remembering that when Lincoln left Springfield, he asked his partner in a country law office to leave his name on the sign hanging out of the office window. He dreamed of coming back and taking up his old life in a small circle.

It must have been his ability to move and feel and live within the small scene that made him so effective in the larger place and that has left him such a vivid figure in our minds.

All of the big world outside was just more and more Springfield to him.

What's the matter with Oak Hill?

Why not Oak Hill?

II

The small town has always been the backbone of the living thing we call America. There is the New England town with its elms and town meetings, in its atmosphere something a little static, even a little pinched. From these tight little towns, with houses set close to the ground, and small stony fields enclosed within stone walls, there came the Adamses, the Emersons, the Thoreaus, indeed the intellectual life of practically all America, the tone that spread out over America. Something there—perhaps the hard stony soil—made life go up into the head, into the brain, made men look at something behind and beneath life, the transcendental, rather more than at life itself, and created a reticent puritanic attitude that for a long while affected the tone in thousands of towns scattered over the Middle West, till out of the place of deeper, richer soil the courage of another, closer approach came into us . . .

Perhaps it is that the small town lies halfway between the cities whence we get the ideas and the soil whence we draw the strength. Perhaps it is that the small-towner remains closer than does the city man to the source of the food he eats, to the ground on which it grows. The hunger for the soil is rooted deeply in man. As George Ade once remarked, 'Our city skyscrapers are filled with men dreaming of some day owning a farm and going into the chicken-raising business.' The small-towner can satisfy this hunger. He may own a farm, perhaps have moved into town from one. A surprising number of small-town men do own farms, merchants, doctors, lawyers. In a few minutes' run, they are out of town. It is a rare small-towner who nowadays doesn't own some kind of a car. Where do you suppose all the second-hand cars go? Even in his town the small-town man knows the famer . . .

Out of the small towns in any case have come most of our governors of states and great numbers of our poets, thinkers, soldiers, and statesmen: besides Abraham Lincoln, R. W. Emerson, Thomas Edison, Mark Twain, Robert Fulton, John Quincy Adams, Robert E. Lee, Stonewall Jackson, William Tecumseh Sherman, U.S. Grant, Susan B. Anthony, Grover Cleveland, Walter Reed. Many names could readily be added to the list.

There has been a new pattern being made in the American towns. In the towns man in his groping, blundering way has been making a new race compounded of all the races of the Old World. The American mixture of many bloods grows constantly into a definite new race.

Do you remember when you, now for so long a city man, your hair graying, were a small-town boy, and what the railroad meant to you? Did you dream of some day being a railroad engineer?

With the coming of that railroad there was a new influx of strange people. England no longer was sending her emigrants here. They went out to England's own colonies. The great Irish immigration began, the Germans came in hundreds of thousands, the Danes, the Swedes, the Norsemen, the Finns came.

It was the great period of building, of town-making, the men of northern Europe pushing up into Wisconsin, Minnesota, the great Northwest, to become lumbermen there, new farmers and town workmen, makers of more towns.

Then the Italians, Greeks, men of all southeastern Europe. Mexicans came up into the Southwest, the Asiatics into the Pacific Coast country. The sons and daughters of all these learning to speak English, helping us in the making of a new language, the American language.

All over America, in the towns, we speak the English language, but the stream of English blood in us grows thinner and thinner. It has been growing thinner ever since the Revolutionary War.

The new race can be seen, studied, understood best in the towns. In the cities, the new people as they came in tended to group themselves. There was a German section, an Italian, a Chinese, a section filled with men from southeastern Europe.

In the small town this couldn't happen. The men who went out along the railroads settled in the towns, became a part of the life of the whole town. The new America was made there. It is still being made there.

III

Our cities are made up of former small-towners.

It has long been a legend that every American small-town boy dreams of some day going away to live in the city. He is supposed to look wistfully at the racing trains passing often without stopping through his little town. Now the new streamline trains go whirling through the towns at eighty, ninety, a hundred miles an hour. There is the soft purr of a mail plane far overhead. He hungers to see the wonders in the world, to be an important figure out there.

New things, new dreams in the heads of the boys of the towns.

However, all boys do not leave their home towns. The boy whose father owns a grocery clerks in his father's store and later becomes a grocer. Or he goes away to college and comes back, sets up in his town as a doctor or law-yer. All his life he goes up and down along the same small-town streets, past the same houses, meets the same men and women. The grown people he sees daily he knew when he wore his first pair of long pants, when he began going to the town school. Like the others, when he was a boy he fell in love with a little girl who lived on his street.

He was afraid to speak to her. He trembled when he passed her on the street. When she was about, he began to show off, wrestled with other little boys in the school yard. He became furiously jealous of another and bolder boy who could walk right up to the girls, speak to them, who could give some girl a bite of his apple.

The town boy grows up, suddenly becomes a young man, begins going about with a small-town girl, takes her to church and to dances and to the moving pictures. He takes her for a ride in the evening in his father's car and presently they are married. They have children.

Friendships are formed. There were two young men, who had known each other since boyhood, seen walking about together evening after eve-ning. They talked. It may be that, after the beginning of such a friendship, between two small-town young men, one of them later went away to some city. His name was mentioned in his smalltown paper.

'Ed Horner has gone to Chicago' (or it may be New York or Cleveland

Early Sunday Morning, Edward Hopper

or Boston or St. Louis). 'He is about to accept a lucrative position in the city.'

If we take the local editor's word for it, all the small-town boys get lucrative positions.

Such a young man may spend the greater part of his life in the city. All his life he will remember the first day or night of his arrival in the city, the strange fear of the vast crowds of people pressing in on him. A kind of terror came. There were too many people. How could he ever find friends, comrades, make a place for himself in the vast herd?

He does not forget his small-town friend. He will, all his life, remember vividly every house along the streets on which is father's house stood. It may be that, as a city man, he will never again form another friendship that will mean to him quite what his remembered small-town friendship meant.

It was with that friend of his youth that he discussed all of his early problems and dreams. To him he confessed his first love, with him smoked his first cigarette, took his first drink of beer. How vividly he remembers the night when he and his friend went together to a near-by larger town! There was something they both wanted intensely or thought they wanted. They went together to a certain notorious house, stood trembling and ashamed before the house, and then came away. They hadn't the courage to enter.

'Gee, Harry, I haven't got the nerve, have you?'

'No, Jim, I guess I've lost my nerve.'

There remains for the city man, raised in an American small town, the memory of the sharing of the experiences, the dreams, the disappointments of youth. He remembers the time he and his friend went with the town ball team to play a team in a neighboring town. Together as boys they discussed the mysteries of life, of death, of love, of religion.

'Do you believe in God? What do you think, Harry?'

'Well, I don't know, John. When a fellow looks up at the sky at night—'

The city man remembers vividly his small-town school-teacher, the place where he with the other town boys built a dam in the creek to make a swimming hole. If he comes from a Southern small town, he remembers a Negro boy with whom he went hunting coons or 'possum at night. The Northern boy remembers the hills on which he went bob-sledding, the ponds on which he learned to skate. There was always another boy who could outstake him, who could cut figure eights and other fancy strokes. When he tried it, he kept falling.

Some times the city man, remembering an old hunger, returns to the town of his youth. He walks about the streets.

The town seems strangely changed to him. It is a constant shock to him that the people of his town have also grown older.

There is a gray-haired man he remembers as a slight youth who played shortstop on the baseball team. Perhaps the main street of his town has been paved since he was a boy. The whole town seems to have shrunk in size. He remembers the long journey when, as a child, he first set off to school. Now it seems but a step from the house where he spent his childhood to the school building.

The city man returning thus to his home town has always a feeling of sadness. He resents the changes in the town, the fact that people of the town have grown older as he has, that strangers have come in.

During all his life in the city, the small town of his boyhood has remained home to him. Every house in the town, the faces of people seen on the street in his boyhood, have all remained sharply in his mind. How clearly he remembers the hill above the waterworks pond, where he, with a troop of other boys, went along a path beside a wheat field to the town swimming hole! He remembers the way the wind played in the wheat. If he is a Southern boy, he remembers the fall days when he gathered persimmons, the fires under the kettles where sorghum molasses was being made at night, Negro women skimming the yellow green froth off the boiling juice.

Or the night when he with a boyhood friend walked home together from a dance or from a spelling bee at a country schoolhouse, the dusty dirt road along which they walked, the wind in the tall fall corn, the rustling sound when the wind played among the broad dry corn leaves, rubbing them together and making a sound like ghosts running whispering through the corn.

He remembers the town's haunted house, the night when he and several other town boys played 'follow-your-leader' and a daring boy led them into the town graveyard.

He is shocked, half-wishing he hadn't returned. 'It would have been better to let my dream, my memory, alone,' he thinks.

But there is a realization in him also that the city in which he has been living for years is made up of men who have come from small towns, who remember vividly the intimacy of life in the towns, who have remained,

112

during all the years of their life as city men, at heart small-towners. Also that city is made up of an infinite number of small towns.

There is something reached for, wanted also by the city-born fellow—to be known and recognized by the clerk in the neighboring drug store, the near-by A. & P., or the news-dealer at the corner. The city man wants also to be known and recognized by the waiters in the restaurant where he goes for his noonday lunch.

It is the old hunger for intimacy.

* * *

V

Something which definitely has changed in the towns is the life of the woman. Who has not heard the story of the American pioneer woman, how she went with her man into the wilderness, worked beside him, often fought beside him, bore her children without skilled medical help, worked with and for him in the newly cleared fields?

It was a hard and lonely life, and only the more hardy of the women survived. Look over old records and you will find that a surprisingly large number of early American men survived three or four wives.

There is a touch of the old life still in great stretches of the country. In little Southern towns and in towns in the mountain country that separates the North from the South, among the hill men and the so-called poor whites of the Southern coastal plains, the women, white and black, still go out of the little towns with their men to work in the fields. They make the gardens in the yards back of the little town houses, in the small communities they feed the pigs and chickens, milk the cow.

See the Southern hill man or the poor white of the South going out of one of the little towns into the fields in the early morning. There is a little procession, the woman and the children following in single file at the heels of the man. Among the Southern cotton tenant farmers, when land is let for the season, it is let, not on the basis of how much land a man can work, but on the basis of the family. The woman of such a man does not walk shoulder to shoulder with him. She trots at his heels. If the wife has a babe in arms, she takes it with her to the fields. It lies on the grass in a fence corner while all day she chops cotton or hoes corn beside her man.

In the American small town of the past there was always a cellar under every house. The fall was the great canning and storing time. Often pits were dug in the yard back of the little frame house, for burying apples, cabbages, and turnips. It was a little trench lined with straw, the apples and turnips and heads of cabbage buried in the straw and then covered with earth. Many women made their own soap. They canned, often, hundreds of cans of fruit and vegetables, sliced apples and hung them in the sun to dry. They made the clothes for their children.

In bins in the cellar under her house were piles of potatoes, pumpkins, and squash. If the woman was the wife of one of the more well-to-do men of the town, she had a sewing woman come in to live for a time with the family. The woman made clothes for the wife and the children. She made shirts for the man of the house. In an earlier day the shoemaker also came to make the shoes for the family.

And then, as it happens in America, suddenly, within a generation, everything changed. The great canneries came into existence. Why go to all the labor of canning fruit and vegetables when, often at less cost, canned food to carry the family through the winter can be had at the store? Clothes for the children, suits for the boys and dresses for the girls, could be bought at the store for less money than it cost to buy the cloth and have in a sewing woman. The clothes fitted better. It became increasingly necessary for the small-town woman or the young girl, as for her sisters in the cities, to be in the fashion.

The fashion magazines came to the small-town women as to city women. With the increased opportunity for movement brought on by the coming of the automobile, it was easier for the more prosperous small-town woman to go to the large stores in near-by cities. She did her shopping there. What had been a great adventure, something looked forward to for years and talked of for years later, a visit to some large American city became just an afternoon jaunt.

And then came the new freedom.

There was talk in the towns, as in the cities, of the rise of women. Women got the vote. More and more they pushed out of the home and began to work in factories and stores. They went into the professions and became lawyers, doctors, and even judges.

The American man had lost his grip on the American woman. His wife and daughter read Freud. They read the novels of Theodore Dreiser, Sinclair Lewis, and William Faulkner. They read Ernest Hemingway's stories. Even by the time the first world war came, they were in full flight.

114

And then came prohibition, bringing drinking into the American home. It happened in the small American town as it did in the American city. There had been the town saloon with its little back room reached through an alleyway. It was the small-town man's club, the place to which he went to escape women, to be alone with other men. It was like the barber shop, a place to lie and brag and play a game of seven-up with other men.

Sometimes, earlier, a woman, accompanied by some loose-living man, slipped into the little room at the back of the saloon. Everyone in town knew about her. It was even said that she smoked cigarettes.

For that matter, even among men, the smoking of cigarettes, Sweet Caporals, was the inevitable mark of the sissy. A real man smoked cigars or a pipe.

There was a man in town who clerked in the town hotel and who smoked the things. He was called Fuzzy.

'The damn sissy, with his coffin nails.'

The lid had, however, suddenly blown off. Women were affected by the movies. They kept getting ideas into their heads. They were out to be men's equals. They got jobs, began to wear bloomers. A young high-school girl, of one of the best families in town, went with a young man to a dance and was seen taking a drink out of a bottle. Women got elected to Congress. There was even one in the United States Senate. They were on juries. They made political speeches. They read books that spoke frankly of things a man of an earlier generation wouldn't have dared whispered in the presence of a 'decent' woman. It was all very puzzling to the American man of the towns, as it was to him of the American cities. Something had got out of his hand. More and more the women of the towns, as of the cities, were pressing into the lead in fields that had formerly been exclusively men's fields. They took the lead in the intellectual and cultural life of the towns. If there was a town library estabished, they did it; if an orchestra was brought from the city to give a concert in the town hall or the auditorium in the high school, it was a woman who got it up; if a lecture were on the boards, some nationally known figure in the intellectual or political world coming to town to speak, the women were back of the program.

It was the women of the towns who organized clubs to beautify the towns. If there was a town park to be built, their hand was in it.

A more prosperous citizen of an American town had sent his daughter off to the state university. Secretly he thought it rather a foolish idea, but

his wife insisted. And then the daughter came home for the summer vaca-
tion. She seemed a very sweet, innocent one. It was in the evening, after
the evening meal and the family had gone to sit on the front porch, darkness
coming, birds chirping sleepily in near-by trees. They were just sitting
there, and then the daughter, taking a cigarette case out of her purse, lit a
cigarette.

'Have one, Dad?' she asked.

It was just plain nonsense, worse than that. It was terrible, a knocking
over of all the old standards of life.

And she did it so casually. There was a tense moment on the porch, the
man's wife sitting there.

See the American small-town man. He wants to explode.

'If it was a son, I'd give him a damn good hiding,' he thinks.

But what's the trouble. A man can't give a hiding to a grown-up daughter sitting there so self-assured, smoking her cigarette.

The American man is out on a limb. He looks at his wife.

'Louise—for God's sake—' he wants to say.

He doesn't get a chance to say it, and now his daughter is offering one of
the things to her mother. Great God! she is taking it.

'Do you know, I believe I will,' she says, smiling.

So there it is—the wife, too. What is the American man to do or say?

Better go downtown, talk it over with some man friend.

'Women sure aren't what they were, but what can a man do? Let them
have it. They are in the saddle. Let them ride.'

It is the story of innumerable American men, who haven't kept up with
the American woman's pace, in the American small town as in the American
city.

•   •   •

IX

The eccentric is a permanent figure in American life. He is in the
cities as in the small town, but in the small town you know him. Curious
enough characters out of life, no doubt, pass you by the thousands in the
city streets, but they come and go swiftly. You do not meet them day after
day in the same streets, the same stores. You do not talk with them, know
intimately their idiosyncrasies.

In every American small town there is the lonely man who seldom

116

leaves his own house. Usually he is a bachelor. He has let a high hedge grow about the yard, almost hiding his house from the street. There are always whispered stories floating about the town concerning his life in the house. It is said that as a young man he was rejected by a beautiful woman. We Americans are born romanticists. Often there are more darkly menacing tales. In his youth it is said that he committeed some mysterious crime. It may be that he came suddenly into town from another place. Year after year his house remains unpainted. The yard before the house is overgrown with weeds. The front porch is rotting away. Occasionally he is seen emerging from his house at night. He hurries furtively along streets. He continually talks to himself.

Sid Smith is the practical joker of the town. He loves to send the town's half-wit on fool errands. He sends him to the hardware store for a left-handed monkey-wrench, to the print shop to see the type lice. He is the fellow who hands out loaded cigars that blow up in your face. When he has been successful with one of his victims, he runs up and down Main Street telling the story, boasting of his cleverness.

The man who loves an argument is downtown on Main Street every afternoon and evening. When he sees a group of men talking together, he joins them. He goes from group to group, listening to talk, and when a statement is made, he immediately challenges it.

He grows angry, he shouts, he waves his arms about. His wife is always scolding him.

'Why are you always making enemies? Why do you do it?'

He doesn't know why. He keeps making up his mind that he will be calm and quiet, talk quietly to others. He can't do it. On the next day he is at it again. He would really like to be a quiet, sensible fellow, leading a quiet, sensible life.

In every town there is the woman who is always having operations. She goes from one doctor to another. Almost everything has been cut out of her. She has grown pale and walks with difficulty, but she is a proud woman. She thinks of herself as a figure in the community. There isn't another woman in town who has been through what she has, she keeps declaring. She is one who enjoys her own suffering.

And there is always that other woman, a born nurse. She is a fat, jolly soul. When someone is sick, she comes to help. She is always Aunt Molly, or Kate, or Sarah—is everyone's aunt. She spreads cheer, has the touch.

117

And the school-teacher who never marries, although she was such a fine-looking younger woman. She goes on, year after year, teaching new crops of children. She has won the respect of the town, but remains, all her life, an oddly lonely-seeming figure.

Henry Horner is the town butt. He is a man of forty-five, and his wife is dead. He lives with his wife's sister in a house out at the edge of town.

Henry once had a little money and went into business. He became a chicken fancier and concocted a chick food to put on the market. He went from town to town trying to sell it, but did not succeed. He spent all his money in the venture.

Now Henry dresses shabbily and has let his hair grow long. He carries a heavy cane, and as he goes through the streets of the town boys crow at him. They imitate the cackle of hens that have been at the business of laying eggs and the clarion cry of the rooster. Henry grows violently angry. He waves his cane about, he swears, he pursues the boys furiously, but never catches them. As he passes through Main Street, some man, standing in a group of men by the post-office, also crows. Henry approaches the group. His hands are trembling. He stands before them demanding justice.

'What man of you did that?'

All the men of the group shake their heads. They look at Henry with blank faces. The town has discovered his weakness. There is a cruel streak in men. They cannot let poor Henry live his life in peace.

A young girl of the town has gone wrong early in life. Some man or boy has got her and has gone about telling the story. Other men and boys begin the pursuit. She is always lying about with men and boys, in fields near the town or in the town graveyard. Hers is a story as old as the Bible. In the town graveyard there is a crude and brutal expression of the meeting of life and death.

Thaddeus is the town's philosopher. He is respected by all the town. The word is out that he is well-read. It is even said that he knows Latin and Greek. Every evening he sits at home reading a book. His wife is a scold, but he pays no attention to her. The men of the town speak of him with admiration and envy.

'Gee, I wish I had his education.'

Thaddeus is a quiet, serene man who is deeply religious, although he never goes to church. He has worked out his own notion of God. He is a merchant, who also owns a farm near town, and is fond of young boys. He is very gentle with them. He has no children of his own, but on summer after-noons he is always taking some boy with him to his farm. Once he caught a clerk stealing money in his store. He did not discharge the clerk.

'If the money is worth more to you than your peace of mind, keep it,' he said.

He is a mystic. 'God,' he says to the boy who has ridden with him to the farm, 'is in the growing corn. He is in the trees over there in that wood, in the grass in that meadow, in the flowering weeds along the road.' The boy does not understand, but feels happy in the presence of the quiet, smiling man.

There is the town bully. He is forever boasting of fights he has won. He goes swaggering about with a half-burned cigar in the corner of his mouth. He declares he has never lost a fight.

'I'll knock your block off! I'll bust your jaw!' he is always shouting to someone. It is the traditions of the towns that he always in the end meets his match. Some smaller man, infuriated by his insults, lights into him and beats him up. It always happens, and when it does it fills the town with joy.

A mysterious woman comes to town. She appears suddenly and rents a house in a quiet residence street. She is one who keeps to herself, makes no acquaintances. When she appears in the streets, she is always well-dressed. All sorts of whispered stories about her run through the town. Young boys hear the stories and walk far out of their way going to and from school to pass her house.

The shades are always drawn, and the town is convinced that she is a wicked, sinful woman. There is a story that she has some connection with a mysterious band of robbers.

Or it is said that she is a kept woman; that she is being kept by a rich man of some distant city. A man of the town who lives on her street declares that often, after midnight, a big expensive-looking car parks before her house and a man enters. To the young boys of the town she becomes a sym-bol of something strange and enticing, out of some mysterious world of sin. It is said that in her house there are luxurious carpets and expensive furni-ture, that she wears jewels that have cost thousands of dollars. The woman stays for a time in the house and then disappears as mysteriously as she came. She also remains in the town's imagination a figure of romance.

Arthur is a thin, wiry little man who is always gay. No matter how gloomy the day, he is full of good cheer. He knows everyone, cries gaily to others as he hurries through the streets. He goes with a half-dancing step.

'Hello! Hello!'

'How are you feeling, Art?'

'Fine! Fine!'

Arthur is as full of life as a squirrel. He hops and dances. Something inside him is always singing and dancing. He is gay, alive, small, an always cheerful streak of sunlight on the town's streets.

There is the man who goes with the same woman year after year. He goes to see her every Sunday evening, takes her to church, drives about with her on week-day evenings, in his car. He is always at her house on one or two evenings during the week, sits with her on the porch of her house. He began going with her when he and she were both in high school. That was nineteen or twenty years ago. He has never paid any attention to any other woman nor has she ever been with any other man. When she began going with him, she was quite pretty, but now she begins to look a little worn. Her mother had died and she is keeping house for her father. The people of the town see the couple going about together year after year. They are a little amused. The word is out that they are engaged. Nothing happens. He just continues to go with her year after year.

There is always the town's stingy man. People say that he gives Abraham Lincoln a headache the way he squeezes a penny. All American towns have a flare for nicknames. He is called Penny Smith, or Penny Jones.

He has a little store at the end of Main Street where he sells knickknacks. It is called a Variety Store.

'Do you know what—I was in Penny Smith's store. He had dropped a penny on the floor. Several customers came in, but he paid no attention to them. They grew tired of waiting and went out. He was down on his hands and knees behind the counter looking for the penny he had dropped. I could have walked off with everything in the store and he wouldn't have known it. He was too absorbed in finding that penny.'

There is a young man who was once called the bright boy of the town. In school he took all of the prizes. His father sent him to college. He was the top man in his classes.

He came home and set up as a lawyer or doctor in the town and presently married. He married a daughter of one of the more well-to-do men of the town. He went along, a steady, successful, quiet man, until he was forty.

120

And then suddenly he went to pieces. Until he was forty, he had never been known to take a drink.

Then he began. He took bottles of whiskey up into his office, was seen on many afternoons reeling through the streets. No one knows what happened to him. He was one kind of man one day and almost on the next day he became something else.

Now he is the town drunkard, and his wife has a frightened look on her face. No one knows what made him do it. It is not explainable, something that fills the town with awe.

Carl is the small-town man who has the gift. He may have been the son of one of the more well-to-do citizens of the town or he may have been a poor man's son. It doesn't matter. Carl was one destined from birth to get on in the world. If he had been a big city man or had lived in one of the industrial cities, he might have become a captain of industry, a millionaire. In his own town he does well enough.

He is a born trader. He began as a boy. He will trade anything. 'He would trade his wife or daughter if he made a profit in the trade,' men say of him. In every trade he makes he comes out ahead.

Often he has no particular business, goes to no office. He walks about, making trades, he lends money, trades in real estate. Dollars stick to his fingers. Every year, in hard times and good times, he keeps getting ahead. He is one who has the gift, who never overlooks a chance. To the people of the town, he seems a good-natured, quiet fellow, but he is not very inclined to make friends. The town secretly admires him.

And then there is the man who throws it away. He keeps inheriting money from dying relatives, but he cannot keep it. He had ten thousand dollars from an aunt who died in Kansas. Every time he makes an investment, something goes wrong with it. He buys a house and forgets to take out insurance and on the next day it burns. He has several well-to-do relatives and keeps inheriting money, but always it slips away from him.

There is a Carrie Nation in almost every American town. She takes it upon her shoulders to look after the town morals. She is always accusing others of some mysterious sin. During the time of prohibition, she became a powerful figure. She was always telephoning to the sheriff, accusing some man of making or selling liquor. A young man is walking along the street smoking a cigarette and she stops before him. She stamps her foot, scolds at him.

121

The Midwest

'Take that cigarette out of your mouth, you filthy thing!' she cries.

She is against the use of tobacco in all forms, against the drinking of any kind of intoxicants, against boys playing baseball or swimming on Sunday, against card-playing. She hates all kinds of expressions of gaiety or joy, is down on dancing. She declares dancing leads young girls straight to ruin. She goes to see the girls' mothers, haunts the town editor. The whole weight of the town's moral life is on her shoulders.

The 'characters' of the towns give the towns their color. In the small towns every man's idiosyncrasies are known. They cannot escape you. Life in the towns can be at times terrible or it can be infinitely amusing and absorbing.

Without quite knowing it, you may yourself be one of the 'characters' of your town. If your neighbors are sometimes odd, it may be that they also think of you as odd. The life in the town is the test of man's ability to adjust himself. It tells the story of his skill in living with others.

●　　●　　●

XV

The church bells are ringing in the towns—Methodist bells, Catholic, Baptist, Presbyterian, Disciples, Lutheran, Episcopal, Congregational bells. Now the cars are parked thick in all the streets before the churches. Men and women are coming afoot, fathers and mothers, followed by their troops of children. The little girls not minding all the fuss, the hair-combing, the scrubbing, the dressing-up. It is an instinct.

It begins early in the female. They like it.

See the little boys with their clean, shining faces, their carefully combed hair. There goes one who seems to like it. 'He is a sissy. That's what he is.'

In the towns the Methodists and Baptists lead the procession in the number of churches. North and South, at the time of the last official count, there were some fifty-three thousand white and Negro Baptist churches. The Methodists ran them a close race. The Baptists lead all the others in the number of Negro churches.

Then there are the Roman Catholics with nearly twenty thousand churches, the Presbyterians with about twelve thousand, the Disciples and the Protestant Episcopalians with some seven or eight thousand each, the Church of Christ with six thousand, the Congregational with five thousand, and the Lutherans, counting both the Missouri Synod, the United and the Norwegian Lutheran, with some eleven thousand.

122

And there are some fifty-five thousand other Protestant churches, the Quakers in many sections strong, the Adventists and the Dunkards, the Christian Scientists, the United Brethren, the Unitarians, the Plymouth Brethren, the Mennonites, not to mention the Great I-Ams, the Zionists, the Two Seeds in the Spirit Baptists, the Christadelphians, the Duck River Baptists, the Shakers, the Holiness churches, the Church of Daniel's Band, the Moravians, and the Defenseless Moravians. The great number and variety of sects, all worshiping the same God, is but another expression of American indivdualism. It is something come down to us out of pioneer days, men and women of many nationalities pouring in, often coming to us to escape religious persecution.

Jim Watson doesn't belong to any church, but his wife does, so Jim contributes to the Baptist church in his town. The Baptist preacher meets Jim on the street.

'Jim, now you tell me, why don't you come to church with your wife?'

Jim says he does.

'I come once a year,' he says, and grins.

'Now you look here, Preacher,' says Jim, 'I chip in fifty dollars a year, don't I? I come to church once a year. That's fifty dollars a sermon. You haven't got another single member in your church who puts up more than that for just one sermon.'

Jim stays at home on Sunday mornings. He reads the Sunday newspaper. It is nice and quiet at home with the wife and kids all gone off to church and Sunday School. Now and then he discusses religion with his special man friend.

'Sure, I believe in God,' Jim says. 'I just think it doesn't make any difference whether a man goes to church or not. I don't think God keeps books on churchgoers, do you, Ed?'

The old Puritanical tightness of the Sabbath has softened a good deal in the American small town. As everyone knows, it never did clamp down hard on the Catholics.

Formerly, in smaller American towns, there were no Sunday afternoon ball games; on summer Sundays no one but the pronounced sinners ever went swimming; there were no shows, no movies. But nowadays, in many American towns, the movies are open on Sunday afternoons; there are ball games with teams from neighboring towns; half the town people are out in cars on summer Sunday afternoons; in the churches there is less insistence on hell fires; somewhat fewer revival meetings are held.

124

The church does, however, exert a tremendous influence on life in the American small town. Many a Catholic priest or a Protestant preacher is first friend to the members of his church when trouble comes.

He is the one who comes into the family circle when things go bad. He performs the marriage ceremony for the son or daughter. You can talk things over with him. He is taken into the family circle and into the confidence of the family when there is sickness or death. He is there with his hand in that of the husband when a man's wife is on her deathbed, when a son has gone bad, when a daughter has been careless and has got herself into a fix. Often he is able to patch up a break threatened between man and wife, hold a breaking family together.

The church you belong to in the American small town fixes the group you belong to. It fixes your social standing in the town life.

It is the church that takes in the newcomers to the town, his fellow church members seeing that the newcomer meets people, is made to feel a part of the town's life. It is a part of the setup of small-town life that enables the young man to meet the girl who will later become his wife.

The church is the center of innumerable activities reaching into many phases of American small-town life. It is and remains the channel through which the average American keeps a kind of touch with the mystery, with the strange fact of birth and death, the mystery of stars, of winds, of the renewal of life in nature in the spring.

The Age*

SHERWOOD ANDERSON

As I remember it, the town of Clyde itself was a fair and a sweet town. There was something of New England—It was in the so-called Western Reserve in the state of Ohio. There were many little white frame houses. All the residence streets were lined with great spreading maples. And at the back of his yard, every citizen with any pretensions had a barn.

The modern world had not come into full flower. Why, look, it is the far-famed horse and buggy age! Of course I shall be accused of nostalgia for speaking of it! But wasn't it Dean Swift who spoke of the man coming back from the world ruled by horses to a world ruled by men, and having a terrible time readjusting himself?

There were always horses tied to hitching-posts along the main street of the town. Sparrows grew fat from the droppings. There were old lady horses with sad eyes, and worn-out geldings: perhaps too many male horses early robbed of malehood.

There were horse races in our main street on winter afternoons, the streets cleared for them, and on winter nights, dances in country barns. Maple trees shedding their winged seeds on spring days when a breeze sprang up, creeks near town where boys went to swim. The terrible passionate curiosity of the young male concerning the young female. Old men, young men already failures in life—inspired ones, who from the beginning accepted failure, embraced it . . . But look! Young fellows of the local baseball team, having won a game from some neighboring town, having got a keg of beer, are going off to Ames's wood, down past the old stave factory, to drink there in the darkness, under trees, to sing ribald songs.

The achievement of a kind of drunkenness. It doesn't all come from the beer. There is the night with shining stars. The keg of beer we have got is sitting on a little platform made of logs or on a stump. We are at the wood's edge, with pasture lands between us and the town. Young men sprawling,

*Selection from Sherwood Anderson's *Memoirs*.

126

lads sprawling. In the pastures nearby, in bright moonlight, cows are grazing. Thoughts weave themselves in and out among spoken thoughts from the others, among the songs.—Now some fellow is boasting of his virility. We have poor little street-tarts in our town. They lie with men and boys under hedges—as they lay with them in the towns told about in the Old Testament, in Greek and Roman towns, in English towns, in French. How but for them do we get our education as young males?

One of the gang is talking. Already we have begun thinking of ourselves as a gang. Suddenly a thought emerges. "Why is it that those among the young men and boys of this town who listen to our elders, remain virtuous, go early to bed, do not associate with our town roughs, or smoke or drink or swear—surely all of them headed onward and upward—everyone says so—why is it that they are almost always such bum ball-players?"

There is that big fellow Jim, lying there on the grass, boasting now. He is very strong. He carried the keg of beer to the wood on his shoulder. Jim belongs to a poor family of the town and already has been arrested for stealing chickens. A doctor of the town, who is a rabid ball-fan, got him out of it by appearing and paying his fine. He carried the keg of beer right down through Main Street, past stores, past people walking, while the rest of us sneaked through alleyways, not wanting it known that we were to share it with him. He is a pitcher with marvelous control. He is a curve ball pitcher. It was his work that enabled us to beat the neighboring town—and last night, when any athlete, to do good work, should have been early to bed, Jim was out with one of our town tarts.

Why, oh, why, in that town of the American Northwest where Sinclair Lewis spent his boyhood, were there no such evenings among other young men and boys! What a different book *Main Street* might have been had a circus ever come to his town, had his town baseball team ever whipped a team from a neighboring one—had springs but come—winter nights under the stars—had he but kissed some high-school girl on a dark porch, her father right inside the house, pretending to read a book in there, thus putting one over on papa. Poor Lewis, he missed a lot! And Henry Mencken, with his trick of making all small-town and country people into one pattern— But of that, more perhaps later. We are in the wood now and Jim is boasting.

"But where did you take her?"

"To the graveyard," he says. Our town graveyard has a national hero buried in it. There is a bronze monument. The United States government put it up . . . But surely, when he, our national hero, was a lad here in this town, he did not go off with other boys for such evenings as this? He did not listen to such ribald songs, hear such talk as is going on here?

Jim laughs. What envy there is in the rest of us! "Oh that I could be such a one." There is the feeling that his boast may not be a boast. There is a nice grass plot about the statue of our national hero. It is on a small hill. "Do you suppose they were lying there, in the moonlight, on the grass, under the monument?"

A butcher's son is sprawling near our mighty virile one. He rolls over on his back and looks up at the stars. He has an ambition, wonderful, gigantic. "Before I die," wistfully he says, "I intend to be with one of every nation on earth."

This scene, and in the distance the lights of the town. The eternal puzzle of life beginning in a boy. "There is this life here, that I am at this moment leading, with these fellows. In spite of all talk, this talk of women, of man's adventures with women, now going on here, in spite of all this, it's a kind of good warm flow." On the ball field during the afternoon, there was a certain play made. You had nothing to do with it. You were playing in the right field and but one fly ball came your way during the game. You muffed that. At bat you did nothing. There was a ball shot down through the infield, very hot, a hard hit one, and little Shorty Grimes raced over. He got it with one hand, turned a quick pivot. He shot it to second . . . a double play. All of the bases full, our side but one run ahead. At that moment you felt something . . . Something of Shorty's quick and so beautifully graceful movement was also in your own body. You felt no jealousy, no envy. There was a strange gladness in you.

The puzzle about all of this as you lie out there under the trees, beneath the stars, the lights of the stars in the distance! There is your own mother. She works hard, is fairly killing herself with work to keep her sons alive. What of her? Suppose she were here now, heard as you did these tales of triumphant sin, heard those songs sung?

That thought put aside as being a bit too uncomfortable. "There is the woman's word, her life, and there is our man's life. There is a world and a time of youth, and a world and a time of maturity. Maybe sometime I may become mature, a man in a man's world. But now I am a boy. There is this happiness, the warm feeling I now have for these others out here with me at the edge of the wood. For everything its time and place."

128

Mary White

WILLIAM ALLEN WHITE

May 17, 1921

The Associated Press reports carrying the news of Mary White's death declared that it came as the result of a fall from a horse. How she would have hooted at that! She never fell from a horse in her life. Horses have fallen on her and with her—"I'm always trying to hold 'em in my lap," she used to say. But she was proud of a few things, and one of them was that she could ride anything that had four legs and hair. Her death resulted not from a fall but from a blow on the head which fractured her skull, and the blow came from the limb of an overhanging tree on the parking.

The last hour of her life was typical of its happiness. She came home from a day's work at school, topped off by a hard grind with the copy on the High School Annual, and felt that a ride would refresh her. She climbed into her khakis, chattering to her mother about the work she was doing, and hurried to get her horse and be out on the dirt roads for the country air and the radiant green fields of the spring. As she rode through the town on an easy gallop she kept waving at passers-by. She knew everyone in town. For a decade the little figure in the long pigtail and the red hair ribbon had been familiar on the streets of Emporia, and she got in the way of speaking to those who nodded at her. She passed the Kerrs, walking the horse, in front of the Normal Library, and waved at them; passed another friend a few hundred feet farther on, and waved at her. The horse was walking, and as she turned into North Merchant Street she took off her cowboy hat, and the horse swung into a lope. She passed the Tripletts and waved her cowboy hat at them, still moving gayly north on Merchant Street. A GAZETTE carrier passed—a High School boy friend—and she waved at him, but with her bridle hand; the horse veered quickly, plunged into the parking where the low-hanging limb faced her, and, while she still looked back waving, the blow came. But she did not fall from the horse; she slipped off, dazed a bit, staggered, and fell in a faint. She never quite recovered consciousness.

129

But she did not fall from the horse, neither was she riding fast. A year or so ago she used to go like the wind. But that habit was broken, and she used the horse to get into the open, to get fresh, hard exercise, and to work off a certain surplus energy that welled up in her and needed a physical outlet. That need has been in her heart for years. It was back of the impulse that kept the dauntless little brown-clad figure on the streets and country roads of the community and built into a strong, muscular body what had been a frail and sickly frame during the first years of her life. But the riding gave her more than a body. It released a gay and hardy soul. She was the happiest thing in the world. And she was happy because she was enlarging her horizon. She came to know all sorts and conditions of men; Charley O'Brien, the traffic cop, was one of her best friends. W. L. Holtz, the Latin teacher, was another. Tom O'Connor, farmer-politician, and Rev. J. H. J. Rice, preacher and police judge, and Frank Beach, music master, were her special friends, and all the girls, black and white, above the track and below the track, in Pepville and Stringtown, were among her acquaintances. And she brought home riotous stories of her adventures. She love to rollick; persiflage was her natural expression at home. Her humor was a continual bubble of joy. She seemed to think in hyperbole and metaphor. She was mischievous without malice, as full of faults as an old shoe. No angel was Mary White, but an easy girl to live with, for she never nursed a grouch five minutes in her life.

With all her eagerness for the out-of-doors, she loved books. On her table when she left her room were a book by Conrad, one by Galsworthy, *Creative Chemistry* by E. E. Slosson, and a Kipling Book. She read Mark Twain, Dickens, and Kipling before she was ten—all of their writings. Wells and Arnold Bennett particularly amused and diverted her. She was entered as a student in Wellesley for 1922; was assistant editor of the High School Annual this year, and in line for election to the editorship next year. She was a member of the executive committee of the High School Y.W.C.A.

Within the last two years she had begun to be moved by an ambition to draw. She began as most children do by scribbling in her schoolbooks, funny pictures. She bought cartoon magazines and took a course—rather casually, naturally, for she was, after all, a child with no strong purposes— and this year she tasted the first fruits of success by having her pictures accepted by the High School Annual. But the thrill of delight she got when Mr. Ecord, of the Normal Annual, asked her to do the cartooning for that book this spring, was too beautiful for words. She fell to her work with all her enthusiastic heart. Her drawings were accepted, and her pride—always repressed by a lively sense of the ridiculous figure she was cutting—was a really gorgeous thing to see. No successful artist ever drank a deeper draft of satisfaction than she took from the little fame her work was getting among her schoolfellows. In her glory, she almost forgot her horse—but never her car.

For she used the car as a jitney bus. It was her social life. She never had a "party" in all her nearly seventeen years—wouldn't have one; but she never drove a block in her life that she didn't begin to fill the car with pick-ups! Everybody rode with Mary White—white and black, old and young, rich and poor, men and women. She liked nothing better than to fill the car with long-legged High School boys and an occasional girl, and parade the town. She never had a "date," nor went to a dance, except once with her brother, Bill, and the "boy proposition" didn't interest her—yet. But young people—great spring-breaking, varnish-cracking, fender-bending, door-sagging carloads of "kids"—gave her great pleasure. Her zests were keen. But the most fun she ever had in her life was acting as chairman of the committee that got up the big turkey dinner for the poor folks at the county home; scores of pies, gallons of slaw, jam, cakes, preserves, oranges, and a wilderness of turkey were loaded into the car and taken to the county home. And, being of a practical turn of mind, she risked her own Christmas dinner to see that the poor folks actually got it all. Not that she was a cynic; she just disliked to tempt folks. While there she found a blind colored uncle, very old, who could do nothing but make rag rugs, and she rustled up from her school friends rags enough to keep him busy for a season. The last engagement she tried to make was to take the guests at the county home out for a car ride. And the last endeavor of her life was to try to get a rest room for colored girls in the High School. She found one girl reading in the toilet, because there was no better place for a colored girl to loaf, and it inflamed her sense of injustice and she became a nagging harpy to those who she thought could remedy the evil. The poor she always had with her and was glad of it. She hungered and thirsted for righteousness; and was the most impious creature in the world. She joined the Church without consulting her parents, not particularly for her soul's good. She never had a thrill of piety in her life, and would have hooted at a "testimony." But even as a little child she felt the church was an agency for helping people to more of life's abundance, and she wanted to help. She never wanted help for herself. Clothes meant little to her. It was a fight to get a new rig on her; but eventually a harder fight to get it off. She never wore a jewel and had no ring but her High School class ring and never asked for anything but a wrist watch. She refused to have her hair up, though she was nearly seventeen. "Mother," she protested, "you don't know how much I get by with, in my braided pigtails, that I could not with my hair up." Above every other passion of her life was her passion not to grow up, to be a child. The tomboy in her, which was big, seemed to loath to be put away forever in skirts. She was a Peter Pan, who refused to grow up.

Her funeral yesterday at the Congregational Church was as she would have wished it; no singing, no flowers except the big bunch of red roses from her brother Bill's Harvard classmen—heavens, how proud that would have made her!—and the red roses from THE GAZETTE forces, in vases at her head and feet. A short prayer; Paul's beautiful essay on "Love" from the Thirteenth Chapter of First Corinthians; some remarks about her democratic spirit by her friend, John H. J. Rice, pastor and police judge, which she would have deprecated if she could; a prayer sent down for her by her friend, Carl Nau; and opening the service the slow, poignant movement from Beethoven's Moonlight Sonata, which she loved; and closing the service a cutting from the joyously melancholy first movement of Tschaikowski's Pathetic Symphony, which she liked to hear in certain moods, on the phonograph; then the Lord's Prayer by her friends in High School.

That was all.

For her pallbearers only her friends were chosen: her Latin teacher, W. L. Holtz; her High School principal, Rice Brown; her doctor, Frank Foncannon; her friend, W. W. Finney; her pal at THE GAZETTE office, Walter Hughes and her brother Bill. It would have made her smile to know that her friend, Charley O'Brien, the traffic cop, had been transferred from Sixth and Commercial to the corner near the church to direct her friends who came to bid her good-by.

A rift in the clouds in a gray day threw a shaft of sunlight upon her coffin as her nervous, energetic little body sank to its last sleep. But the soul of her, the glowing, gorgeous, fervent soul of her, surely was flaming in eager joy upon some other dawn.

The Illinois Village

VACHEL LINDSAY

O you who lose the art of hope,
Whose temples seem to shrine a lie,
Whose sidewalks are but stones of fear,
Who weep that Liberty must die,
Turn to the little prairie towns,
Your higher hope shall yet begin.
On every side awaits you there
Some gate where glory enters in.

Yet when I see the flocks of girls,
Watching the Sunday train go thro'
(As tho' the whole wide world went by)
With eyes that long to travel too,
I sigh, despite my soul made glad
By cloudy dresses and brown hair,
Sigh for the sweet life wrenched and torn
By thundering commerce, fierce and bare.
Nymphs of the wheat these girls should be:
Kings of the grove, their lovers, strong.
Why are they not inspired, aflame?
This beauty calls for valiant song—
For men to carve these fairy-forms
And faces in a fountain-frieze;
Dancers that own immortal hours;
Painters that work upon their knees;
Maids, lovers, friends, so deep in life,
So deep in love and poet's deeds,

133

The Midwest

The railroad is a thing disowned,
The city but a field of weeds.

Who can pass a village church
By night in these clean prairie lands
Without a touch of Spirit-power?
So white and fixed and cool it stands—
A thing from some strange fairy-town,
A pious amaranthine flower,
Unsullied by the winds, as pure
As jade or marble, wrought this hour:—
Rural in form, foursquare and plain,
And yet our sister, the new moon,
Makes it a praying wizard's dream.
The trees that watch at dusty noon
Breaking its sharpest lines, veil not
The whiteness it reflects from God,

Flashing like Spring on many an eye,
Making clean flesh, that once was clod.

Who can pass a district school
Without the hope that there may wait
Some baby-heart the books shall flame
With zeal to make his playmates great,
To make the whole wide village gleam
A strangely carved celestial gem,
Eternal in its beauty-light,
The Artist's town of Bethlehem!

Normal Love

JOYCE CAROL OATES

Downtown

I park my car in a high-rise garage, three floors up. Everything is silent. The garage is gray, the color of concrete blocks and metal. Many cars are parked here, in silence, but no one is around. A small tension rises in me, an alarm. Is there anyone around? Anyone? Our city is not a large city, there is no danger. There might be danger late at night for a woman alone. Now it is a winter afternoon, a weekday, overcast, too cold for anyone to make trouble. . . . I lock the car door, I put the keys in my purse, I walk quickly to the elevator and press the button for Down.

The elevator is slow. Is it out of order? Why is there no one around? A sudden noise behind me . . . behind me a man is walking this way, putting something in his pocket. Car keys, probably. His footsteps make brisk noises on the concrete. The air is cold. My heart begins to pound absurdly, I know there is no danger and yet my muscles stiffen as if in expectation of danger, the very shape of my skeleton tensing as if to receive a blow. . . . The man waits with me for the elevator. I don't look at him. He doesn't look at me. He is wearing a fairly good overcoat, he is no danger to me. There is no danger in this city; the very coldness of the air on this December day makes everything abrupt and undramatic, there is no tension, nothing. The elevator comes. The door opens. I step inside, the man steps quickly inside, for a moment I feel a sense of panic, as if inside me a door is opening suddenly upon nothing, upon blackness. The elevator takes us down. The man says nothing, makes no movement, does not take his hands out of his pockets as if . . . as if to take them out would be a sign, and he dare not make a sign. I wait with my heart hammering. I wait. The elevator stops, the door opens, a woman and some children are waiting to get inside, I step out quickly and escape. . . .

I spend the afternoon shopping. I am not followed.

The Midwest

My husband

sits alone downstairs after we have all gone to bed. This is a sacred time for him, I think. Secrets rise in him at this time. If I come to the landing to say, "It's after two o'clock," he will stare up at me, startled. He sits on the sofa with an ashtray beside him. He is smoking and thinking. He is sitting there in a kind of troubled peace, a man of forty, six feet two and lean, unmuscular, a city man with dark hair thinning on top, the tension and bewilderment of the city in the lines of his face. His face is lined, yes. Why is his face lined? He has not the power of true amazement any longer, yet his face, in the light of two o'clock in the morning, in the fuzzy beige light from our lamp, shows a bewilderment that should be stronger. He is thinking, dreaming, a terrible sadness fills him, he is sitting there alone and will glance up at me, startled, if I come to the landing. The newspaper is out back, folded to be thrown out tomorrow, the newspaper with the story about the missing girl.

My children

are eager to get out of the doors of the house and eager to get back through them again. They jerk one way, scrambling for freedom. Then they are hurrying back. They are hungry. The boys have long unpredictable legs. They are always knocking against tables. They spill milk, drop plates, their nostrils have been raw with colds for weeks. They like hot dogs and hamburgers. The meat comes processed in strange shapes they never notice—tied neatly with a tiny knot of intestine, pink, or ground to an intricate maze of wormlike red tissue. It is all tissue. The boys like this meat very much. One of my daughters is melancholy and selfish, remote and spiteful, thirteen years old . . . the corners of her eyes narrow at things I can't imagine. She is always thinking. She looks like her father, with the same pinched calculating face; a smile can transform such a face. The other girl is only nine, a good-natured child, she loves us all and can't understand why her father is drifting from us, at the age of forty, a mysterious stubborn drifting we can't understand.

My neighborhood supermarket

has a tinsel Christmas tree inside. A fluffy angel blows a horn at its very top. The tree is pretty but difficult to look at, the metallic branches catch light and reflect it painfully. A radio is playing "Jingle Bells" but the rhythm is very fast, speeded up. . . . Which day of the week is this? I do

136

most of my shopping on Tuesday. But sometimes on Wednesday we have already run out of something, or I forgot to buy something, and I go back to the store. By the time Thursday comes I need something more, usually milk, and on Friday I have my hair done and the hairdresser is just down the block so it's no trouble to drop in again; the store is very pleasant. Christmas carols are being played now. But the sounds are filmy and vague, in the distance, as if the angels singing such songs are distracted, glancing over their shoulders at something. During the week the supermarket is not very crowded. Sometimes I come back again on Saturday and it's crowded then, but more girls are stationed at the check-out counters, so I suppose everything works out. I suppose they have it all figured out.

It is necessary for me to look carefully at everything. Most things are familiar—these cans and packages—but still I look carefully, to see if there is any change, to see if there are special things that I want. I have to buy a lot of groceries. Two shopping carts are necessary sometimes, so one of the boys comes along. As long as he doesn't knock anything over, he's helpful. I should be proud of him, a son of my own, but I don't have time to be proud of him. His nose is running, he wipes it on the side of his hand . . . on his sleeve. . . . "Take this," I tell him and give him a Kleenex. He accepts it. He wipes his nose as if his nose had become suddenly delicate.

But I prefer to shop alone. I take my time with everything. I take my time buying meat, inspecting the shapes of meat. The radio is now playing "Let It Snow." Far beyond my hearing are the cries of amazed animals stunned by hammer blows, their hoofs skidding in the dirt, their shoulders and heads wrenching to get free of the horns that imprison them—men have hold of these horns! They are herded into trucks. Their flanks and sides are carried frozen out of trucks, big refrigerated trucks so long they can hardly make the turns of our old-fashioned little intersections.

Our house

is on a street that is partly good, partly bad. There are boarding houses at the corner. This is a college town, quiet and unexciting, a nice place to live; only in the last several years has the crime rate begun to rise, but nothing has happened to us. Students living in those boarding houses sometimes make trouble, but inside the houses only; they have never bothered us. The street has potholes. I drive automatically around them now, not even seeing them.

The university's president lives a few blocks away, in a large, old home.

137

Mornings in our house are quiet. All my children go to school now. The telephone rings suddenly and my mouth goes dry; I hurry to answer the phone, I am anxious, wondering . . . could it be a wrong number? Or is it a friend? Is it someone inviting us out? There is so much cruel power in that person calling me, in his anonymity! But the telephone must ring also when I am not home and then, then I am the one who is in power, then the caller (probably another wife, like myself) must stand listening sadly to the ringing of a telephone in an empty house, denied a few minutes' conversation. All my children go to school now. They walk to school. When the telephone rings in the empty house I go blank with anxiety, with hope. The noise rings through me. When no one calls I do housework, laundry or vacuuming, making all the beds, straightening things out; then I go out shopping. I work around my house thinking to myself about the mystery of a house, the lives dreamed out in it. My children are eager to get away in the morning and eager to come back in the afternoon. I catch myself up quickly, dreaming of them, their bouncing impatient limbs somehow inside me, damaging me. . . . Do they want to damage me, my flesh? No. Does my husband want to damage me? No. The house, which I wanted so badly eight years ago, is very silent in the morning. I walk through the rooms, buttoning my car coat, getting ready to go out and shop . . . I am thinking with part of my mind about what I must buy today, clothes for one of the kids, a shower curtain to replace the ripped one, some of those new dark stockings, maybe a new pair of shoes. . . . I like to shop, I go shopping every day. I cannot locate myself precisely in this house, so I go out. I have bought everything for the rooms myself, choosing the pieces of furniture carefully, worrying over them, studying magazines like *House Beautiful*. Our sofa is dark brown, our rug is light beige. The coffee table is a long modern oval, of dark walnut. The room used to seem striking to me, even beautiful, but now it looks a little worn and cheap, I don't know why. I picked out all this furniture and my husband and I argued over its cost but isn't it the furniture of a strange family, something another woman has chosen? My husband shows no sign of himself here. He puts everything of his away, as his own father did. Nothing remains of him downstairs, he is a professor at the university and most of his books are at school, his real life is somewhere else, not here. He is invisible here, in this house.

I look out the front window. Across the street is a house like this one, of dark red brick, two stories high with a big attic where, as in our house, two boys have their room. These houses were built in the forties. I look out the window. It seems to me that something moves against the window of that house—another woman, looking out? Is she looking across the street at me?

The purse

came into our lives by accident. My husband took the car to have the brakes fixed and on his way home, walking back home, he cut across a vacant lot. I have seen him out walking, alone, and the strength of his walk has always impressed me—a man with somewhere to get to, a stubbornness that women need in men. But he is not really like that. He was wearing his trench coat, a soiled tan coat, his hands were stuck in his pockets, he was walking fast and with his head bowed as usual (thinking of what? of his students? of the bill for the car?), his eyes drifting along the ground . . . and something caught his eye, the corner of his eye. It happened that way.

He saw a woman's purse. It had been thrown into the frozen grass, a few yards from the path, a black patent-leather purse. He paused. He leaned over and picked it up. . . .

Around him in the field was frozen milkweed.

"I found this," he said to me, coming in the back door. He looked worried, slightly embarrassed, as if I would blame him for something. Inside the purse was a wallet of some brown cheap plastic material, and inside the wallet some snapshots, a few dollar bills, some change, an identification card. Crumpled tissue stained with pink lipstick, and a comb, and a tube of lipstick, a few loose pennies . . . keys on a chain with a small fake rabbit's foot. . . .

Linda Slater, 1463 St. Clair. In case of emergency notify Mr. and Mrs. Frank Slater, 1463 St. Clair.

At the dentist's   at the hairdresser's   at the supermarket

Betty has three cavities this time. She won't brush her teeth. I check her toothbrush at night: sometimes it is wet, but what does that mean? All my children tell lies.

The dental assistant is about nineteen years old, with her hair in a big frothy mess, bleached. I glance through my checkbook ahead of time and see that I have forgotten already today to record one check . . . what was that check? A small storm rises in me, irritation and alarm. My husband never makes mistakes with the checkbook or with money or figures of any

139

kind, he does them in his head, he never makes mistakes. He doesn't make much money as a professor but he never makes mistakes adding up that money or subtracting it.

Outside in the waiting room while I wait for Betty I notice last night's newspaper still here. From across the room I can see the headline on the left-hand side of the page: GIRL MISSING. Last night we read that story. Linda Slater, 20, was reported missing and her whereabouts not known. Her purse was found in a vacant lot late Monday afternoon by Dr. Norman York, Professor of History at the University. He telephoned her parents. He brought the purse over to them. My eye darted at his name again and again—his name is my name, that is my name in the newspaper, about a man who found a girl's purse. The girl is now missing. She is five feet three inches tall, weighs one hundred ten pounds, dark brown hair, blue eyes, I can't remember. . . .

I leaf through a magazine and look at the photographs of food. Christmas is coming. We will all make Christmas cookies, the children and I. I will plan meals, a week of meals for Christmas week, I will make up things ahead of time and freeze them . . . and on Christmas day we will have a ham, I think, instead of a turkey. . . . The table settings in the magazine are very beautiful, decorated with holly and pine boughs.

Finally I pick up the newspaper and look at her picture again—Linda Slater, 20, dark hair and firm, staring, curious eyes, a very short upper lip. A posed photograph. It probably exaggerates her beauty.

Friday, the hairdresser's. Glenda does my hair. She is a big cheerful girl. She washes my hair enthusiastically, scrubbing my scalp. One time her fingers slipped and one of them, or a knuckle, went into my eye. The soap stung but I didn't make any fuss, I don't mind pain, I usually laugh it off in embarrassment.

Glenda pins my hair up in big rollers. There are four chairs before the big mirror, two others occupied, women having their hair pinned up. This place is not very clean, but it is reasonable. The air is chatty and warm. All the girls are friendly. Glenda has a big, robust air about her, I can smell the gum she is chewing. Her diamond ring looks much too big to be real; I know her husband is a factory worker.

"Hey, you ever seen a thalidomide baby?" Glenda asks the girl who is working next to her.

"What kind?"

"Thalidomide, you know—that sleeping pill they had."

"Oh yeah. No. Where is there one?"

"He's not a baby now, he's pretty grown-up."

"Where?"

"My mother-in-law's street, across the street from her."

The woman whose hair is being done next to me twists her head around. I see her here often, she has a bleached-out, staring face, a redhead with pale freckles. She is about my age, forty. "There's a thalidomide girl lives down the street from us," she said.

"How old?"

"Twelve."

"This boy, this one I was telling you about, is real nasty. He's maybe six feet tall, he goes to high school already and is a real brat. His mother spoiled him."

"The girl has little arms, real short arms, little flippers."

"*He's* got flippers. He wears some wool things, like mittens, up around them in the winter. He can use them flippers like they were arms."

"Is he smart?"

"He's a smart aleck."

"The girl is pretty smart, I guess. But she's a show-off too; I seen her once in a store downtown acting up. Her and two other girls. They're about in seventh grade, these girls, and flirting with some guy. This girl's got real short little flippers, just like baby arms, and she was touching some salesguy's chin with one of them. It was a shoe store."

"She was what?"

"She was kidding around, flirting—that guy's face was so red, it wasn't even funny."

"Flirting, she was flirting?"

"Yeah, with those little arms of hers. They say she's real smart, but she's nasty."

"*He's* nasty. Down at school the girls are just crazy for him and they call him up all the time, because he's cute, and they don't seem to care about the flippers or anything. But around the house his mother has to do everything for him . . . he can't even go to the bathroom by himself, he thinks he's so smart but he has to have help. They asked him if he would like some artificial arms but he wouldn't. He said no. They tried to get him to take them but he wouldn't. He gets all this attention because of them short arms. . . ."

At the supermarket I go back to the dairy products and get a carton of milk, lifting it up to see if it's leaking underneath. It seems all right. I buy some cottage cheese. I didn't bother with a grocery cart but it occurs to me that I need other things, so my arms get full, it's awkward carrying everything. I carry the items pressed up against my chest. At the check-out counter I notice some watery milk on my coat.

The texture of wet snow

is stubborn, won't melt. It has turned gray and wet. I was not always forty years old. I remember looking out the front window of my parents' house in Indiana, watching the rain. I had long blond hair, I always dressed well, I was waiting for something to happen to me, and it happened. Once I went for a walk, alone, when I was visiting my grandmother in West Bend. I went for a walk into a little park. I looked at the roses because they had gone to all that trouble to plant roses; I stopped and looked at a sundial . . . but the sun was not shining, I couldn't see what time it was.

When I get home Susan says, "Betty is sort of sick."

Betty is throwing up in the bathroom upstairs. While I am with her the telephone rings, one of the children answers it. I wait but no one calls me; it must be for one of the children.

Dinner

always takes place at six. Everyone is ready to eat. My husband has been home since five, has had a drink, has looked through the paper. His name no longer appears in those stories about Linda Slater. I want to ask him about it, how does he feel, what is he thinking? . . . but his silence baffles me. I resent this silence in him, though it has always been in him, since we met twenty years ago.

He comes into the kitchen when Susan gets him. Susan hangs onto him, teasing. She loves him and her love is a torment to all of us and to herself, making her forehead rise in childish angry frowns. "Daddy you're not listening!" she often says, throwing herself around as if trying to damage herself; or she gets up from the table with dignity and walks away, and Norman calls her back, and she says *no*, and he makes a sudden movement to push his chair back and get her and, pretending to be frightened, perhaps a little frightened, she does come back. . . .

We sit. Tonight we are having creamed chicken with carrots and peas. It is a familiar dish, they like it, they are hungry. Now we are beginning dinner at last, sitting around the big kitchen table, all of us eased into our places as if at the start of a boat race . . . floating with difficulty on the element of our lives, which is love. Is it love? We are here, around this particular table, because two people love each other and got married. On that day I stared at the sundial I was positive no one would marry me . . . but I needn't have worried, like most women. It happened.

Sometimes I lean over the bathroom sink, alone, feeling nauseated, clutching my head and thinking *What is going to happen?* Am I going to throw up? But I never throw up. I can't bring it up out of me, whatever is inside. Even when I was pregnant I had a strong stomach. The nausea passes and my head is filled suddenly with activity, the pictures of things I must use—the colored sponges I use in the kitchen, one for dishes exclusively and the other for wiping counters and the table, the sheets and pillowcases I must fold, fold, again and again, the beds I must make, the small rugs I must straighten, the cans I must open with the can opener, rinse, and put under the sink in the garbage can. My head is filled suddenly with a love for these things. I must go downstairs and open cupboards and the refrigerator to seek out certain packages and cans and jars, the containers of love. Every day I must do this. I must go down into the kitchen and prepare meals for my family, with love, careful of the delicate shapes of love. Plates, forks, spoons, knives, paper napkins, glasses . . . these achieve a secret meaning, placed on the table. Will one of the boys knock his milk glass over? No matter. Mop it up. Norman will mop it up, he takes care of emergencies, a tradition. Everyone sits. A Friday-night dinner. Do they understand this bouquet of love I have set out for them? What, precisely, do they see? If the carrots were missing from the main dish and there were only peas in it, along with pepper and salt and a few other spices, would this make any difference? I should have put pimiento in the cream sauce, but what was left in the jar had spoiled. In the salad I have put two kind of lettuce, tomatoes, radishes, cucumber slices, bits of celery and green pepper. If I had left out the green pepper would they notice? Do they notice that it is there? I have made biscuits from a mix. They all put the biscuits on their plates and the chicken and sauce over them, except for Susan, who can't stand soggy things; if the biscuits were missing? . . . Bobby drops his fork onto the floor. No matter, wipe it off. The dinner has begun. The race is on, no going back. My husband is saying something. Stern, or smiling? He smiles. Good. My husband is saying something to me about

143

this evening. "What time are they coming?" He always asks that question when we have someone over for the evening; they are alway invited for 8:30. "Eight-thirty," I tell him. My husband is an intelligent man and his intelligence is kindly, gentle; over the years he has perfected small attentions while his imagination drifts from me.

What can I say to him?

Around the table everyone is chattering, jiggling, reaching out, eating noisily. The boys bump elbows accidentally on purpose. Susan says, "Oh you're a little pig!" Jamie says, "Mind your own business!" Susan says, "Shut up!" Jamie says, "You shut up!" Susan says, "*You* shut up!" Around the table everyone is eating . . . they are jockeying for position, anxious to finish dinner and get away. Susan will finish first. She has left all the peas on her plate, carefully picked out. Is this to anger me, or do the peas really sicken her?

After they are finished I gather up the plates, the forks, the spoons, the knives, the smudged glasses . . . the cream sauce is hardening, I hate to get it on my fingers, its coldness appalls me . . . the table is wet, someone has spilled sauce on it, but no matter; we have a table nothing can hurt. Nothing can hurt it. I gather everything up, taking away that night's pattern on the table, and put it on the kitchen counter, a mess, setting it down and feeling suddenly very strange. . . .

Friends

come in, smile at us, take off their coats. Norm makes drinks. Scotch and water. We sit. Arnold and Brenda look a little tired? No, Brenda looks good. She is wearing those new stockings that have a wet look to them, and her shoes look new too. People sometimes mistake Brenda for me, and me for Brenda, though my hair is lighter than hers and I am taller than she is. I don't mind being mistaken for someone else. We are both faculty wives. Our husbands talk together, we talk together. I look over at Norman to see if he is still so distracted, but I can't tell. He avoids people's eyes, an old habit of his. Around eleven I go out into the kitchen and Brenda comes with me, carrying her drink. I take slices of cheese and meat out of the refrigerator, which I have prepared earlier and wrapped in cellophane. I put some bread in a little wicker basket with a cloth napkin in it. I set out some pickles and olives. Brenda leans her stomach against the counter, looking into her drink. "I'm sorry Arnold is acting so funny tonight," she says. She has creases in her neck that show when she looks down, her chin creasing

144

into her throat. "He started drinking when he got home from school. He thinks they're easing him out. . . ."

We talk about Brenda's exercise sessions at the YWCA, the hour of routines she and ten other housewives go through. They wear leotards. They meet every Wednesday morning. We talk about the wife of another professor, an older woman who never goes out any longer, is never seen at school or in town. She had had an operation this summer. "You'd think it would be enough to get it removed successfully and to survive," Brenda says. Her face is screwed up into a look of sympathy and bewilderment. "I mean, a woman can wear all kinds of things now, nobody could tell. . . . How could anybody tell?"

Nobody could tell.

Norm and I sleep heavily at night, in the two halves of our bed. Vividly I can remember the past years, those months when I was pregnant. But I can't remember how it came to be that I was pregnant. I can remember being in my earlier twenties, a new wife, sitting in an erotic daze somewhere . . . on a train? . . . my loins dazzled with the memory of our love, the unbearable dazzling of what my young husband had done to me, again and again, but the girl on the train seems to be in a movie, on film, being taken away from me and not me at all . . . she stares dreamily out the window, in a trance, enchanted. I am not that girl.

I could never remember why I was pregnant, precisely. It had seemed important, it had seemed sacred, that I remember the precise day, the precise night . . . but I never could. I didn't have time. Everything fell away. I had a small baby, I was going to have another; I had two babies and I was going to have another; we had to pack, I was pregnant and afraid of a miscarriage, we couldn't afford to pay movers, we spent all day packing dishes and books . . . we drove across the country to a school where Norm taught for one year, then we drove back across the country to another school where he taught for five years, thinking he had found his place, then he decided that that school wasn't good enough for him and so we came to this school, nine years ago, or perhaps ten years ago, a school that seems to me precisely like the other two we were at.

"We heard on the radio coming over that part of a woman's torso was found on the shore, down river," Brenda says, making a face. "Some kids found it. Wouldn't that be awful to have one of our own kids find something like that? They were playing down by the river. . . ."

So she is dead.

The Midwest

Saturday

I take Betty to the doctor. Asian flu. That means they will all get it, all the children. Susan goes for her piano lessons. The car heater is broken, I must tell Norman, I am afraid to tell Norman . . . we can't afford to pay for it. I have started to buy Christmas presents. My head is dazzled suddenly with the thought of presents, Christmas presents, it makes me a little dizzy to think of them . . . I am dazzled as if by a sudden streaming of light, lovely light! Days of buying presents stretch out before me. And then Christmas week. Some presents I will mail all the way back to Indiana; it is important to keep up these traditions. Even my old uncles, they appreciate being remembered. Everyone appreciates being remembered. It is terrible not to be remembered.

. . . A roast, roast beef. Wild rice. Gravy. Rolls from the bakery, hard rolls and soft rolls . . . salad . . . carrots? Not carrots. Cauliflower with cheddar-cheese sauce. Spiced apples. Tonight I will put spiced apples out in a white dish, on a white platter, spiced apples looking like lovely dark red wheels. . . .

The supermarket is crowded. Everyone is in a hurry, but it is a pleasant hurry. Music from somewhere. The floor seems to be rocking beneath me with this music, like the floor of a boat, but it is a pleasant sensation. I float along the aisles. The cans on the shelves stretch up over my head, so many different sizes and colors—I put cans in the cart, I put in boxes, packages, bottles, I put in heads of lettuce—the lettuce isn't very good today and it costs 39¢—and then on to the dairy counter—four cartons of milk—I check the bottoms of the cartons to see if they are leaking—bottles of orange juice with a special groove for a human hand to fit into! On another counter are bathroom things. Pills, shampoo, soap, deodorants . . . the pills remind me of an advertisement on television for cold tablets. The capsules detonate gradually over a period of twelve hours, I think. They release themselves in tiny fragments into the bloodstream. I think of the cells of my body with the seeds of my future inside them, unreadable. They have the seeds of cancer inside them, death itself, the particular way in which I will wear out and die, everything contained secretly in them and ready to go off at a certain time. But that time is a secret.

At the drugstore there is a pile of newspapers and one of the headlines is GIRL'S BODY FOUND IN RIVER. The picture of that girl appears again, a beautiful girl, staring out at the camera with her perky upper lip, lipsticked and pretty, very sure of herself. Parts of a body were found along the river

146

and in the river, a woman's torso, a head. The face mutilated. And so her face is no longer that face, the one in the paper? . . . I stare down at her and I feel panic inside me, in the back of my head, behind my knees. What is this threat to me? Am I going to break down? Am I going to scream? A yellowish cell threatens to burst inside me; like sperm, it is yellow and living.

A man

in the corner of a woman's eye paralyzes the entire eye. A woman wants to rake her body with her nails, streaming blood, she wants to gash her face so that no man need look at it, she wants to be finished and safe. But why does my heart pound so? We are not at war. Yes, we are at war somewhere, soldiers somewhere "at war," but we ourselves are not at war and should therefore be at peace. Why am I not at peace, being forty years old?

This man has a weak face, he looks very young. The photograph is blurred. Why, he is only a boy, his eyes are a boy's eyes . . . but there is no youth in him, only finality. He has come to the end of something. Identified by a motel proprietor, last seen with Linda Slater on Saturday evening; the two of them came to a certain motel out on the highway and there, in a room, they argued, and then they left. . . . What did they argue about? Why will it never be known precisely what they argued about on that night?

Imagine the strength behind a knife that could sever a head from a body, so beautiful a head! Imagine the torrents of blood that would gush from the throat! There must have been confusion at the end, madness, not love or hate. Things are speeded up as they approach the end of something. The boy must have been hurried, making mistakes, whimpering to himself, everything speeded up and dazzling and crazy beyond his imagination. . . . At one o'clock neither of them, the girl or the boy, knew what would happen at two o'clock. Perhaps they knew that something would happen, some strange thing, but perhaps they had sensed such events earlier in their lives, falsely, when nothing did happen. This time it happened.

My husband

lets the newspaper fall from him. A stunned, vacuous sorrow shows in his face; I watch him from the darkened dining room. From another room the television noise continues, someone is laughing, a great crowd of people

147

laughing over a machine. I don't have time for my huband's sorrow. I see
the dreaminess in him, the stunned clarity of some final perception—I
would like to shout in his face, "Why are you surprised? She had to die like
everyone else!" But I say nothing. He came home late from school today,
looking a little sick. If he gets the flu along with Betty I will have to take
care of him as if he were a child, worse than a child, and a stab of pleasure
comes to me . . . but no, no, it's more trouble than anything else, he has
been sick many times like a child, worse than a child; I can't feel pleasure. I
am in a hurry, I can't feel anything. Time is snatched from me in handfuls.
The people who laugh over the television set, in the other room, are laughing in a terrible unison, like tiny people with tiny lungs, laughing at me. I
stand here watching a man I have been married to for many years and I can
never possess him, my husband. I have lived with him for twenty years but
I can never possess him. I can never be that girl's age. My head and torso
are connected. He will never look at me as he has looked at her, at her photograph.

I have to run out to the store before six. The metallic Christmas tree
looks the same, the angel looks the same, I don't bother with a cart but
hurry back to the dairy counter. A few housewives are there, in a hurry like
me. Three children are fooling around but it is not possible to tell whose
they are. I pick up a carton of eggs, Grade A eggs I forgot to buy earlier,
and a few other things; I hurry back to the check-out counter.

The parking lot is nearly empty at this time of day. Rough ice on the
pavement, a white and blue container marked "Salvation Army Pick-Up," a
kid's jalopy idling nosily at the curb with some high-school kids in it, frozen
weeds and trash between the parking lot and the sidewalk. . . . I hurry to
my car.

I am not followed.

The South

Writers of the southern small town experience have created fiction within a complex set of variables. The turbulent events of southern history have bespoken innumerable human dramas: the traditions and values of the "Old South"; the agony and defeat of The Civil War; the clash between rich and poor; the smoldering tensions between blacks and whites; the challenges of progress.

In the 1930s writers such as Erskine Caldwell, William Faulkner, Katherine Ann Porter, and Thomas Wolfe realistically portrayed the tragic and comic aspects of southern life. They were central figures in a literary movement which became known as the Southern Literary Renaissance. In their fiction they evoked a strong sense of the southern past and the changes being visited upon it by the present. Their fiction is considered some of the most important American literature of this century.

William Faulkner, whose writing gives exceptional insight into the southern experience, based the Jefferson of his novels on his home town of Oxford, Mississippi. The decaying mansions and ramshackle hovels of his works emphasized the southern ambience of Jefferson, underscoring its poverty and racial isolation. The useless, futile lives of the Jefferson aristocracy reflected their sense of guilt, frustration, and failure.

However, the South was undergoing enormous changes during the formative years of the Southern Literary Renaissance, not the least of which was the intrusion of industrial America upon what had heretofore been an easy-going, agrarian society. In *The Web and the Rock* Thomas Wolfe described life in Libya Hill, a fictional counterpart of his hometown of Asheville, North Carolina:

149

. . . New people were coming to town all the time, new faces were being seen upon the streets. There was quite a general feeling in the air that great events were just around the corner, and that a bright destiny was in store for Libya Hill.

It was the time when they were just hatching from the shell, when the place was changing from a little isolated mountain village, lost to the world, with its few thousand native population, to a briskly-moving modern world, with its railway connections to all parts, and with a growing population of wealthy people who had heard about the beauties of the setting and were coming there to live.

This, then, was the changing South, recorded by modern writers such as Jesse Stuart and James Agee. Agee eloquently described Knoxville as a town becoming a city—a city marked by industrial progress, but still retaining its traditional southern atmosphere. In another part of the South, Jesse Stuart's story "Sunday Afternoon Hanging" tells of the legally sanctioned public lynchings which took place in the hill country of Kentucky long after they had been outlawed elsewhere.

The greatest change in the South, however, has been in racial relations. William Faulkner wrote that there was "a curse on the land" brought on by years of slavery; the curse has been lifted, but the affliction is deep. It was white supremacy that traditionally had ordered and controlled the black experience; and although this is no longer true in the sense and to the extent that it once was, the South is still burdened by the effects of a biracial social structure. In literature this has meant the emergence of a unique identity and the development of black literature: literature of protest that has at its center the affirmation of all human struggles for freedom.

In 1951 Ralph Ellison, a black and a southerner, produced *Invisible Man,* a novel which was not exclusively a work of social protest. The small town experiences of his boyhood dealt with Oklahoma—but his story of the black boy entering manhood must be read as a universal statement of small-town race relations. Chapter one, reprinted here, recounts the humiliation and torture Ellison and his friends were subjected to the night they were called upon to provide "entertainment" for the white males of the town.

Arna Bontemps' selection, "Saturday Night," provides a striking portrait of small town southern life in 1933. Bontemps' restrained, journalistic style masterfully highlights the constant tensions—racial, economic, social—that permeate the small town environment.

William Faulkner's fictional Jefferson is the setting for "That Evening Sun." The blacks lived in the squalor of "The Hollow" or "Freedom Town." He describes the black environment there as a group of ". . . small cabins whose weathered roofs were on a level with the crown of the road. They were set in small grassless plots littered with broken things, bricks, planks, crockery, things of a once utilitarian value, . . ."

Since the publication of Ellison's *Invisible Man,* other blacks have written about their experiences in the small town. Maya Angelou, who creatively expresses the black heritage in many different forms of art, wrote that perhaps the most prominent aspect of the black's life was not its shabbiness, but its total segregation and alienation from the white life of the town:

> . . . the segregation was so complete that most black children didn't really, absolutely know what whites looked like. Other than that they were different, to be dreaded, and in that dread was included the hostility of the powerless against the powerful, the poor against the rich, the worker against the worked for and the ragged against the well dressed . . .

That Evening Sun

WILLIAM FAULKNER

I

Monday is no different from any other weekday in Jefferson now.
The streets are paved now, and the telephone and electric companies are
cutting down more and more of the shade trees—the water oaks, the maples
and locusts and elms—to make room for iron poles bearing clusters of
bloated and ghostly and bloodless grapes, and we have a city laundry which
makes the rounds on Monday morning, gathering the bundles of clothes
into bright-colored, specially-made motor cars: the soiled wearing of a
whole week now flees apparitionlike behind alert and irritable electric
horns, with a long diminishing noise of rubber and asphalt like tearing silk,
and even the Negro women who still take in white people's washing after
the old custom, fetch and deliver it in automobiles.

But fifteen years ago, on Monday morning the quiet, dusty, shady
streets would be full of Negro women with, balanced on their steady, tur-
baned heads, bundles of clothes tied up in sheets, almost as large as cotton
bales, carried so without touch of hand between the kitchen door of the
white house and the blackened washpot beside a cabin door in Negro Hollow.

Nancy would set her bundle on the top of her head, then upon the
bundle in turn she would set the black straw sailor hat which she wore
winter and summer. She was tall, with a high, sad face sunken a little where
her teeth were missing. Sometimes we would go a part of the way down the
lane and across the pasture with her, to watch the balanced bundle and the
hat that never bobbed nor wavered, even when she walked down into the
ditch and up the other side and stooped through the fence. She would go
down on her hands and knees and crawl through the gap, her head rigid,
uptilted, the bundle steady as a rock or a balloon, and rise to her feet again
and go on.

Sometimes the husbands of the washing women would fetch and deliver

153

the clothes, but Jesus never did that for Nancy, even before father told him to stay away from our house, even when Dilsey was sick and Nancy would come to cook for us.

And then about half the time we'd have to go down the lane to Nancy's cabin and tell her to come on and cook breakfast. We would stop at the ditch, because father told us to not have anything to do with Jesus—he was a short black man, with a razor scar down his face—and we would throw rocks at Nancy's house until she came to the door, leaning her head around it without any clothes on.

"What yawl mean, chunking my house?" Nancy said. "What you little devils mean?"

"Father says for you to come on and get breakfast," Caddy said. "Father says it's over a half an hour now, and you've got to come this minute."

"I aint studying no breakfast," Nancy said. "I going to get my sleep out."

"I bet you're drunk," Jason said. "Father says you're drunk. Are you drunk, Nancy?"

"Who says I is?" Nancy said. "I got to get my sleep out. I aint studying no breakfast."

So after a while we quit chunking the cabin and went back home. When she finally came, it was too late for me to go to school. So we thought it was whisky until that day they arrested her again and they were taking her to jail and they passed Mr Stovall. He was the cashier in the bank and a deacon in the Baptist church, and Nancy began to say:

"When you going to pay me, white man? When you going to pay me, white man? It's been three times now since you paid me a cent—" Mr Stovall knocked her down, but she kept on saying, "When you going to pay me, white man? It's been three times now since—"until Mr Stovall kicked her in the mouth with his heel and the marshall caught Mr Stovall back, and Nancy lying in the street, laughing. She turned her head and spat out some blood and teeth and said, "It's been three times now since he paid me a cent."

That was how she lost her teeth, and all that day they told about Nancy and Mr Stovall, and all that night the ones that passed the jail could hear Nancy singing and yelling. They could see her hands holding to the window bars, and a lot of them stopped along the fence, listening to her and to the jailer trying to make her stop. She didn't shut up until almost daylight,

when the jailer began to hear a bumping and scraping upstairs and he went up there and found Nancy hanging from the window bar. He said that it was cocaine and not whisky, because no nigger would try to commit suicide unless he was full of cocaine, because a nigger full of cocaine wasn't a nigger any longer.

The jailer cut her down and revived her; then he beat her, whipped her. She had hung herself with her dress. She had fixed it all right, but when they arrested her she didn't have on anything except a dress and so she didn't have anything to tie her hands with and she couldn't make her hands let go of the window ledge. So the jailer heard the noise and ran up there and found Nancy hanging from the window, stark naked, her belly already swelling out a little, like a little balloon.

When Dilsey was sick in her cabin and Nancy was cooking for us, we could see her apron swelling out; that was before father told Jesus to stay away from the house. Jesus was in the kitchen, sitting behind the stove, with his razor scar on his black face like a piece of dirty string. He said it was a watermelon that Nancy had under her dress.

"It never come off your vine, though," Nancy said.

"Off of what vine?" Caddy said.

"I can cut down the vine it did come off of," Jesus said.

"What makes you want to talk like that before these children?" Nancy said. "Whyn't you go on to work? You done et. You want Mr Jason to catch you hanging around his kitchen, talking that way before these chillen?"

"Talking what way?" Caddy said. "What vine?"

"I cant hang around white man's kitchen," Jesus said. "But white man can hang around mine. White man can come in my house, but I cant stop him. When white man want to come in my house, I aint got no house. I cant stop him, but he cant kick me outen it. He cant do that."

Dilsey was still sick in her cabin. Father told Jesus to stay off our place. Dilsey was still sick. It was a long time. We were in the library after supper.

"Isn't Nancy through in the kitchen yet?" mother said. "It seems to me that she has had plenty of time to have finished the dishes."

"Let Quentin go and see," father said. "Go and see if Nancy is through, Quentin. Tell her she can go on home."

I went to the kitchen. Nancy was through. The dishes were put away and the fire was out. Nancy was was sitting in a chair, close to the cold stove. She looked at me.

"Mother wants to know if you are through," I said.

156

"Yes," Nancy said. She looked at me. "I done finished." She looked at me.

"What is it?" I said. "What is it?"

"I aint nothing but a nigger," Nancy said. "It aint none of my fault."

She looked at me, sitting in the chair before the cold stove, the sailor hat on her head. I went back to the library. It was the cold stove and all, when you think of a kitchen being warm and busy and cheerful. And with a cold stove and the dishes all put away, and nobody wanting to eat at that hour.

"Is she through?" mother said.

"Yessum," I said.

"What is she doing?" mother said.

"She's not doing anything. She's through."

"I'll go and see," father said.

"Maybe she's waiting for Jesus to come and take her home," Caddy said.

"Jesus is gone," I said. Nancy told us how one morning she woke up and Jesus was gone.

"He quit me," Nancy said. "Done gone to Memphis, I reckon. Dodging them city *po*-lice for a while, I reckon."

"And a good riddance," father said. "I hope he stays there."

"Nancy's scaired of the dark," Jason said.

"So are you," Caddy said.

"I'm not," Jason said.

"Scairy cat," Caddy said.

"I'm not," Jason said.

"You, Candace!" mother said. Father came back.

"I am going to walk down the lane with Nancy," he said. "She says that Jesus is back."

"Has she seen him?" mother said.

"No. Some Negro sent her word that he was back in town. I wont be long."

"You'll leave me alone, to take Nancy home?" mother said. "Is her safety more precious to you than mine?"

"I wont be long," father said.

"You'll leave these children unprotected, with that Negro about?"

"I'm going too," Caddy said. "Let me go, Father."

"What would he do with them, if he were unfortunate enough to have them?" father said.

"I want to go, too," Jason said.

"Jason!" mother said. She was speaking to father. You could tell that by the way she said the name. Like she believed that all day father had been trying to think of doing the thing she wouldn't like the most, and that she knew all the time that after a while he would think of it. I stayed quiet, because father and I both knew that mother would want him to make me stay with her if she just thought of it in time. So father didn't look at me. I was the oldest. I was nine and Caddy was seven and Jason was five.

"Nonsense," father said. "We wont be long."

Nancy had her hat on. We came to the lane. "Jesus always been good to me," Nancy said. "Whenever he had two dollars, one of them was mine." We walked in the lane. "If I can just get through the lane," Nancy said, "I be all right then."

The lane was always dark. "This is where Jason got scared on Hallowe'en," Caddy said.

"I didn't," Jason said.

"Cant Aunt Rachel do anything with him?" father said. Aunt Rachel was old. She lived in a cabin beyond Nancy's, by herself. She had white hair and she smoked a pipe in the door, all day long; she didn't work any more. They said she was Jesus' mother. Sometimes she said she was and sometimes she said she wasn't any kin to Jesus.

"Yes, you did," Caddy said. "You were scairder than Frony. You were scairder than T. P even. Scairder than niggers."

"Cant nobody do nothing with him," Nancy said. "He say I done woke up the devil in him and aint but one thing going to lay it down again."

"Well, he's gone now," father said. "There's nothing for you to be afraid of now. And if you'd just let white men alone."

"Let what white men alone?" Caddy said. "How let them alone?"

"He aint gone nowhere," Nancy said. "I can feel him. I can feel him now, in this lane. He hearing us talk, every word, hid somewhere, waiting. I aint seen him, and I aint going to see him again but once more, with that razor in his mouth. That razor on that string down his back, inside his shirt. And then I aint going to be even surprised."

"I wasn't scaired," Jason said.

"If you'd behave yourself, you'd have kept out of this," father said. "But it's all right now. He's probably in St. Louis now. Probably in St. Louis now. Probably got another wife by now and forgot all about you."

"If he has, I better not find out about it," Nancy said. "I'd stand there right over them, and every time he wropped her, I'd cut that arm off. I'd cut his head off and I'd slit her belly and I'd shove—"

"Hush," father said.

"Slit whose belly, Nancy?" Caddy said.

"I wasn't scaired," Jason said. "I'd walk right down this lane by myself."

"Yah," Caddy said. "You wouldn't dare to put your foot down in it if we were not here too."

II

Dilsey was still sick, so we took Nancy home every night until mother said, "How much longer is this going on? I to be left alone in this big house while you take home a frightened Negro?"

We fixed a pallet in the kitchen for Nancy. One night we waked up, hearing the sound. It was not singing and it was not crying, coming up the dark stairs. There was a light in mother's room and we heard father going down the hall, down the back stairs, and Caddy and I went into the hall. The floor was cold. Our toes curled away from it while we listened to the sound. It was like singing and it wasn't like singing, like the sounds that Negroes make.

Then it stopped and we heard father going down the back stairs, and we went to the head of the stairs. Then the sound began again, in the stairway, not loud, and we could see Nancy's eyes halfway up the stairs, against the wall. They looked like cat's eyes do, like a big cat against the wall, watching us. When we came down the steps to where she was, she quit making the sound again, and we stood there until father came back up from the kitchen, with his pistol in his hand. He went back down with Nancy and they came back with Nancy's pallet.

We spread the pallet in our room. After the light in mother's room went off, we could see Nancy's eyes again. "Nancy," Caddy whispered, "are you asleep, Nancy?"

Nancy whispered something. It was oh or no, I dont know which. Like nobody had made it, like it came from nowhere and went nowhere, until it was like Nancy was not there at all; that I had looked so hard at her eyes on the stairs that they had got printed on my eyeballs, like the sun does when you have closed your eyes and there is no sun. "Jesus," Nancy whispered, "Jesus."

"Was it Jesus?" Caddy said. "Did he try to come into the kitchen?"

"Jesus," Nancy said. Like this: Jeeeeeeeeeeeeeeeesus, until the sound went out, like a match or a candle does.

"It's the other Jesus she means," I said.

"Can you see us, Nancy?" Caddy whispered. "Can you see our eyes too?"

"I ain't nothing but a nigger," Nancy said. "God knows. God knows."

"What did you see down there in the kitchen?" Caddy whispered. "What tried to get in?"

"God knows," Nancy said. We could see her eyes. "God knows."

Dilsey got well. She cooked dinner. "You'd better stay in bed a day or two longer," father said.

"What for?" Dilsey said, "If I had been a day later, this place would be to rack and ruin. Get on out of here now, and let me get my kitchen straight again."

Dilsey cooked supper too. And that night, just before dark, Nancy came into the kitchen.

"How do you know he's back?" Dilsey said. "You aint seen him."

"Jesus is a nigger," Jason said.

"I can feel him," Nancy said. "I can feel him laying yonder in the ditch."

"Tonight?" Dilsey said. "Is he there tonight?"

"Dilsey's a nigger too," Jason said.

"You try to eat something," Dilsey said.

"I dont want nothing," Nancy said.

"I aint a nigger," Jason said.

"Drink some coffee," Dilsey said. She poured a cup of coffee for Nancy. "Do you know he's out there tonight? How come you know it's tonight?"

"I know," Nancy said. "He's there, waiting. I know. I done lived with him too long. I know what he is fixing to do fore he know it himself."

"Drink some coffee," Dilsey said. Nancy held the cup to her mouth and blew into the cup. Her mouth pursed out like a spreading adder's, like a rubber mouth, like she had blown all the color out of her lips with blowing the coffee.

"I aint a nigger," Jason said. "Are you a nigger, Nancy?"

"I hellborn, child," Nancy said. "I won't be nothing soon. I going back where I come from soon."

III

She began to drink the coffee. While she was drinking, holding the cup in both hands, she began to make the sound again. She made the sound into the cup and the coffee sploshed out onto her hands and her dress. Her eyes looked at us and she sat there, her elbows on her knees, holding the cup in both hands, looking at us across the wet cup, making the sound. "Look at Nancy," Jason said. "Nancy cant cook for us now. Dilsey's got well now."

"You hush up," Dilsey said. Nancy held the cup in both hands, looking at us, making the sound, like there were two of them: one looking at us and the other making the sound. "Whyn't you let Mr Jason telefoam the marshal?" Dilsey said. Nancy stopped then, holding the cup in her long brown hands, She tried to drink some coffee again, but it sploshed out of the cup, onto her hands and her dress, and she put the cup down. Jason watched her.

"I cant swallow it," Nancy said. "I swallows but it wont go down me."

"You go down to the cabin," Dilsey said. "Frony will fix you a pallet and I'll be there soon."

"Wont no nigger stop him," Nancy said.

"I aint a nigger," Jason said. "Am I, Dilsey?"

"I reckon not," Dilsey said. She looked at Nancy. "I dont reckon so. What you going to do, then?"

Nancy looked at us. Her eyes went fast, like she was afraid there wasn't time to look, without hardly moving at all. She looked at us, at all three of us at one time. "You member that night I stayed in yawls' room?" she said. She told about how we waked up early the next morning, and played. We had to play quiet, on her pallet, until father woke up and it was time to get breakfast. "Go and ask your maw to let me stay here tonight," Nancy said. "I wont need no pallet. We can play some more."

Caddy asked mother. Jason went too. "I cant have Negroes sleeping in the bedrooms," mother said. Jason cried. He cried until mother said he couldn't have any dessert for three days if he didn't stop. Then Jason said he would stop if Dilsey would make a chocolate cake. Father was there.

"Why dont you do something about it?" mother said. "What do we have officers for?"

"Why is Nancy afraid of Jesus?" Caddy said. "Are you afraid of father, mother?"

"What could the officers do?" father said. "If Nancy hasn't seen him, how could the officers find him?"

"Then why is she afraid?" mother said.

"She says he is there. She says she knows he is there tonight."

"Yet we pay taxes," mother said. "I must wait here alone in this big house while you take a Negro woman home."

"You know that I am not lying outside with a razor," father said.

"I'll stop if Dilsey will make a chocolate cake," Jason said. Mother told us to go out and father said he didn't know if Jason would get a chocolate cake or not, but he knew what Jason was going to get in about a minute. We went back to the kitchen and told Nancy.

"Father said for you to go home and lock the door, and you'll be all right," Caddy said, "All right from what, Nancy? Is Jesus mad at you?" Nancy was holding the coffee cup in her hands again, her elbows on her knees and her hands holding the cup between her knees. She was looking into the cup. "What have you done that made Jesus mad?" Caddy said. Nancy let the cup go. It didn't break on the floor, but the coffee spilled out, and Nancy sat there with her hands still making the shape of the cup. She began to make the sound again, not loud. Not singing and not unsinging. We watched her.

"Here," Dilsey said. "You quit that, now. You get aholt of yourself. You wait here. I going to get Versh to walk home with you." Dilsey went out.

We looked at Nancy. Her shoulders kept shaking, but she quit making the sound. We watched her. "What's Jesus going to do to you? Caddy said. "We went away."

Nancy looked at us. "We had fun that night I stayed in yawls' room, didn't we?"

"I didn't," Jason said. "I didn't have any fun."

"You were asleep in mother's room," Caddy said. "You were not there."

"Let's go down to my house and have some more fun," Nancy said.

"Mother wont let us," I said. "It's too late now."

"Don't bother her," Nancy said. "We can tell her in the morning. She wont mind."

"She wouldn't let us," I said.

"Dont ask her now," Nancy said. "Dont bother her now."

"She didn't say we couldn't go," Caddy said.

"We didn't ask," I said.

"If you go, I'll tell," Jason said.

"We'll have fun," Nancy said. "They won't mind, just to my house. I been working for yawl a long time. They wont mind."

"I'm not afraid to go," Caddy said. "Jason is the one that's afraid. He'll tell."

"I'm not," Jason said.

"Yes, you are," Caddy said. "You'll tell."

"I won't tell," Jason said. "I'm not afraid."

"Jason ain't afraid to go with me," Nancy said. "Is you, Jason?"

"Jason is going to tell," Caddy said. The lane was dark. We passed the pasture gate. "I bet if something was to jump out from behind that gate, Jason would holler."

"I wouldn't," Jason said. We walked down the lane. Nancy was talking loud.

"What are you talking so loud for, Nancy?" Caddy said.

"Who; me?" Nancy said. "Listen at Quentin and Caddy and Jason saying I'm talking loud."

"You talk like there was five of us here," Caddy said. "You talk like father was here too."

"Who; me talking loud, Mr. Jason?" Nancy said.

"Nancy called Jason 'Mister,' " Caddy said.

"Listen how Caddy and Quentin and Jason talk," Nancy said.

"We're not talking loud," Caddy said. "You're the one that's talking like father—"

"Hush," Nancy said; "Hush, Mr. Jason."

"Nancy called Jason 'Mister' aguh—"

"Hush," Nancy said. She was talking loud when we crossed the ditch and stooped through the fence where she used to stoop through with the clothes on her head. Then we came to her house. We were going fast then. She opened the door. The smell of the house was like the lamp and the smell of Nancy was like the wick, like they were waiting for one another to begin to smell. She lit the lamp and closed the door and put the bar up. Then she quit talking loud, looking at us.

"What're we going to do" Caddy said.

"What do yawl want to do?" Nancy said.

"You said we would have some fun," Caddy said.

There was something about Nancy's house; something you could smell besides Nancy and the house. Jason smelled it, even. "I don't want to stay here," he said. "I want to go home."

"Go home, then," Caddy said.

"I don't want to go by myself," Jason said.

"We're going to have some fun," Nancy said.

"How?" Caddy said.

Nancy stood by the door. She was looking at us, only it was like she had emptied her eyes, like she had quit using them. "What do you want to do?" she said.

"Tell us a story," Caddy said. "Can you tell a story?"

"Yes," Nancy said.

"Tell it," Caddy said. We looked at Nancy. "You don't know any stories."

"Yes," Nancy said. "Yes, I do."

She came and sat in a chair before the hearth. There was a little fire there. Nancy built it up, when it was already hot inside. She built a good blaze. She told a story. She talked like her eyes looked, like her eyes watching us and her voice talking to us did not belong to her. Like she was living somewhere else, waiting somewhere else. She was outside the cabin. Her voice was inside and the shape of her, the Nancy that could stoop under a barbed wire fence with a bundle of clothes balanced on her head as though without weight, like a balloon, was there. But that was all. "And so this here queen come walking up to the ditch, where that bad man was hiding. She was walking up to the ditch, and she say, 'If I can just get past this here ditch,' was what she say . . ."

"What ditch?" Caddy said. "A ditch like that one there? Why did a queen want to go into a ditch?"

"To get to her house," Nancy said. She looked at us. "She had to cross the ditch to get into her house quick and bar the door."

"Why did she want to go home and bar the door?" Caddy said.

IV

Nancy looked at us. She quit talking. She looked at us. Jason's legs stuck straight out of his pants where he sat on Nancy's lap. "I don't think that's a good story," he said. "I want to go home."

"Maybe we had better," Caddy said. She got up from the floor. "I bet they are looking for us right now." She went toward the door.

164

"No," Nancy said. "Don't open it." She got up quick and passed Caddy. She didn't touch the door, the wooden bar.

"Why not?" Caddy said.

"Come back to the lamp," Nancy said. "We'll have fun. You don't have to go."

"We ought to go," Caddy said. "Unless we have a lot of fun." She and Nancy came back to the fire, the lamp.

"I want to go home," Jason said. "I'm going to tell."

"I know another story," Nancy said. She stood close to the lamp. She looked at Caddy, like when your eyes look up at a stick balanced on your nose. She had to look down to see Caddy, but her eyes looked like that, like when you are balancing a stick.

"I won't listen to it," Jason said. "I'll bang on the floor."

"It's a good one," Nancy said. "It's better than the other one."

"What's it about?" Caddy said. Nancy was standing by the lamp. Her hand was on the lamp, against the light, long and brown.

"Your hand is on that hot globe," Caddy said. "Don't it feel hot to your hand?"

Nancy looked at her hand on the lamp chimney. She took her hand away, slow. She stood there, looking at Caddy, wringing her long hand as though it were tied to her wrist with a string.

"Let's do something else," Caddy said.

"I want to go home," Jason said.

"I got some popcorn," Nancy said. She looked at Caddy and then at Jason and then at me and then at Caddy again. "I got some popcorn."

"I don't like popcorn," Jason said. "I'd rather have candy."

Nancy looked at Jason. "You can hold the popper." She was still wringing her hand; it was long and limp and brown.

"All right," Jason said. "I'll stay a while if I can do that. Caddy can't hold it. I'll want to go home again if Caddy holds the popper."

Nancy built up the fire. "Look at Nancy putting her hands in the fire," Caddy said. "What's the matter with you, Nancy?"

"I got popcorn," Nancy said. "I got some." She took the popper from under the bed. It was broken. Jason began to cry.

"Now we can't have any popcorn," he said.

"We ought to go home, anyway," Caddy said. "Come on, Quentin."

"Wait," Nancy said; "wait. I can fix it. Don't you want to help me fix it?"

"I don't think I want any," Caddy said. "It's too late now."

"You help me, Jason," Nancy said. "Don't you want to help me?"

"No," Jason said. "I want to go home."

"Hush," Nancy said; "hush. Watch. Watch me. I can fix it so Jason can hold it and pop the corn." She got a piece of wire and fixed the popper.

"It won't hold good," Caddy said.

"Yes, it will," Nancy said. "Yawl watch. Yawl help me shell some corn."

The popcorn was under the bed too. We shelled it into the popper and Nancy helped Jason hold the popper over the fire.

"It's not popping," Jason said. "I want to go home."

"You wait," Nancy said. "It'll begin to pop. We'll have fun then." She was sitting close to the fire. The lamp was turned up so high it was beginning to smoke.

"Why don't you turn it down some?" I said.

"It's all right," Nancy said. "I'll clean it. Yawl wait. The popcorn will start in a minute."

"I don't believe it's going to start," Caddy said. "We ought to start home, anyway. They'll be worried."

"No," Nancy said. "It's going to pop. Dilsey will tell um yawl with me. I been working for yawl long time. They won't mind if yawl at my house. You wait, now. It'll start popping any minute now."

Then Jason got some smoke in his eyes and he began to cry. He dropped the popper into the fire. Nancy got a wet rag and wiped Jason's face, but he didn't stop crying.

"Hush," she said. "Hush." But he didn't hush. Caddy took the popper out of the fire.

"It's burned up," she aaid. "You'll have to get some more popcorn, Nancy."

"Did you put all of it in?" Nancy said.

"Yes," Caddy said. Nancy looked at Caddy. Then she took the popper and opened it and poured the cinders into her apron and began to sort the grains, her hands long and brown, and we watching her.

"Haven't you got any more?" Caddy said.

"Yes," Nancy said; "yes. Look. This here ain't burnt. All we need to do is—"

"I want to go home," Jason said. "I'm going to tell."

"Hush," Caddy said. We all listened. Nancy's head was already turned

166

toward the barred door, her eyes filled with red lamplight. "Somebody is coming," Caddy said.

Then Nancy began to make that sound again, not loud, sitting there above the fire, her long hands dangling between her knees; all of a sudden water began to come out on her face in big drops, running down her face, carrying in each one a little turning ball of firelight like a spark until it dropped off her chin. "She's not crying," I said.

"I ain't crying," Nancy said. Her eyes were closed. "I ain't crying. Who is it?"

"I don't know," Caddy said. She went to the door and looked out. "We've got to go now," she said. "Here comes father."

"I'm going to tell," Jason said. "Yawl made me come."

The water still ran down Nancy's face. She turned in her chair. "Listen. Tell him. Tell him we going to have fun. Tell him I take good care of yawl until in the morning. Tell him to let me come home with yawl and sleep on the floor. Tell him I won't need no pallet. We'll have fun. You member last time how we had so much fun?"

"I didn't have fun," Jason said. "You hurt me. You put smoke in my eyes. I'm going to tell."

v

Father came in. He looked at us. Nancy did not get up.

"Tell him," she said.

"Caddy made us come down here," Jason said. "I didn't want to."

Father came to the fire. Nancy looked up at him. "Can't you go to Aunt Rachel's and stay?" he said. Nancy looked up at father, her hands between her knees. "He's not here," father said. "I would have seen him. There's not a soul in sight."

"He in the ditch," Nancy said. "He waiting in the ditch yonder."

"Nonsense," father said. He looked at Nancy. "Do you know he's there?"

"I got the sign," Nancy said.

"What sign?"

"I got it. It was on the table when I come in. It was a hogbone, with blood meat still on it, laying by the lamp. He's out there. When yawl walk out that door, I gone."

"Gone where, Nancy?" Caddy said.

"I'm not a tattletale," Jason said.

"Nonsense," father said.

"He out there," Nancy said. "He looking through that window this minute, waiting for yawl to go. Then I gone."

"Nonsense," father said. "Lock up your house and we'll take you on to Aunt Rachel's."

" 'Twont do no good," Nancy said. She didn't look at father now, but he looked down at her, at her long, limp, moving hands, "Putting it off wont do no good."

"Then what do you want to do?" father said.

"I don't know," Nancy said. "I can't do nothing. Just put it off. And that don't do no good. I reckon it belong to me. I reckon what I going to get ain't no more than mine."

"Get what?" Caddy said. "What's yours?"

"Nothing," father said. "You all must get to bed."

"Caddy made me come," Jason said.

"Go on to Aunt Rachel's," father said.

"It won't do no good," Nancy said. She sat before the fire, her elbows on her knees, her long hands between her knees. "When even your own kitchen wouldn't do no good. When even if I was sleeping on the floor in the room with your chillen, and the next morning there I am, and blood—"

"Hush," father said. "Lock the door and put out the lamp and go to bed."

"I scared of the dark," Nancy said. "I scared for it to happen in the dark."

"You mean you're going to sit right here with the lamp lighted?" father said. Then Nancy began to make the sound again, sitting before the fire, her long hands between her knees. "Ah, damnation," father said. "Come along, chillen. It's past bedtime."

"When yawl go home, I gone," Nancy said. She talked quieter now, and her face looked quiet, like her hands. "Anyway, I got my coffin money saved up with Mr. Lovelady." Mr. Lovelady was a short, dirty man who collected the Negro insurance, coming around to the cabins or the kitchens every Saturday morning, to collect fifteen cents. He and his wife lived at the hotel. One morning his wife committed suicide. They had a child, a little girl. He and the child went away. After a week or two he came back alone. We would see him going along the lanes and the back streets on Saturday mornings.

168

"Nonsense," father said. "You'll be the first thing I'll see in the kitchen tomorrow morning."

"You'll see what you'll see, I reckon," Nancy said. "But it will take the Lord to say what that will be."

VI

We left her sitting before the fire.

"Come and put the bar up," father said. But she didn't move. She didn't look at us again, sitting quietly there between the lamp and the fire. From some distance down the lane we could look back and see her through the open door.

"What, Father?" Caddy said. "What's going to happen?"

"Nothing," father said. Jason was on father's back, so Jason was the tallest of all of us. We went down into the ditch. I looked at it, quiet. I couldn't see much where the moonlight and the shadows tangled.

"If Jesus is hid here, he can see us, cant he?" Caddy said.

"He's not there," father said. "He went away a long time ago."

"You made me come," Jason said, high; against the sky it looked like father had two heads, a little one and a big one. "I didn't want to."

We went up out of the ditch. We could still see Nancy's house and the open door, but we couldn't see Nancy now, sitting before the fire with the door open, because she was tired. "I just done got tired," she said. "I just a nigger. It ain't no fault of mine."

But we could hear her, because she began just after we came up out of the ditch, the sound that was not singing and not unsinging. "Who will do our washing now, Father?" I said.

"I'm not a nigger," Jason said, high and close above father's head.

"You're worse," Caddy said, "you are a tattletale. If something was to jump out, you'd be scairder than a nigger."

"I wouldn't," Jason said.

"You'd cry," Caddy said.

"Caddy," father said.

"I wouldn't!" Jason said.

"Scairy cat," Caddy said.

"Candace!" father said.

The Lost Boy

THOMAS WOLFE

I

Light came and went and came again, the booming strokes of three
o'clock beat out across the town in thronging bronze from the courthouse
bell, light winds of April blew the fountain out in rainbow sheets, until the
plume returned and pulsed, as Grover turned into the Square. He was a
child, dark-eyed and grave, birthmarked upon his neck—a berry of warm
brown—and with a gentle face, too quiet and too listening for his years. The
scuffed boy's shoes, the thick-ribbed stockings gartered at the knees, the
short knee pants cut straight with three small useless buttons at the side,
the sailor blouse, the old cap battered out of shape, perched sideways up on
top of the raven head, the old soiled canvas bag slung from the shoulder,
empty now, but waiting for the crisp sheets of the afternoon—these
friendly, shabby garments, shaped by Grover, uttered him. He turned and
passed along the north side of the Square and in that moment saw the union
of Forever and of Now.

Light came and went and came again, the great plume of the fountain
pulsed and winds of April sheeted it across the Square in a rainbow gos-
samer of spray. The fire department horses drummed on the floors with
wooden stomp, most casually, and with dry whiskings of their clean, coarse
tails. The street cars ground into the Square from every portion of the
compass and halted briefly like wound toys in their familiar quarter-hourly
formula. A dray, hauled by a boneyard nag, rattled across the cobbles on
the other side before his father's shop. The courthouse bell boomed out its
solemn warning of immediate three, and everything was just the same as it
had always been.

He saw that haggis of vexed shapes with quiet eyes—that hodgepodge of
ill-sorted architectures that made up the Square, and he did not feel lost.
For "Here," thought Grover, "here is the Square as it has always been—
and papa's shop, the fire department and the City Hall, the fountain pulsing

170

with its plume, the street cars coming in and halting at the quarter hour, the hardware store on the corner there, the row of old brick buildings on this side of the street, the people passing and the light that comes and changes and that always will come back again, and everything that comes and goes and changes in the Square, and yet will be the same again. And here," the boy thought, "is Grover with his paper bag. Here is old Grover, almost twelve years old. Here is the month of April, 1904. Here is the courthouse bell and three o'clock. Here is Grover on the Square that never changes. Here is Grover, caught upon this point of time.

It seemed to him that the Square, itself the accidental masonry of many years, the chance agglomeration of time and of disrupted strivings, was the center of the universe. It was for him, in his soul's picture, the earth's pivot, the granite core of changelessness, the eternal place where all things came and passed, and yet abode forever and would never change.

He passed the old shack on the corner—the wooden fire-trap where S. Goldberg ran his wiener stand. Then he passed the Singer place next door, with its gleaming display of new machines. He saw them and admired them, but he felt no joy. They brought back to him the busy hum of house-work and of women sewing, the intricacy of stitch and weave, the mystery of style and pattern, the memory of women bending over flashing needles, the pedaled tread, the busy whir. It was women's work: it filled him with unknown associations of dullness and of vague depression. And always, also, with a moment's twinge of horror, for his dark eye would always travel toward that needle stitching up and down so fast the eye could never follow it. And then he would remember how his mother once had told him she had driven the needle through her finger, and always, when he passed this place, he would remember it and for a moment crane his neck and turn his head away.

He passed on then, but had to stop again next door before the music store. He always had to stop by places that had shining perfect things in them. He loved hardware stores and windows full of accurate geometric tools. He loved windows full of hammers, saws, and planing boards. He liked windows full of strong new rakes and hoes, with unworn handles, of white perfect wood, stamped hard and vivid with the maker's seal. He loved to see such things as these in the windows of hardware stores. And he would fairly gloat upon them and think that some day he would own a set himself.

171

General Store, Moundville, Alabama, 1936

Also, he always stopped before the music and piano store. It was a splendid store. And in the window was a small white dog upon his haunches, with head cocked gravely to one side, a small white dog that never moved, that never barked, that listened attentively at the flaring funnel of a horn to hear "His Master's Voice"—a horn forever silent, and a voice that never spoke. And within were many rich and shining shapes of great pianos, an air of splendor and of wealth.

And now, indeed, he *was* caught, held suspended. A waft of air, warm, chocolate-laden, filled his nostrils. He tried to pass the white front of the little eight-foot shop; he paused, struggling with conscience; he could not go on. It was the little candy shop run by old Crocker and his wife. And Grover could not pass.

"Old stingy Crockers!" he thought scornfully. "I'll not go there any more. But—" as the maddening fragrance of rich cooking chocolate touched him once again—"I'll just look in the window and see what they've got." He paused a moment, looking with his dark and quiet eyes into the window of the little candy shop. The window, spotlessly clean, was filled with trays of fresh-made candy. His eyes rested on a tray of chocolate drops. Unconsciously he licked his lips. Put one of them upon your tongue and it just melted there, like honeydew. And then the trays full of rich home-made fudge. He gazed longingly at the deep body of the chocolate fudge, reflectively at maple walnut, more critically, yet with longing, at the mints, the nougatines, and all the other dainties.

"Old stingy Crockers!" Grover muttered once again, and turned to go. "I wouldn't go in *there* again."

And yet he did not go away. "Old stingy Crockers" they might be; still, they did make the best candy in town, the best, in fact, that he had ever tasted.

He looked through the window back into the little shop and saw Mrs. Crocker there. A customer had gone in and had made a purchase, and as Grover looked he saw Mrs. Crocker, with her little wrenny face, her pinched features, lean over and peer primly at the scales. She had a piece of fudge in her clean, bony, little fingers, and as Grover looked, she broke it, primly, in her little bony hands. She dropped a morsel down into the scales. They weighted down alarmingly, and her thin lips tightened. She snatched the piece of fudge out of the scales and broke it carefully once again. This time the scales wavered, went down very slowly, and came back again. Mrs.

173

Crocker carefully put the reclaimed piece of fudge back in the tray, dumped the remainder in a paper bag, folded it and gave it to the customer, counted the money carefully and doled it out into the till, the pennies in one place, the nickels in another.

Grover stood there, looking scornfully. "Old stingy Crocker—afraid that she might give a crumb away!"

He grunted scornfully and again he turned to go. But now Mr. Crocker came out from the little partitioned place where they made all their candy, bearing a tray of fresh-made fudge in his skinny hands. Old Man Crocker rocked along the counter to the front and put it down. He really rocked along. He was a cripple. And like his wife, he was a wrenny, wizened little creature, with bony hands, thin lips, a pinched and meager face. One leg was inches shorter than the other, and on this leg there was an enormous thick-soled boot, with a kind of wooden, rocker-like arrangement, six inches high at least, to make up for the deficiency. On this wooden cradle Mr. Crocker rocked along, with a prim and apprehensive little smile, as if he were afraid he was going to lose something.

"Old stingy Crocker!" muttered Grover. "Humph! He wouldn't give you anything!"

And yet—he did not go away. He hung there curiously, peering through the window, with his dark and gentle face now focused and intent, alert and curious, flattening his nose against the glass. Unconsciously he scratched the thick-ribbed fabric of one stockinged leg with the scuffed and worn toe of his old shoe. The fresh, warm odor of the new-made fudge was delicious. It was a little maddening. Half consciously he began to fumble in one trouser pocket, and pulled out his purse, a shabby worn old black one with a twisted clasp. He opened it and prowled about inside.

What he found was not inspiring—a nickel and two pennies and—he had forgotten them—the stamps. He took the stamps out and unfolded them. There were five twos, eight ones, all that remained of the dollar-sixty-cents' worth which Reed, the pharmacist, had given him for running errands a week or two before.

"Old Crocker," Grover thought, and looked somberly at the grotesque little form as it rocked back into the shop again, around the counter, and up the other side. "Well—" again he looked indefinitely at the stamps in his hand—"he's had all the rest of them. He might as well take these."

So, soothing conscience with this sop of scorn, he went into the shop and stood looking at the trays in the glass case and finally decided. Pointing with a slightly grimy finger at the fresh-made tray of chocolate fudge, he said, "I'll take fifteen cents' worth of this, Mr. Crocker." He paused a moment, fighting with embarrassment, then he lifted his dark face and said quietly, "And please, I'll have to give you stamps again."

Mr. Crocker made no answer. He did not look at Grover. He pressed his lips together primly. He went rocking away and got the candy scoop, came back, slid open the door of the glass case, put fudge into the scoop, and, rocking to the scales, began to weigh the candy out. Grover watched him as he peered and squinted, he watched him purse and press his lips together, he saw him take a piece of fudge and break it in two parts. And then old Crocker broke two parts in two again. He weighed, he squinted, and he hovered, until it seemed to Grover that by calling *Mrs.* Crocker stingy he had been guilty of a rank injustice. But finally, to his vast relief, the job was over, the scales hung there, quivering apprehensively, upon the very hair-line of nervous balance, as if even the scales were afraid that one more move from Old Man Crocker and they would be undone.

Mr. Crocker took the candy then and dumped it in a paper bag and, rocking back along the counter toward the boy, he dryly said: "Where are the stamps?" Grover gave them to him. Mr. Crocker relinquished his claw-like hold upon the bag and set it down upon the counter. Grover took the bag and dropped it in his canvas sack, and then remembered. "Mr. Crocker—" again he felt the old embarrassment that was almost like strong pain—"I gave you too much," Grover said. "There were eighteen cents in stamps. You—you can just give me three ones back."

Mr. Crocker did not answer. He was busy with his bony little hands, unfolding the stamps and flattening them out on top of the glass counter. When he had done so, he peered at them sharply for a moment, thrusting his scrawny neck forward and running his eye up and down, like a book-keeper who totes up rows of figures.

When he had finished, he said tartly: "I don't like this kind of business. If you want candy, you should have the money for it. I'm not a post office. The next time you come in here and want anything, you'll have to pay me money for it."

Hot anger rose in Grover's throat. His olive face suffused with angry color. His tarry eyes got black and bright. He was on the verge of saying: "Then why did you take my other stamps? Why do you tell me now, when you have taken all the stamps I had, that you don't want them?"

But he was a boy, a boy of eleven years, a quiet, gentle, gravely thoughtful boy, and he had been taught how to respect his elders. So he just stood there looking with his tar-black eyes. Old Man Crocker, pursing at the mouth a little, without meeting Grover's gaze, took the stamps up in his thin, parched fingers and, turning, rocked away with them down to the till.

He took the twos and folded them and laid them in one rounded scallop, then took the ones and folded them and put them in the one next to it. Then he closed the till and started to rock off, down toward the other end. Grover, his face now quiet and grave, kept looking at him, but Mr. Crocker did not look at Grover. Instead he began to take some stamped cardboard shapes and fold them into boxes.

In a moment Grover said, "Mr. Crocker, will you give me the three ones, please?"

Mr. Crocker did not answer. He kept folding boxes, and he compressed his thin lips quickly as he did so. But Mrs. Crocker, back turned to her spouse, also folding boxes with her birdlike hands, muttered tartly: "Hm! I'd give him nothing!"

Mr. Crocker looked up, looked at Grover, said, "What are you waiting for?"

"Will you give me the three ones, please?" Grover said.

"I'll give you nothing," Mr. Crocker said.

He left his work and came rocking forward along the counter. "Now you get out of here! Don't you come in here with any more of those stamps," said Mr. Crocker.

"I should like to know where he gets them—that's what I should like to know," said Mrs. Crocker.

She did not look up as she said these words. She inclined her head a little to the side, in Mr. Crocker's direction, and continued to fold the boxes with her bony fingers.

"You get out of here!" said Mr. Crocker. "And don't you come back here with any stamps. . . . Where did you get those stamps?" he said.

"That's just what I've been thinking," Mrs. Crocker said. "I've been thinking all along."

"You've been coming in here for the last two weeks with those stamps," said Mr. Crocker. "I don't like the look of it. Where did you get those stamps?" he said.

"That's what I've been thinking," said Mrs. Crocker, for a second time.

Grover had got white underneath his olive skin. His eyes had lost their luster. They looked like dull, stunned balls of tar. "From Mr. Reed," he said. "I got the stamps from Mr. Reed." Then he burst out desperately: "Mr. Crocker—Mr. Reed will tell you how I got the stamps. I did some work for Mr. Reed, he gave me those stamps two weeks ago."

"Mr. Reed," said Mrs. Crocker acidly. She did not turn her head. "I call it mighty funny."

"Mr. Crocker," Grover said, "if you'll just let me have three ones——"

"You get out of here!" cried Mr. Crocker, and he began rocking forward toward Grover. "Now don't you come in here again, boy! There's something funny about this whole business! I don't like the look of it," said Mr. Crocker. "If you can't pay as other people do, then I don't want your trade."

"Mr. Crocker," Grover said again, and underneath the olive skin his face was gray, "if you'll just let me have those three——"

"You get out of here!" Mr. Crocker cried, rocking down toward the counter's end. "If you don't get out, boy——"

"*I'd* call a policeman, that's what I'd do," Mrs. Crocker said.

Mr. Crocker rocked around the lower end of the counter. He came rocking up to Grover. "You get out," he said.

He took the boy and pushed him with his bony little hands, and Grover was sick and gray down to the hollow pit of his stomach.

"You've got to give me those three ones," he said.

"You get out of here!" shrilled Mr. Crocker. He seized the screen door, pulled it open, and pushed Grover out. "Don't you come back in here," he said, pausing for a moment, and working thinly at the lips. He turned and rocked back in the shop again. The screen door slammed behind him. Grover stood there on the pavement. And light came and went and came again into the Square.

The boy stood there, and a wagon rattled past. There were some people passing by, but Grover did not notice them. He stood there blindly, in the watches of the sun, feeling this was Time, this was the center of the universe, the granite core of changelessness, and feeling, this is Grover, this the Square, this is Now.

But something had gone out of day. He felt the overwhelming, soul-sickening guilt that all the children, all the good men of the earth, have felt since Time began. And even anger had died down, had been drowned out, in this swelling tide of guilt, and "This is the Square"—thought Grover as

177

before—"This is Now. There is my father's shop. And all of it is as it has always been—save I."

And the Square reeled drunkenly around him, light went in blind gray motes before his eyes, the fountain sheeted out to rainbow iridescence and returned to its proud, pulsing plume again. But all the brightness had gone out of day, and "Here is the Square, and here is permanence, and here is Time—and all of it the same as it has always been, save I."

The scuffed boots of the lost boy moved and stumbled blindly. The numb feet crossed the pavement—reached the cobbled street, reached the plotted central square—the grass plots, and the flower beds, so soon to be packed with red geraniums.

"I want to be alone," thought Grover, "where I cannot go near him. . . . Oh God, I hope he never hears, that no one ever tells him——"

The plume blew out, the iridescent sheet of spray blew over him. He passed through, found the other side and crossed the street, and—"Oh God, if papa ever hears!" thought Grover, as his numb feet started up the steps into his father's shop.

He found and felt the steps—the width and thickness of old lumber twenty feet in length. He saw it all—the iron columns on his father's porch, painted with the dull anomalous black-green that all such columns in this land and weather come to; two angels, fly-specked, and the waiting stones. Beyond and all around, in the stonecutter's shop, cold shapes of white and marble, rounded stone, the languid angel with strong marble hands of love.

He went on down the aisle, the white shapes stood around him. He went on to the back of the workroom. This he knew—the little cast-iron stove in left-hand corner, caked, brown, heat-blistered, and the elbow of the long stack running out across the shop; the high and dirty window looking down across the Market Square toward Niggertown; the rude old shelves, plank-boarded, thick, the wood not smooth but pulpy, like the strong hair of an animal; upon the shelves the chisels of all sizes and a layer of stone dust; an emery wheel with pump tread; and a door that let out on the alleyway, yet the alleyway twelve feet below. Here in the room, two trestles of this coarse spiked wood upon which rested gravestones, and at one, his father at work.

The boy looked, saw the name was Creasman: saw the carved analysis of John, the symmetry of the s, the fine sentiment that was being polished off beneath the name and date: "John Creasman, November 7, 1903."

Gant looked up. He was a man of fifty-three, gaunt-visaged, mustache cropped, immensely long and tall and gaunt. He wore good dark clothes—heavy, massive—save he had no coat. He worked in shirt-sleeves with his vest on, a strong watch chain stretching across his vest, wing collar and black tie, Adam's apple, bony forehead, bony nose, light eyes, gray-green, undeep and cold, and, somehow, lonely-looking, a striped apron going up around his shoulders, and starched cuffs. And in one hand a tremendous rounded wooden mallet like a butcher's bole; and in his other hand, a strong cold chisel.

"How are you, son?"

He did not look up as he spoke. He spoke quietly, absently. He worked upon the chisel and the wooden mallet, as a jeweler might work on a watch, except that in the man and in the wooden mallet there was power too.

"What is it, son?" he said.

He moved around the table from the head, started up on "J" once again.

"Papa, I never stole the stamps," said Grover.

Gant put down the mallet, laid the chisel down. He came around the trestle.

"What?" he said.

As Grover winked his tar-black eyes, they brightened, the hot tears shot out. "I never stole the stamps," he said.

"Hey? What is this?" his father said. "What stamps?"

"That Mr. Reed gave me, when the other boy was sick and I worked there for three days. . . . And Old Man Crocker," Grover said, "he took all the stamps. And I told him Mr. Reed had given them to me. And now he owes me three ones—and Old Man Crocker says he don't believe that they were mine. He says—he says—that I must have taken them somewhere," Grover blurted out.

"The stamps that Reed gave you—hey?" the stonecutter said. "The stamps you had—" He wet his thumb upon his lips, threw back his head and slowly swung his gaze around the ceiling, then turned and strode quickly from his work-shop out into the storeroom.

Almost at once he came back again, and as he passed the old gray painted-board partition of his office he cleared his throat and wet his thumb and said, "Now, I tell you——"

Then he turned and strode up toward the front again and cleared his throat and said, "I tell you now—" He wheeled about and started back, and as he came along the aisle between the marshaled rows of gravestones he said beneath his breath, "By God, now——"

He took Grover by the hand and they went out flying. Down the aisle they went by all the gravestones, past the fly-specked angels waiting there, and down the wooden steps and across the Square. The fountain pulsed, the plume blew out in sheeted iridescence, and it swept across them; an old gray horse, with a peaceful look about his torn lips, swucked up the cool mountain water from the trough as Grover and his father went across the Square, but they did not notice it.

They crossed swiftly to the other side in a direct line to the candy shop. Gant was still dressed in his long striped apron, and he was still holding Grover by the hand. He opened the screen door and stepped inside.

"Give him the stamps," Gant said.

Mr. Crocker came rocking forward behind the counter, with the prim and careful look that now was somewhat like a smile. "It was just—" he said.

"Give him the stamps," Gant said, and threw some coins down on the counter.

Mr. Crocker rocked away and got the stamps. He came rocking back. "I just didn't know—" he said.

The stonecutter took the stamps and gave them to the boy. And Mr. Crocker took the coins.

"It was just that—" Mr. Crocker began again, and smiled.

Gant cleared his throat: "You never were a father," he said. "You never knew the feelings of a father, or understood the feelings of a child; and that is why you acted as you did. But a judgment is upon you. God has cursed you. He has afflicted you. He has made you lame and childless as you are— and lame and childless, miserable as you are, you will go to your grave and be forgotten!"

And Crocker's wife kept kneading her bony little hands and said, imploringly, "Oh, no—oh don't say that, please don't say that."

The stone cutter, the breath still hoarse in him, left the store, still holding the boy tightly by the hand. Light came again into the day.

"Well, son," he said, and laid his hand on the boy's back. "Well, son," he said, "now don't you mind."

They walked across the Square, the sheeted spray of iridescent light swept out on them, the horse swizzled at the water-trough, and "Well, son," the stonecutter said.

And the old horse sloped down, ringing with his hoofs upon the cobble-stones.

"Well, son," said the stonecutter once again, "be a good boy."

And he trod his own steps then with his great stride and went back again into his shop.

The lost boy stood upon the Square, hard by the porch of his father's shop.

"This is Time," thought Grover. "Here is the Square, here is my father's shop, and here am I."

And light came and went and came again—but now not quite the same as it had done before. The boy saw the pattern of familiar shapes and knew that they were just the same as they had always been. But something had gone out of day, and something had come in again. Out of the vision of those quiet eyes some brightness had gone, and into their vision had come some deeper color. He could not say, he did not know through what transforming shadows life had passed within that quarter hour. He only knew that something had been lost—something forever gained. . . .

Sunday Afternoon Hanging

JESSE STUART

Boy, you don't know anything about it. Let yer grandpa tell you a little about this hanging business in Kentucky. You set around here and talk about the hot seat for a man that kills another man in cold blood. Hot seat ain't nothing. People can't go and see a body killed in the hot seat. Just a little bunch allowed in to write up a few of the poor devil's last words. When they used to kill a man everybody got to see it and laugh and faint, cuss or cry, do just as he damn pleased about it. It used to be that way here in Kentucky. Now let me tell you, there's no fun to giving a man the hot seat or giving him gas or a lot of stuff like that, giving him the pen for life. Didn't keep 'em up there and feed 'em for life when I was a boy. They took 'em out and swung 'em to a limb and people from all over the country came to see 'em swing.

Let me tell you how it was. That was before the days of baseball. People came for forty miles to see a hanging. We had one every weekend in Blakesburg for the people to come and see. You know that's how Blakesburg got the name Hang-Town. God, I remember well as if it was yesterday. Used to be an old elm in the lower end of town where they hung 'em. It was upon a little hill where everybody could get an eyeful of the man they swung to the elm limb. Pa and Ma and me, we used to go every Sunday of the world after church was out. We could hardly wait to get to the hanging. It was as much fun to see a hanging them days as it is to see a baseball game nowadays here in Kentucky. God, do I remember the old days. I was just a boy then but I remember it just like it was yesterday. I can see the crowd yet that gathered at the hangings, and all the hollering you ever heard in your life it was put up at one of them hangings when a poor devil was swung up to the old elm limb.

That old tree just fell three years ago. God Almighty got rid of it. Must a been some of them innocent men they swung up there and in Heaven they got after God Almighty to do something about that tree. And God Almighty got rid of it. He looks after his people. He'll do a lot too, I guess, of what his angels in Heaven wants him to do. Son, I am an old man and I believe I know. Well, of all the trees in the lower end of Blakesburg, the old elm where they hung all them men was the only one the lightnin' hit and split from limb to roots. Tree must have been five feet through the middle, too. And don't you know the people wouldn't burn a stick of that wood in their stoves and fireplaces. They just rolled it over the bank into the Ohio River and let it float away. People was afraid that if they burnt it they would be haunted the rest of their days.

You've heard about poor old Jim Murphy and his wife gettin' killed that time. I know you've seen the hickory club they've got over there in the Blakesburg Courthouse with poor old Jim's tooth stuck in it—that hard white hickory club—no, don't guess you did see it. The 1913 flood got up in the courthouse and carried it off. Had poor old Jim's tooth in it. See, here is the way it was. It happened up there in Sand Bottom. Right up there where that foul murder happened two years ago when that old strollop and that man tortured the little girl to death with a red-hot poker. Foulest things that have ever happened in this country have happened right up there in Sand Bottom. To go on with my story. A bunch of Sixeymores up there then. God, they's rotten eggs too. Well, there was two Sixeymore brothers well as I remember, a Dudley Toms, a Winslow, and a Grubb into that scrape. The Sixeymore brothers planned the murder of these two old people for their money. They had heard by a woman that went there and cooked for them that they had eleven hundred dollars hid in a old teakettle in the pantry. Well, the Sixeymore brothers—Tim and Jake—promised Freed Winslow Jim Murphy's mules if he would help kill him and his wife. They promised Dudley Toms the two cows and Work Grubb his thirty acres of land if he would help kill them.

They went to the little log house down by the Sandy River one dark rainy night when there was no moon. It was in the dark of the moon. They had the whole thing planned. They thought that if they killed the old people and throwed them in Sandy in the dark of the moon the bodies would never come to the top of the water. So they cut a hickory club; Tim Sixeymore cut it with a poleax up on Flint Sneed's pint, up where the old furnace used to be. People used to go there and see the stump. It all come out in Tim's confession before they swung him. They cut the club—all went there that dark night. Jim made a chicken squall and old man Murphy—game man as ever drawed a breath of wind—run out against his old lady's will. She said: "Somebody to kill us, Jim. Don't go out there." You know how a woman can just about tell things; God gives 'em the power to pertect themselves just like he does a possum or a horse. They can almost smell danger. Old Jim run out and—whack—Sixeymore hit him in the mouth with the hickory club. Killed him dead as a mackrel. That one lick finished him. He just walled his eyes back and died. Then all five of the men went in where old Lizzie Murphy was a settin' before the fire smokin' her pipe and she said: "Give me time to pray once more to God Almighty." She begged to pray but they didn't give her time. Dudley Toms said the hardest thing he ever tried to do was to kill that old woman and her a-beggin' to just get to pray to God Almighty just one more time. He hit her over the head with a fire shovel and to make sure she was dead he beat out her brains with the shovel. Then they carried them down and throwed them in the dark waters of Little Sandy on that dark night. But nature don't hold things and uphold dirty work. That water give up the dead bodies down at Cedar Riffles. Some fishermen caught them there. And Dudley Toms didn't know that there was a speck of blood left on his hatband. But there was. See, there's always a clue. Can't do a thing like that and get by with it, not even if the law is on your side. Boy, you suffer for what you do in this old world. Talk about men suffering before they died. I was right there at the hanging. Everybody in the county came to it. It was the biggest hanging we ever had. Had a hanging of five that Sunday. Hung these five and they was the kind of fellows the people liked to see swing to a limb. Was a lot better than just going out and getting somebody for stealing a horse and hanging him, or a man for abusing his wife; somebody like that hardly had enough against him to hang. I've seen many a poor devil hang over almost nothing. Today he wouldn't have to go to jail for it. Used to hang him for the same thing. The people wanted a hanging every week and the sheriff and judge had better have a hanging at least once a month or they would never get elected again. If they didn't have hangings often enough the people would go to them and say, "Look here, you'll not get my vote next time if this is the way you intend to do. Lay down on the job, never have a hanging. Damn poor Law. You'll never be elected again."

Well, the day these five men was hung I was just a boy. I remember it just like it was yesterday. I was up to the jail that morning after the confession and saw them getting their breakfast. Jailer Wurt Hammons said:

"Boys, eat hearty. This will be your last grub here on this earth. The devil will serve your breakfast tomorrow morning. You have the chance to have anything that you want to eat that I can get for you."

Well, the Sixeymore boys took a stewed turkey apiece and a biler of black coffee without sugar or cream. Dudley Toms wouldn't eat a bite. Tim said to him: "Hell, take your hanging like a man. Go to the gallows on a full stummick. Get that much off the county before you die." Work Grubb took twelve hard-fried eggs and a pint of licker to wash 'em down with. Winslow took fried eggs and licker—don't remember how many eggs and how much licker. But that is what they had for breakfast. Well, the county carpenter, Jake Tillman, had the county make coffins for them. He was hired to make the coffins for the men the county hung. He had five good county coffins made—took their measurements and made them to fit. Had one awfully big for Tim Sixeymore. He was six feet and seven inches tall and weighed some over three hundred pounds. Biggest man I believe I ever saw. He wasn't dough-bellied either. Weighed a lot and was hard as the butt of a shell-barked hickory. His brother was about as big and powerful. God, old Tim was a man and not afraid of God Almighty hisself. God would have to watch him at the jedgment bar. If he got half a chance he'd do something to God Almighty.

I remember the two excursion boats that come down the river that day to the hanging and the one that come up the river. They was just loaded with people hollering and waving handkerchiefs around the deck. There was a double-decker come up the river with a load of people. And of all the people that ever come to Blakesburg they were there that day. Mules tied to the trees along the streets—not many houses in Blakesburg them days but there was a thicket of trees through the town. Wagons of all descriptions. Hug-me-tight buggies—them things had just come out then—people looked at the new contraption and quarreled about the indecency of men and women riding in them little narrow seats all loved up. Said they ought to be hung for an example for doing it. And there was a lot of two-horse surreys and rubber-tired hacks and jolt wagons there that day. Jolt wagons with whole families riding in wagon beds full of straw. People and people everywhere you looked. Never was such a crowd in Blakesburg as there was that day. Little children crying and dogs that followed the wagons to town out fighting in the streets and the horses neighing to each other and rearing up in the collar, mules biting and kicking each other! It was the awfulest time I ever saw. If a dark cloud would a riz over that town I would a swore the world was coming to an end. But it was a pretty day for a crowd and for a hanging. Sun in the sky. June wind blowing. Roses in bloom. One of the prettiest days I believe I ever saw. The reason that I remember it so well was that they hung 'em at sunup. Some of the people had come all night to be there in time to see the hanging in the morning.

Well, the band got there. You know they always had a band at the hangings to furnish the music. Had a seven-piece band at this hanging. Always before we just had a drummer, a pot beater, and a fifer. About everybody likes a fife. It puts madness in their bones and bodies and helps drown the screams of the women and the fighting of the dogs and the whinnying of the horses. The band had on the gayest suits you ever saw for this occasion. Just like a political rally where they used to butcher five or six steers to feed the people. These band players had on bright yaller pants and red sashes and pea-green jackets and them old three-cornered hats. God, but they did look nifty.

Well as I remember the band struck up a tune that day. It was "Dixie." Some of the horses broke loose and took down through the town but the people let 'em go. They stayed still for the hanging. It was the biggest thing we'd had in many a day. Horses broke loose without riders on them and took out through the crowd among the barking dogs, running over them and the children. People didn't pay attention to that. It was a hanging and people wanted to see every bit of it. They didn't care if a child did get run over so it wasn't their own. And it took five or six sheriffs; they had big guns on 'em to keep any fights from starting and they wore bright yaller jackets. Lord, all the people there. And you could always tell a mountaineer them days from the back country. He always had the smell of wood smoke on him and barnyard manure. Big bony devils! Hairy as all get out! Never would shave their bony faces!

I remember seeing the first horse and express come into sight. Dudley Toms was sitting on his coffin with a rope around his neck, the hangman's knot already tied. Bert Blevins always did that for the county. One of his knots never did slip. It always flew up in the right place and hit 'em one on the jaw and broke their necks. Bert was a whiz on this hanging business. And when the horse come in sight and Dudley was a sittin' up there on the coffin—God, the people nearly tore the limbs out of the trees with their jumpin' and screamin' and they had that big shell-bark hickory club that

Tim hit Jim Murphy with back there the night he made the chicken squall. That had just been three weeks before. They really brought men to justice back in them days when they had to have someone to hang every Sunday after church. Screams was so loud that you had to hold your fingers in your ears. Here was that big shell-bark hickory club held up in the air by a big man while Dudley stood on his coffin and made his confession. They wanted to hear it. They wanted all out of a hanging that there was in one.

At first Dudley Toms wouldn't talk. The jailer said, "Tell them, Dudley. They want your confession before you give it to the devil. We want it first-handed here. You can give it second-handed to the devil." And Dudley he stood up there on his coffin while that horse—a new one they was breakin' in to haul men to the gallows—he just ripped and snorted.

And Dudley said, "First time I ever killed anybody. Was hard to kill Lizzie Murphy with that shovel. But I had to do it. No use to cry over spilt milk. I hate like hell to hang. I do. But I'd rather do it right now and see what all this after death is that I've heard so much about. I hate to die. But take me out of all this—take me out!" And he kinda broke down.

Well, they unfastened his hands from behind him so they could see him kick and pull on the rope with his tongue turnin' black and hangin' out of his mouth. They just made him stand on the coffin and they tied the rope that went around his neck to the rope that was already fastened to the old hangin'-tree and just drove the wagon out from under him while the band struck up a tune. I'll never forget seein' him swing there and kick—that expression on the dyin' man's face. The band was a-playin', the children a-screamin' because it was the first hangin' a lot of them had ever seen. Some of the women started shouting. Never saw anything like it in my life. But Dudley's kinfolk was there to get him. Some of the women fainted and they just had a couple of barrels of water there so they could throw cold water in the faces of the fainting women. That's what they done. Had boys hired right ready to throw water on the faces of the fainting women or the fighting dogs when they got in the way of the hangin'.

The next to ride up was Freed Winslow. He was up on top of his coffin and the horse that hauled him wasn't so afraid of the suits that the bandmen wore. The horse had been to many a hangin'. Well, while the kinsfolk was claimin' the body of Dudley Toms, Freed Winslow was standing on top of his coffin making his confession. It was a fine confession, too, if there was ever a good hangin' confession made. Said Freed Winslow: "Ladies and

187

gentlemen, I have made peace with my God. I am not afraid to die. I prayed all night last night. I been prayin' ever since I got in this mess. That very first night after I helped do this killing I saw so many devils around my bed that I had to get up and light the lamp. They was cuttin' all kinds of shines. They even run across my stummick. God, it was awful. I hope to meet you all in Heaven where there ain't no devils to run across your stummick and grin at you. Good-by, folks. Sorry for what I have done and I hope you won't hold it against me. I ought to die."

So they put the knot over his head and drove the wagon out from under him and he fell off his own coffin and the band struck up a tune. While he was in the air struggling for breath and glomming at the wind with his hands, the band players kept pumping harder. That fife kept screaming above the cries of the women. Talking of fainting of pretty girls. They sure did faint. Freed Winslow was a handsome man. There his tongue went out of his mouth. His face black. His curly hair flying in the wind, black as a frostbit pawpaw in the early fall, and he died strugglin' just like a possum struggles for breath after its neck has been broke under a mattock handle.

The next to come up to the hang-tree was Work Grubb. He was thought to be a fine man in the neighborhood. He was a-ridin' on his coffin, hairiest man you ever saw. Looked like one of them men in the days of old with all the beard on his face. He looked kindly like he was ashamed when the wagon rolled up under the tree. I never can forget all them knotholes in his coffin. Bet he wasn't more than under the ground till the water started seepin' and the dirt and these worms started crumbling through these knotholes. Well, the band struck up a tune and the people screamed. Just like a man when he makes a score nowdays in baseball. It was a score with death then. The band had to play while the people screamed and waited for his confession. He waited calmly as I ever saw a man waiting for death. He wasn't scared, not one iotum. He just waited and when the people screamed till they were hoarse he stood up on his coffin and said, "What I got to say to you is: Go on and kill me. Remember the killer pays. I was guilty and I deserve to die but you don't deserve to kill me."

One old fat snaggle-toothed woman up and hollered, "You won't get pore old Uncle Jim Murphy's thirty acres of land, will ye? Might get some hot land to farm in hell. Say they've got a lot of desert land down there!" And she just hollered and laughed at the condemned man going to the elm limb.

Well, the band struck up "Dixie." And the wagon drove out from under him soon as the rope was fastened. And Work swung there with his thin legs dangling in the air. Didn't use a cap on their faces in them days. People wanted to see their faces while they was dyin'. The band played while he dangled at the end of the rope and clutched for thin air. Of all the cries that ever went up from the people it did there. Then Doc Turner went up and stopped the swinging body and put his hand on the heart. He said, "He's dead. He's gone to the other world."

The next they brought up on the wagon was Jake Sixeymore. He was a-laughing. They asked him if he wanted to make any confession. And he laughed and said, "All I want is a pint of Rock and Rye to stick in my hip pocket for old Satan and a good homemade twist. He's going to have hell, with me and my brother Tim both with him. We'll both want jobs and we'll get into it. I want to get on the good side of him first. I'm not a damn bit sorry over anything I've done. Just one life to live, one death to die, something beyond or nothing beyond and I'll hold my own any goddam place they put me. So, swing your goddam rope to me soon as you give me that half-pint of Rock and Rye and that twist of Kentucky-burley terbacker."

"Sure thing," said the sheriff. "Give it to him. I'm afraid it's the last he'll ever get."

So the fellow just give one of them big horse-pints with just one little dram taken out of it. He give him a twist that looked as big as my arm at the elbow. He took it, thanked the fellow in the gray with the long handle-bar mustache and dough-belly that shook as he walked, and then he said, "I'm ready, gentlemen. Pull your goddam rope."

Well, the crowd was kindly quiet for a few minutes, then the band struck up a tune. And he was riding on the highest wagon and the highest coffin. The rope broke his neck the first crack. Of all the screams! His tongue just come out of his mouth, a twisted tongue, and where he bit it, it was bleeding. God, what a sight. And his face black as a pawpaw leaf. He swung there low against the ground, the limb sagging and the rope swinging. Doc Smith run out and put his ear to his heart. He said, "Dead man. He is in the other world by now or gettin' mighty close."

Well, people—just his old dad and mammy there in their rags. God, I felt sorry for them. I couldn't help it. Had two boys there that day to hang. They took him off in the coffin and carried him a little ways and put him down in the grass. They waited for Tim to die so they could haul them both to the same double grave on the same wagon. Her gray hair flying in the wind, him a mountain man with the smell of wood smoke and cow manure on him. He had shed tears. He was a man stout as a rock. His sons were no stronger-looking than their old white-haired father.

Well, the last wagon come up there that day. It had one of the biggest coffins I ever saw on it. The biggest man I ever saw was riding on top of that box. His big hands looked like shovels folded up there on his chest. He looked mean as the devil out of his eyes. They were black eyes and they had beads of fire shining from them. You could see them from the crowd. His hair looked like briers around a stump: a big mop of it, and it looked like a comb had never been run through it in his life. Clay still on his knuckles where he had worked in the mines. He'd kill and he'd rob and he'd work. He was a great worker. Could do as much work as four ordinary men and lift more than any two men in the mines. Lord, he was a sight to look at. He looked like a mountain man. He could eat the side of a hog's ribs at one meal and a whole pone of corn bread and drink a gallon of buttermilk. He could eat three dozen fried eggs and drink a whole biler of strong coffee. Now he was facing the gallows. He just set there like a rock. I heard one old whiskered man with a willow cane say: "Now, if he confesses all his guilt we'll get a good confession."

The band struck up a tune. "Dixie," I believe. Nearly played it and "Old Kentucky Home" to death that day. It was one of the songs. And the people started screaming. It was the last one of the five and they just tried to see how much noise they could make. God, it was awful to hear. I remember his pore old mother fainting and how they dashed two buckets of cold water in her face. I remember the tears that come from his pore old pap's wrinkled eyes . . . it was a sight to see! I have often wished I'd never seen it. God, it was awful to think about.

When the band stopped the sheriff said, "Let's hear your confession, Tim Sixeymore."

Well, that great big man got up and stood on his coffin. And he looked like a giant to me. Great big devil, unafraid of the whole crowd.

And he said, "Yes, I've got a big confession to make. I got plenty to tell you bastard men and wench women, goddam you!"

You could a heard a pin drop there that day till some strange dogs started fighting and then the babies started crying. Well, they throwed water on the dogs and got them stopped and the women started nursing the babies and got them stopped. If they didn't want to nurse, the women just made 'em nurse. And they soon stopped crying. They wanted to get the whole confession.

"Gentlemen bastards and sonofabitches. Women wenches and hussies and goddam you all. Get this, the whole crowd of you that's come here to see me hang. I've done a whole hell of a sight more that I ought to hang for than this. But you—you come here to laugh at a man that meets death. All I got to say is goddam every blessed one of you and I hope to hand every one of you a cup of water in hell. You low-down brindle house-cats, come here to hang a man when he ain't done a single damn thing to you. I've killed seventeen men, raped five women, stole more than I can tell you about. Got a good mother and a good father. Don't hold a thing against them, you lousy bastards and wenches and young babies that nurse your mother's milk. This will be something for you to tell the generations about yet to come. And that is not all. I planned to kill Jim Murphy and Lizzie Murphy. It was all my work and yet all these fellows had to die. I hope God Almighty burns this sonofabitchen tree with lightning before another hundred years roll by. Poor devils without a chance. Die for you to laugh at and see struggle on the scaffold. Die for you to laugh at as you would a chicken fight. You lowdown cowardly sonofabitches. Now laugh at me. I'll show you, by God, how a man can die. I'm not a bit afraid of whatever is to come. I'll be ready soon as I get one more good drink of Kentucky whisky and a chaw of terbacker in my jaw. Then you can give me the rope, goddam you. Strike up your goddam band. You people whoop and holler as much as you damn please, you low-lifed lousy bastards. I can whip any four fair-fisted in the crowd. Will fight you right up here on top of my coffin. Want to try it, any of you? None—"

There was silence in the crowd. Not a voice was lifted.

"Well, then, give me a drink of licker and a chaw of terbacker and I'm ready for the Happy Hunting Ground."

The sheriff stepped up and give him a drink out of a full horse-pint and give him a chaw of his own twist of terbacker. I'll bet twenty men offered him a drink of licker but the sheriff took charge because it was his duty under the sharp eyes of the Law.

When he got the rope around his neck I remember he said, "Look here, you bunch of wenches. Let me show you how to die. I'll hope to give your tail a couple of kicks in hell. I'll just get there first. So long, you goddam bellering crowd."

Well, a lot of the old men held their heads. The women sniffed and the band struck up the last tune, they thought, for the day. But it wasn't the last tune. They put the rope around his neck and tied it to the rope in the tree, and drove the wagon out from under him. Well, he just snapped that rope like it was twine and laughed till you could a heared him for a mile. The limb swayed with him, too. No well rope would hold him after it was wore the way it was, hanging so many people. Somebody went and got another rope. It was a brand new rope. And they fixed a new rope up in the elm and caught another limb so the two of them wouldn't give. And the seventh time, the rope held him. Well, the sheriff had to arrest his father and mother. They started fighting in the crowd. They's lots of people started taking it up for them and if they hadn't got him hung when they did it would have been a pitched battle by three o'clock. People started taking sides. You know what that meant in them days.

It wasn't long before the band started playing a retreat. It must have been Napoleon Bonaparte's retreat or some big general's—maybe George Washington's. That was what happened at the end of the hangings. Had to have some soft music to soften the people up a little bit. God, it had been an awful day. Women pulling hair and shouting and praying, singing, screaming till you couldn't hear your ears. God, Kentucky used to have her hangings. And that was the biggest one I ever saw in Kentucky. Lauria and Kent Sixeymore riding on their son's coffins. Lauria was a-setting on the end of one and Kent was a-setting on the end of the other. It was a sad thing to see. Pore old man and woman! Their hair white as cotton fleece flyin' in the spring wind, the dogs a-barking and a-fighting. And the band, just about petered out on fast music, started playing that slow soft kind. People almost in tears! Big day was over. People getting at the little restaurant where it said, "Good lodging for a man and brute and a glass of licker and a night's lodging for a quarter." People trying to get something to eat. Women and children hungry and old skinny hounds running up to the back porches to the slop barrels and fighting over them. People fighting in the streets. Wagons going out of Blakesburg with the dead. No wonder they call that place Hang-Town! It was a hang-town. If you could just a seen, son, that crowd a-breaking up and leaving. It was a sight. People getting acquainted and talking about the hanging, talking about their crops and the cattle and the doings of the Lord to the wicked people for their sins. That was the biggest hanging I ever saw. Used all them two barrels of cold water on the fighting dogs and the fainting women. When the crowd left, all the gardens and flowers had been tromped under. Town looked awful and limbs broke out of the trees where people couldn't see out of the crowd and climbed the trees and got up in them like birds! God, but it was awful!

Then a little later on they got to building a scaffold an' just letting a body see their bodies before they dropped down into a trap door and a sawdust bottom. They even put a cap over their face till people couldn't see their faces. Just kept a-gettin' it easier and easier till they didn't hang 'em at all. Got to having baseball games instead and then people got bad in these parts. Law got to be a joke! Something like it is now. Give 'em just as easy a death as possible, like the hot seat. They used to let 'em hang in Kentucky!

Knoxville: Summer of 1915

JAMES AGEE

We are talking now of summer evenings in Knoxville, Tennessee in the time that I lived there so successfully disguised to myself as a child. It was a little bit mixed sort of block, fairly solidly lower middle class, with one or two juts apiece on either side of that. The houses corresponded: middle-sized gracefully fretted wood houses built in the late nineties and early nineteen hundreds, with small front and side and more spacious back yards, and trees in the yards, and porches. These were softwooded trees, poplars, tulip trees, cottonwoods. There were fences around one or two of the houses, but mainly the yards ran into each other with only now and then a low hedge that wasn't doing very well. There were few good friends among the grown people, and they were not poor enough for the other sort of intimate acquaintance, but everyone nodded and spoke, and even might talk short times, trivially, and at the two extremes of the general or the particular, and ordinarily next door neighbors talked quite a bit when they happened to run into each other, and never paid calls. The men were mostly small businessmen, one or two very modestly executives, one or two worked with their hands, most of them clerical, and most of them between thirty and forty-five.

But it is of these evenings, I speak.

Supper was at six and was over by half past. There was still daylight, shining softly and with a tarnish, like the lining of a shell; and the carbon lamps lifted at the corners were on in the light, and the locusts were started, and the fire flies were out, and a few frogs were flopping in the dewy grass, by the time the fathers and the children came out. The children ran out first hell bent and yelling those names by which they were known; then the fathers sank out leisurely in crossed supenders, their collars removed and their necks looking tall and shy. The mothers stayed back in the kitchen washing and drying, putting things away, recrossing their traceless

194

footsteps like the lifetime journeys of bees, measuring out the dry cocoa for breakfast. When they came out they had taken off their aprons and their skirts were dampened and they sat in rockers on their porches quietly.

It is not of the games children play in the evening that I want to speak now, it is of a contemporaneous atmosphere that has little to do with them: that of the fathers of families, each in his space of lawn, his shirt fishlike pale in the unnatural light and his face nearly anonymous, hosing their lawns. The hoses were attached at spigots that stood out of the brick foundations of the houses. The nozzles were variously set but usually so there was a long sweet stream of spray, the nozzle wet in the hand, the water trickling the right forearm and the peeled-back cuff, and the water whishing out a long loose and low-curved cone, and so gentle a sound. First, an insane noise of violence in the nozzle, then the still irregular sound of adjustment, then the smoothing into steadiness and a pitch as accurately tuned to the size and style of stream as any violin. So many qualities of sound out of one hose; so many choral differences out of those several hoses that were in earshot. Out of any one hose, the almost dead silence of the release, and the short still arch of the separate big drops, silent as a held breath, and the only noise the flattering noise on leaves and the slapped grass at the fall of each big drop. That, and the intense hiss with the intense stream; that, and that same intensity not growing less but growing more quiet and delicate with the turn of the nozzle, up to that extreme tender whisper when the water was just a wide bell of film. Chiefly, though, the hoses were set much alike, in a compromise between distance and tenderness of spray (and quite surely a sense of art behind this compromise, and a quiet, deep joy, too real to recognize itself), and the sounds therefore were pitched much alike; pointed by the snorting start of a new hose; decorated by some man playful with the nozzle; left empty, like God by the sparrow's fall, when any single one of them desists; and all, though near alike, of various pitch; and this in unison. These sweet pale streamings in the light lift out their pallors and their voices all together, mothers hushing their children, the hushing unnaturally prolonged, the men gentle and silent and each snaillike withdrawn into the quietude of what he singly is doing, the urination of huge children stood loosely military against an invisible wall, and gently happy and peaceful, tasting the mean goodness of their living like the last of their suppers in their mouths; while the locusts carry on this noise of hoses on their much higher and sharper key. The noise of the locust is dry, and it seems not to

195

be rasped or vibrated but urged from him as if through a small orifice by a
breath that can never give out. Also there is never one locust but an illusion
of at least a thousand. The noise of each locust is pitched in some classic
locust range out of which none of them varies more than two full tones; and
yet you seem to hear each locust discrete from all the rest, and there is a
long, slow, pulse in their noise, like the scarcely defined arch of a long and
high set bridge. They are all around in every tree, so that the noise seems
to come from nowhere and everywhere at once, from the whole shell
heaven, shivering in your flesh and teasing your eardrums, the boldest of all
the sounds of night. And yet it is habitual to summer nights, and is of the
great order of noises, like the noises of the sea and of the blood her preco-
cious grandchild, which you realize you are hearing only when you catch
yourself listening. Meantime from low in the dark, just outside the swaying
horizons of the hoses, conveying always grass in the damp of dew and its
strong green-black smear of smell, the regular yet spaced noises of the
crickets, each a sweet cold silver noise threenoted, like the slipping each
time of three matched links of a small chain.

But the men by now, one by one, have silenced their hoses and drained
and coiled them. Now only two, and now only one, is left, and you see only
ghostlike shirt with the sleeve garters, and sober mystery of his mild face
like the lifted face of large cattle enquiring of your presence in a pitch-dark
pool of meadow; and now he too is gone; and it has become that time of evening when people sit on their porches, rocking gently and talking gently and
watching the street and the standing up into their sphere of possession of
the trees, of birds hung havens, hangars. People go by; things go by. A
horse, drawing a buggy, breaking his hollow iron music on the asphalt: a
loud auto: a quiet auto: people in pairs, not in a hurry, scuffling, switching
their weight of aestival body, talking casually, the taste hovering over them
of vanilla, strawberry, pasteboard and starched milk, the image upon them
of lovers and horsemen, squared with clowns in hueless amber. A street car
raising its iron moan; stopping; belling and starting, stertorous; rousing and
raising again its iron increasing moan and swimming its gold windows and
straw seats on past and past and past, the bleak spark crackling and cursing
above it like a small malignant spirit set to dog its tracks; the iron whine
rises on rising speed; still risen, faints; halts; the faint stinging bell; rises
again, still fainter; fainting, lifting, lifts, faints forgone: forgotten. Now is the
night one blue dew.

Now is the night one blue dew, my father has drained, he has coiled the hose.

Low on the length of lawns, a frailing of fire who breathes.

Content, silver, like peeps of light, each cricket makes his comment over and over in the drowned grass.

A cold toad thumpily flounders.

Within the edges of damp shadows of side yards are hovering children nearly sick with joy of fear, who watch the unguarding of a telephone pole.

Around white carbon corner lamps bugs of all sizes are lifted elliptic, solar systems. Big hardshells bruise themselves, assailant: he is fallen on his back, legs squiggling.

Parents on porches: rock and rock. From damp strings morning glories: hang their ancient faces.

The dry and exalted noise of the locusts from all the air at once enchants my eardrums.

On the rough wet grass of the back yard my father and mother have spread quilts. We all lie there, my mother, my father, my uncle, my aunt, and I too am lying there. First we were sitting up, then one of us lay down, and then we all lay down, on our stomachs, or on our sides, or on our backs, and they have kept on talking. They are not talking much, and the talk is quiet, of nothing in particular, of nothing at all in particular, of nothing at all. The stars are wide and alive, they seem each like a smile of great sweetness, and they seem very near. All my people are larger bodies then mine, quiet, with voices gentle and meaningless like the voices of sleeping birds. One is an artist, he is living at home. One is a musician, she is living at home. One is my mother who is good to me. One is my father who is good to me. By some chance, here they are, all on this earth; and who shall ever tell the sorrow of being on this earth, lying, on quilts, on the grass, in a summer evening, among the sounds of the night. May God bless my people, my uncle, my aunt, my mother, my good father, oh, remember them kindly in their time of trouble; and in the hour of their taking away.

After a little I am taken in and put to bed. Sleep, soft smiling, draws me unto her: and those receive me, who quietly treat me, as one familiar and well-beloved in that home: but will not, oh, will not, not now, not ever; but will not ever tell me who I am.

197

Saturday Night

Portrait of a Small Southern Town, 1933

ARNA BONTEMPS

Day ends abruptly here. The Alabama twilight is as brief and lovely as a rainbow. A host of excited chimney-swifts leave the broken flues of a ruined old mansion, waver upward, fleck the mauve sky for an instant, then disappear.

Suddenly we become aware of wagons—mule carts—on the red-dirt county road. In one there is a family of black share farmers; four girls, three boys, and the old couple. The girls and the woman wear blood-red dresses made of identical cloth; and the boys, under their overall straps, have on blouses cut from the same tawdry bolt. The wizened old father has on a shirt of a suspiciously similar complexion, but fortunately it is pretty well covered by an overall jumper. All the faces are as round as full moons. At the moment they wear smiles. In another wagon a smaller family of poor whites rides behind a team of leaner mules. Two men sit in the front seat with necks thrust out, their cheeks bulging with tobacco. There is an old woman and a young one in the second seat, and a small boy on the floor. These folks have things to sell: a coop of half-grown chickens, several bushels of sweet potatoes, some green vegetables. And there is a bundle of fodder for the restless, waiting team when it reaches the square in the heart of town. Other wagons follow.

In passing our gate not one of them fails to pause long enough to notice the license plates on the battered Chevrolet in the driveway. Thanks to the Scottsboro case and the reports of more recent Communistic activities here, all New Yorkers, black or white, are held in suspicion—this in addition to the traditional distrust of strangers. We wave our arms from the doorsteps.

"Good evening."

"H'm. 'Evenin', p'fesser. 'Evenin'."

It is hard to explain the title they have given me so confidently on first sight. Maybe it is because I am dressed too well for a share farmer and too poorly for a rural doctor.

198

A few moments later we are in the procession, our light car leaping joyously on the sorry road. It does not occur to us till we turn onto the paved pike that none of the wagons carry lanterns. When we are driving at forty or better, they materialize like ghosts out of the darkness and we are obliged to slam on brakes and skid for our lives. It is the same with the people walking on the pavement; they never step off the concrete to favor a passing automobile. We drop down to twenty and comment bitterly on this attitude. Some night a reckless young fellow, momentarily blinded perhaps by the lights of an approaching car, is going to pick one of them off. Before reaching the city limits we have occasion to swerve perilously in order to miss a wandering cow, and at another point we stop dead still while a small herd of goats crosses the pike. Another brief spurt and we come into the aged little town. Where shall we go now?

In New York or Chicago we would never ask that question. There one leaves home with a fixed purpose, accomplishes it, and returns. The going is incidental to the objective. Here the going is the thing. Whatever one does, the romance of the journey is unpremeditated. One does not even decide what groceries he will buy on a Saturday night. Since we *shall* buy, however, and since the principal stores face the courthouse square, it might be well to begin there.

The white stone building with its wide austere steps on four sides sits on a green knoll, surrounded by giant oaks. On the grassy slopes there are the usual cannon mounted. Apparently the Confederacy has never disarmed; the South, the stranger gathers, is still in rebellion. Was it H. L. Mencken who first made this observation? It is charmingly true. On the steps of one side a political stump speaker is in action; he is seeking a petty office in the county. He has drawn a strictly riffraff crowd by his strident oratory.

". . . Take Macon County fer'n instance. Down yonder there's seven niggers to every white man. Why, if anything was to happen . . . Yet 'n still they got heap better roads 'n we got here in Madison County."

A swarm of hucksters surrounds the square. A few of them have forsaken their carts to join the crowd on the steps, but the larger number are not interested. It does not disturb them that there are seven niggers to one white man in Macon County; they know that there are less than seven customers, black or white, to one huckster in Madison County, and that is the real issue. It is a tribute to these that now, even in this county, a man is not certain to be swept into office on the rebound of such a speech.

199

A picturesque old editor in a black frock coat, with flowing silver hair, a cane, a ten-gallon hat, and a mysterious reputation, pauses a moment to re-light his cigar and to catch a few words from the speaker. We are told that before the war this editor owned and published the town's first string news-paper. Then something happened, something. . . . Now he is publishing a rival paper. He is the only man we have seen who *looks* Southern, and he manifests a melodramatic interest in the story of the seven niggers to one white man. It is easy to believe that the genesis of racial antagonism is with just such men—petty politicians, rural editors, and their like. The poor whites have taken too much blame. The white peasantry and the black are at peace except when harried and driven by these.

Gradually the streets have become crowded, but everyone seems to be idle, soberly gawking into shop windows to pass the time. In the next block we learn that the local Ford agency has gone out of business—"after all these years." That is the first vivid mark of the depression we discover. Somehow it is hard to realize that Fords are not selling. No wonder the rustics in overalls gawk into lighted windows, no wonder there is pain and defeat on their faces. No wonder the town is sick.

· · ·

We wander from shop to shop, buying apples and popcorn balls and hamburgers, but the horror of that comparison stays with us, and we know in our hearts that we have touched the nerve of this town's sore. Medieval-ism. Medieval serfs. Medieval lords. Medieval poverty. Medieval religion. Medieval thoughts. Medieval woes. There is no modern doubt here, no robust skepticism. This town takes its traditions without a quibble. It has never stopped to question its axioms, its institutions, its prejudices, its poli-tics. Medieval credulity. And hence, in this black time, it has now accepted defeat. The peasants gawk stupidly into shop windows.

Fortunately, the earth is good. There are bushel baskets on the cobble-stones, overflowing with fine potatoes. Corn is too cheap to sell. The small farmers are keeping theirs for home use. Green vegetables abound. There is no want of food.

Fortunately, too (prohibition to the contrary), there are still ways in which a poor man may brace his courage and make brave gestures. Old Badfoot Tyson is a case. A solitary, eccentric farmer, he had a decent crop of watermelons last summer. But Badfoot made the mistake of planting his

200

melons too near the road. They were discovered by the boys of one of the colored schools. They made away with most of the crop, and the little game-legged man swore bitterly. One day a few weeks later when he was in the Negro barber shop getting a bottle of the particular hair tonic he had learned to drink, he heard that a crowd of students from the colored school had gone up the pike on a truck for a day's outing. This information evidently remained in his thought even after he had emptied the bottle of "hair tonic," for he went home, got his double-barreled shotgun, and started up the road. He found a jutting rock that hung over a high embankment and sat there to await the return of the students. Then when the truck did return, as it reached the turn where Badfoot was perched on the overhanging rock, he raised his gun, leveled it, and cut loose with both barrels. Half a dozen youngsters were swept from the flat bed of the truck. The old half-witted and drunken farmer cackled hoarsely and tumbled into the weeds below the embankment.

Our groceries bought, we drift over to the Negro street where our car is parked. The chauffeur of a local millionaire family, who looks enough like Paul Robeson to be his twin brother, flashes his Packard into the block, stops before the pool hall, and gets out leisurely. There is no gawking or despair in this block. It is true that Cynthe, the professional beggar woman, is a medievalism, but the depression has plainly hurt these folks but little. They have never had plenty; and want is only a trifle sharper than before. On the other hand the big men of the town have been softened. The business houses are especially kind.

We walk very slowly. In the Italian market there is a beautiful display of fresh red fish. In another place there is a pyramid of Florida oranges. The Negroes are all indolently ambling along. A little troop of backwoods musicians has stopped at the lunch counter. We can hear their guitars, their voices.

> Back that train an' git yo'
> Heavy load, O Lawdy;
> Back that train an' git yo'
> Heavy load.

Suddenly a black boy hurries by, consternation on his face. He enters the colored drug store. Presently, folks begin leaving the place. There is no

201

indolence or ambling now. The Negroes walk rapidly. One, in his excitement, cuts across the street in the middle of the block. Another breaks into a run. All of them are getting off the main street, trying to make it to the darkened side-streets. A crowd starts pouring out of the pool hall. Men slip along the fronts of the buildings like shadows. We hear a whip pop; wagon wheels grind on the cobble stones.

What's up? What's it all about? Just a minute; tell me.

The best we get is a wild side glance. Terror is on the street. Out of the starry evening a warning has gone forth, something as tacit and ominous perhaps as the evidence that told Chicken Little the sky was falling. The result (on a more heroic scale) is the same. Not an audible word is spoken on the sidewalks—just the mute communication of animal to animal, then terror and flight. And while they scurry feverishly, we stand beneath the yellow blossom of the swaying street lamp and gesture vainly with our hands. Still they pass. The disdain, the utter scorn they have for us as outsiders is clearly manifest now. We are jostled roughly by a fat blubbery fellow whose breath we hear wheezing between his teeth, and when he turns to beg pardon, I take his arm firmly. The two of us plant our heels and shake our fingers in his face.

"You've got to tell us. We don't know what to do."

His eyes seem as round and flat as silver dollars. But he perceives our earnestness and submits to the inquisition.

"A white man been kilt on the pike jes outa town."

"Murdered?"

"Nah, run over. Somebody hit him wid a car."

We cannot hide the fact that the news is less stirring than we had expected, and we are more perplexed than ever.

"Well. What about it?"

"They don't know who kilt him. That's what. The car ain't stopped."

The town's motorcycle cop, a short barrel-chested fellow with baby cheeks, a cigar dangling from his mouth, and a gun hanging from his belt, pops his motor, swings around the corner where we are standing, and dashes out toward the pike. A moment later an autombile careens dangerously on the same turn. There are two young men hanging on the running board. We restrain our prisoner with difficulty.

"Well . . ."

"It might o'been a cullud man what did that killin."

"Oh."

The light breaks. We know right well that it *was* a colored man who was driving that car. The others know it instinctively. We had to be told enough to put our minds on the right track. That driver refused to stop because he feared a mob.

The suave nut-brown pharmacist stands in the door of his place with hands thrust nervously into the pockets of his freshly laundered white coat. We go inside, order sodas, and sit down with him at one of the little round tables. All of us try hard to show ourselves unshaken by the panic on the streets. The druggist tells us that he studied at the Meharry Medical school in Nashville. We are glad to know him.

We can hear the sharp deliberate ticks of a small clock on a shelf. Presently the streets are empty.

Saturday night again—and again things to buy. The clerk in the chain store offers to bring our box of groceries out to the curb. *Hurry back!* We need meat, perhaps veal. . . . A few years ago in certain small towns of the South colored folks could not buy veal. The limited supply was frankly reserved for white customers. That seems far away; here we even have the effrontery to be exceedingly critical of that which is offered us.

On again; more shops, more purchases. The short bald man in the Jewish variety store stands against the glass door with hands in his pockets. He wears a dark sweater coat. The two or three Jews in this town are strangely unpleasant to Negroes. The blacks hold no malice, however. They feel that they understand. Even the illiterate blacks imagine they comprehend the psychological subtleties of race prejudice. They are amused by its vagaries. And in this one matter, we actually believe, the gods have in fun blessed them with an Olympian viewpoint.

But we have not forgotten the breathless pandemonium that filled these streets on the night of our last visit to town. Apparently the incident is forgotten. The huge good-looking chauffeur is standing beside his glistening Packard, a cigar held elegantly between his long fingers. Cynthe is on the street again, a snuff brush hanging from her lips, and her hand cupped in an attitude of medieval humility as she asks for a coin. The motor cop, cruising the streets leisurely, wears a big smile. Somehow we can't accept this tranquility. It is not natural that a night so charged with peril and drama should pass so lightly. Perhaps we need to adjust ourselves. There is a peculiar nervous preparation that we do not have, a certain diffidence. These black folks live on the very edges of a crater, and the grave danger that stops our breath merely to observe has ceased to terrify them. And we can see now that the excitement that drove them from the streets a week ago was no more than a good rain would have caused. They are neither tired nor depressed after that vigorous drain on their emotions.

The barber shop is crowded. The air is heavy with smoke and rustic political comment. Still we are unable to get an answer when we ask about the accident on the road. The decision of the Supreme Court in favor of a new trial for the Scottsboro boys still creates a lively stir, however. The black middle-aged barber, who seems to have a genius for catching the consensus of opinion, makes a whispered summary when the others have become quiet.

"The Alabama co't is gonna kill them boys for meanness, now. You can bet yo' bottom dollar on that. Either they is gonna kill 'em or they's gonna give 'em life—an' that's worser."

At a soda fountain we meet the rosy, buff-colored mulatto girl who operates the elevator in a local department store. What about that accident on the road last week? There is nothing to hide now. She looks up from her glass with the stain of dark grapes on her teeth.

"Sure they got him. You see, there was two other folks in the car with him: all colored. He was just seventeen. He was giving the other two a ride. They turned him up to the sheriff. He would of stopped, he said, but he was afraid of a mob. That's good sense. They had his trial yesterday. Ten years. Better'n being lynched, I say."

She is in a hurry. There is going to be a dance. Of course we can't detain her; anyway we would be misunderstood if we persisted in buying her sodas. There are only straight lines in the reasoning of these folks. There is a limit to the number of sodas you may buy a yellow girl on Saturday night. We are too fatigued and depressed to care much.

Upstairs the colored doctors and dentists have offices on the same floor with the black fortune teller who calls himself "Kid Wonder." The latter is away—he has also an office in Birmingham—but the doctors, dentists, and lawyers can be seen through their glass doors. All of them smoke cigars and recline majestially behind their desks. One doctor has an ironing board for an examination table; the wicker bottoms are broken out of the chairs. He has large fan-like hands that he holds before his face as he talks, and we notice that the fingernails wear vivid black rims. A black peasant in overalls and jumper is listening to his words, following his gestures with round-eyed wonder.

204

We had intended to have a word with the doctor, but we decide not to wait. On the street again. We are forced to admit that the caricatures of Octavus Roy Cohen are less absurd than we had formerly credited them with being. It is interesting that the medicine men and the fortune tellers should have offices on the same floor of the same building, that here these two professions should be inclined to flow together as they did in the middle ages. Let us walk awhile; there is no hurry.

A quick wind blows up a few clouds. There is a brief flurry of rain, then again the small white moon; let us walk awhile. The pool hall is filled with voices, laughter. The barber puts his head out the door and tells us a picturesque bit of gossip about the rosy, buff-colored girl and a certain prominent rich man. He smiles: well, what do you make of it? We do not answer because that is the same question we have been asking ourselves all evening. Again the moon slips into a pocket of clouds.

It is raining when we get on the pike, the windy gusts coming first from one side and then the other. What do you make of it? Certainly there is beauty here, plus quality: the undismayed peasantry, the fruitful land, the many-colored rain, the melancholy of old moss-covered buildings and moss-covered traditions, the crushed and broken soldiers who have never surrendered, much loveliness. But it is all wrong. The beauty of this town is solely the beauty of its sins, its feudal injustices, its peaceful paupers, its colorful hangovers. Cynthe with her bowed head and cupped hand, the giant chauffeur taking pride in his authority as a favored menial, the yellow girl with her purple stained teeth and her flowing ribbons of gossip, the meretricious medicine men, the clean young druggist with his hopeless eyes, the silver-haired rural editor, the strident-voiced stump speaker, the bitter Jewish shopkeepers.

The rain increases. At the turn of the Pike there is an automobile stuck in the heavy mud. We slow down. The white driver beckons to two backs who are about to pass him without stopping. "Come here boys, give me a push." They do not speak but come quietly and set their muscles against the weight of the car. Prsently it gets away. The driver does not pause or look back. No matter. They would not see his gesture anyway. Their caps are pulled over their faces, their heads bowed against the driving rain. Apparently neither they nor the driver have been aware of anything irregular in the episode that summoned them to push a carload of able men out of the mud and left them ankle deep in the spot as the others drove away. Apparently there is no pang, no tragedy.

206

CHAPTER ONE FROM *Invisible Man*

RALPH ELLISON

It goes a long way back, some twenty years. All my life I had been looking for something, and everywhere I turned someone tried to tell me what it was. I accepted their answers too, though they were often in contradiction and even self-contradictory. I was naïve. I was looking for myself and asking everyone except myself questions which I, and only I, could answer. It took me a long time and much painful boomeranging of my expectations to achieve a realization everyone else appears to have been born with: That I am nobody but myself. But first I had to discover that I am an invisible man!

And yet I am no freak of nature, nor of history. I was in the cards, other things having been equal (or unequal) eighty-five years ago. I am not ashamed of my grandparents for having been slaves. I am only ashamed of myself for having at one time been ashamed. About eighty-five years ago they were told that they were free, united with others of our country in everything pertaining to the common good, and, in everything social, separate like the fingers of the hand. And they believed it. They exulted in it. They stayed in their place, worked hard, and brought up my father to do the same. But my grandfather is the one. He was an odd old guy, my grandfather, and I am told I take after him. It was he who caused the trouble. On his deathbed he called my father to him and said, "Son, after I'm gone I want you to keep up the good fight. I never told you, but our life is a war and I have been a traitor all my born days, a spy in the enemy's country ever since I give up my gun back in the Reconstruction. Live with your head in the lion's mouth. I want you to overcome 'em with yeses, undermine 'em with grins, agree 'em to death and destruction, let 'em swoller you till they vomit or bust wide open." They thought the old man had gone out of his mind. IIe had been the meekest of men. The younger children were rushed from the room, the shades drawn and the flame of the lamp turned so low that it sputtered on the wick like the old man's breathing. "Learn it to the younguns," he whispered fiercely; then he died.

But my folks were more alarmed over his last words than over his dying. It was as though he had not died at all, his words caused so much anxiety. I was warned emphatically to forget what he had said and, indeed, this is the first time it has been mentioned outside the family circle. It had a tremendous effect upon me, however. I could never be sure of what he meant. Grandfather had been a quiet old man who never made any trouble, yet on his deathbed he had called himself a traitor and a spy, and he had spoken of his meekness as a dangerous activity. It became a constant puzzle which lay unanswered in the back of my mind. And whenever things went well for me I remembered my grandfather and felt guilty and uncomfortable. It was as though I was carrying out his advice in spite of myself. And to make it worse, everyone loved me for it. I was praised by the most lily-white men of the town. I was considered an example of desirable conduct—just as my grandfather had been. And what puzzled me was that the old man had defined it as *treachery*. When I was praised for my conduct I felt a guilt that in some way I was doing something that was really against the wishes of the white folks, that if they had understood they would have desired me to act just the opposite, that I should have been sulky and mean, and that that really would have been what they wanted, even though they were fooled and thought they wanted me to act as I did. It made me afraid that some day they would look upon me as a traitor and I would be lost. Still I was more afraid to act any other way because they didn't like that at all. The old man's words were like a curse. On my graduation day I delivered an oration in which I showed that humility was the secret, indeed, the very essence of progress. (Not that I believed this—how could I, remembering my grandfather?—I only believed that it worked.) It was a great success. Everyone praised me and I was invited to give the speech at a gathering of the town's leading white citizens. It was a triumph for our whole community.

It was in the main ballroom of the leading hotel. When I got there I discovered that it was on the occasion of a smoker, and I was told that since I was to be there anyway I might as well take part in the battle royal to be fought by some of my schoolmates as part of the entertainment. The battle royal came first.

All of the town's big shots were there in their tuxedoes, wolfing down the buffet foods, drinking beer and whiskey and smoking black cigars. It was a large room with a high ceiling. Chairs were arranged in neat rows around three sides of a portable boxing ring. The fourth side was clear, revealing a

Main Street, Greensboro, Alabama, 1936

gleaming space of polished floor. I had some misgivings over the battle royal, by the way. Not from a distaste for fighting, but because I didn't care too much for the other fellows who were to take part. They were tough guys who seemed to have no grandfather's curse worrying their minds. No one could mistake their toughness. And besides, I suspected that fighting a battle royal might detract from the dignity of my speech. In those pre-in-visible days I visualized myself as a potential Booker T. Washington. But the other fellows didn't care too much for me either, and there were nine of them. I felt superior to them in my way, and I didn't like the manner in which we were all crowded together into the servants' elevator. Nor did they like my being there. In fact, as the warmly lighted floors flashed past the elevator we had words over the fact that I, by taking part in the fight, had knocked one of their friends out of a night's work.

We were led out of the elevator through a rococo hall into an anteroom and told to get into our fighting togs. Each of us was issued a pair of boxing gloves and ushered out into the big mirrored hall, which we entered looking cautiously about us and whispering, lest we might accidentally be heard above the noise of the room. It was foggy with cigar smoke. And already the whiskey was taking effect. I was shocked to see some of the most important men of the town quite tipsy. They were all there—bankers, lawyers, judges, doctors, fire chiefs, teachers, merchants. Even one of the more fashionable pastors. Something we could not see was going on up front. A clarinet was vibrating sensuously and the men were standing up and moving eagerly forward. We were a small tight group, clustered together, our bare upper bodies touching and shining with anticipatory sweat; while up front the big shots were becoming increasingly excited over something we still could not see. Suddenly I heard the school superintendent, who had told me to come, yell, "Bring up the shines, gentlemen! Bring up the little shines!"

We were rushed up to the front of the ballroom, where it smelled even more strongly of tobacco and whiskey. Then we were pushed into place. I almost wet my pants. A sea of faces, some hostile, some amused, ringed around us, and in the center, facing us, stood a magnificent blonde—stark naked. There was dead silence. I felt a blast of cold air chill me. I tried to back away, but they were behind me and around me. Some of the boys stood with lowered heads, trembling. I felt a wave of irrational guilt and fear. My teeth chattered, my skin turned to goose flesh, my knees knocked. Yet I was strongly attracted and looked in spite of myself. Had the price of looking been blindness, I would have looked. The hair was yellow like that of a circus kewpie doll, the face heavily powdered and rouged, as though to form an abstract mask, the eyes hollow and smeared a cool blue, the color of a baboon's butt. I felt a desire to spit upon her as my eyes brushed slowly over her body. Her breasts were firm and round as the domes of East Indian temples, and I stood so close as to see the fine skin texture and beads of pearly perspiration glistening like dew around the pink and erected buds of her nipples. I wanted at one and the same time to run from the room, to sink through the floor, or go to her and cover her from my eyes and the eyes of the others with my body; to feel the soft thighs, to caress her and destroy her, to love her and murder her, to hide from her, and yet to stroke where below the small American flag tattooed upon her belly her thighs formed a capital V. I had a notion that of all in the room she saw only me with her impersonal eyes.

And then she began to dance, a slow sensuous movement; the smoke of a hundred cigars clinging to her like the thinnest of veils. She seemed like a fair bird-girl girdled in veils calling to me from the angry surface of some gray and threatening sea. I was transported. Then I became aware of the clarinet playing and the big shots yelling at us. Some threatened us if we looked and others if we did not. On my right I saw one boy faint. And now a man grabbed a silver pitcher from a table and stepped close as he dashed ice water upon him and stood him up and forced two of us to support him as his head hung and moans issued from his thick bluish lips. Another boy began to plead to go home. He was the largest of the group, wearing dark red fighting trunks much too small to conceal the erection which projected from him as though in answer to the insinuating low-registered moaning of the clarinet. He tried to hide himself with his boxing gloves.

And all the while the blonde continued dancing, smiling faintly at the big shots who watched her with fascination, and faintly smiling at our fear. I noticed a certain merchant who followed her hungrily, his lips loose and drooling. He was a large man who wore diamond studs in a shirtfront which swelled with the ample paunch underneath, and each time the blonde swayed her undulating hips he ran his hand through the thin hair of his bald head and, with his arms upheld, his posture clumsy like that of an intoxicated panda, wound his belly in a slow and obscene grind. This creature was completely hypnotized. The music had quickened. As the dancer flung herself about with a detached expression on her face, the men began reaching out to touch her. I could see their beefy fingers sink into the soft flesh. Some of the others tried to stop them and she began to move around the floor in graceful circles, as they gave chase, slipping and sliding over the polished floor. It was mad. Chairs went crashing, drinks were spilt, as they ran laughing and howling after her. They caught her just as she reached a door, raised her from the floor, and tossed her as college boys are tossed at a hazing, and above her red, fixed-smiling lips I saw the terror and disgust in her eyes, almost like my own terror and that which I saw in some of the other boys. As I watched, they tossed her twice and her soft breasts seemed to flatten against the air and her legs flung wildly as she spun. Some of the more sober ones helped her to escape. And I started off the floor, heading for the anteroom with the rest of the boys.

Some were still crying and in hysteria. But as we tried to leave we were stopped and ordered to get into the ring. There was nothing to do but what we were told. All ten of us climbed under the ropes and allowed ourselves to be blindfolded with broad bands of white cloth. One of the men seemed to feel a bit sympathetic and tried to cheer us up as we stood with our backs against the ropes. Some of us tried to grin. "See that boy over there?" one of the men said. "I want you to run across at the bell and give it to him right in the belly. If you don't get him, I'm going to get you. I don't like his looks." Each of us was told the same. The blindfolds were put on. Yet even then I had been going over my speech. In my mind each word was as bright as flame. I felt the cloth pressed into place, and frowned so that it would be loosened when I relaxed.

But now I felt a sudden fit of blind terror. I was unused to darkness. It was as though I had suddenly found myself in a dark room filled with poisonous cottonmouths. I could hear the bleary voices yelling insistently for the battle royal to begin.

"Get going in there!"

"Let me at that big nigger!"

I strained to pick up the school superintendent's voice, as though to squeeze some security out of that slightly more familiar sound.

"Let me at those black sonsabitches!" someone yelled.

"No, Jackson, no" another voice yelled. "Here, somebody, help me hold Jack."

"I want to get at that ginger-colored nigger. Tear him limb from limb," the first voice yelled.

I stood against the ropes trembling. For in those days I was what they called ginger-colored, and he sounded as though he might crunch me between his teeth like a crisp ginger cookie.

Quite a struggle was going on. Chairs were being kicked about and I could hear voices grunting as with a terrific effort. I wanted to see, to see more desperately than ever before. But the blindfold was as tight as a thick skin-puckering scab and when I raised my gloved hands to push the layers of white aside a voice yelled, "Oh, no you don't, black bastard! Leave that alone!"

"Ring the bell before Jackson kills him a coon!" someone boomed in the sudden silence. And I heard the bell clang and the sound of the feet scuffling forward.

A glove smacked against my head. I pivoted, striking out stiffly as someone went past, and felt the jar ripple along the length of my arm to my shoulder. Then it seemed as though all nine of the boys had turned upon me at once. Blows pounded me from all sides while I struck out as best I could. So many blows landed upon me that I wondered if I were not the only blindfolded fighter in the ring, or if the man called Jackson hadn't succeeded in getting me after all.

Blindfolded, I could no longer control my motions. I had no dignity. I stumbled about like a baby or a drunken man. The smoke had become thicker and with each new blow it seemed to sear and further restrict my lungs. My saliva became like hot bitter glue. A glove connected with my head, filling my mouth with warm blood. It was everywhere. I could not tell if the moisture I felt upon my body was sweat or blood. A blow landed hard against the nape of my neck. I felt myself going over, my head hitting the floor. Streaks of blue light filled the black world behind the blindfold. I lay prone, pretending that I was knocked out, but felt myself seized by hands and yanked to my feet. "Get going, black boy! Mix it up!" My arms were like lead, my head smarting from blows. I managed to feel my way to the ropes and held on, trying to catch my breath. A glove landed in my midsection and I went over again, feeling as though the smoke had become a knife jabbed into my guts. Pushed this way and that by the legs milling around me, I finally pulled erect and discovered that I could see the black, sweat-washed forms weaving in the smoky-blue atmosphere like drunken dancers weaving to the rapid drum-like thuds of blows.

Everyone fought hysterically. It was complete anarchy. Everybody fought everybody else. No group fought together for long. Two, three, four, fought one, then turned to fight each other, were themselves attacked. Blows landed below the belt and in the kidney, with the gloves open as well as closed, and with my eye partly opened now there was not so much terror. I moved carefully, avoiding blows, although not too many to attract attention, fighting from group to group. The boys groped about like blind, cautious crabs crouching to protect their mid-sections, their heads pulled in short against their shoulders, their arms stretched nervously before them, with their fists testing the smoke-filled air like the knobbed feelers of hypersensitive snails. In one corner I glimpsed a boy violently punching the air and heard him scream in pain as he smashed his hand against a ring post. For a second I saw him bent over holding his hand, then going down as a blow caught his unprotected head. I played one group against the other, slipping in and throwing a punch then stepping out of range while pushing the others into the melee to take the blows blindly aimed at me. The smoke was agonizing and there were no rounds, no bells at three minute intervals to relieve our exhaustion. The room spun round me, a swirl of lights, smoke, sweating bodies surrounded by tense white faces. I bled from both nose and mouth, the blood spattering upon my chest.

The men kept yelling, "Slug him, black boy! Knock his guts out!"

"Uppercut him! Kill him ! Kill that big boy!"

Taking a fake fall, I saw a boy going down heavily beside me as though we were felled by a single blow, saw a sneaker-clad foot shoot into his groin as the two who had knocked him down stumbled upon him. I rolled out of range, feeling a twinge of nausea.

The harder we fought the more threatening the men became. And yet, I had begun to worry about my speech again. How would it go? Would they recognize my ability? What would they give me?

I was fighting automatically when suddenly I noticed that one after another of the boys was leaving the ring. I was surprised, filled with panic, as though I had been left alone with an unknown danger. Then I understood. The boys had arranged it among themselves. It was the custom for the two men left in the ring to slug it out for the winner's prize. I discovered this too late. When the bell sounded two men in tuxedoes leaped into the ring and removed the blindfold. I found myself facing Tatlock, the biggest of the gang. I felt sick at my stomach. Hardly had the bell stopped ringing in my ears than it clanged again and I saw him moving swiftly toward me. Thinking of nothing else to do I hit him smash on the nose. He kept coming, bringing the rank sharp violence of stale sweat. His face was a black blank of a face, only his eyes alive—with hate of me and aglow with a feverish terror from what had happened to us all. I became anxious. I wanted to deliver my speech and he came at me as though he meant to beat it out of me. I smashed him again and again, taking his blows as they came. Then on a sudden impulse I struck him lightly and as we clinched, I whispered, "Fake like I knocked you out, you can have the prize."

"I'll break your behind," he whispered hoarsely.

"For *them?*"

"For *me,* sonofabitch!"

They were yelling for us to break it up and Tatlock spun me half around with a blow, and as a joggled camera sweeps in a reeling scene, I saw the howling red faces crouching tense beneath the cloud of blue-gray smoke. For a moment the world wavered, unraveled, flowed, then my head cleared and Tatlock bounced before me. That fluttering shadow before my eyes was his jabbing left hand. Then falling forward, my head against his damp shoulder, I whispered.

"I'll make it five dollars more."

"Go to hell!"

But his muscles relaxed a trifle beneath my pressure and I breathed, "Seven?"

"Give it to your ma," he said, ripping me beneath the heart.

And while I still held him I butted him and moved away. I felt myself bombarded with punches. I fought back with hopeless desperation. I wanted to deliver my speech more than anything else in the world, because I felt that only these men could judge truly my ability, and now this stupid clown was ruining my chances. I began fighting carefully now, moving in to punch him and out again with my greater speed. A lucky blow to his chin and I had him going too—until I heard a loud voice yell, "I got my money on the big boy."

Hearing this, I almost dropped my guard. I was confused: Should I try to win against the voice out there? Would not this go against my speech, and was not this a moment for humility, for nonresistance? A blow to my head as I danced about sent my right eye popping like a jack-in-the-box and settled my dilemma. The room went red as I fell. It was a dream fall, my body languid and fastidious as to where to land, until the floor became im-

215

patient and smashed up to meet me. A moment later I came to. An hypnotic voice said FIVE emphatically. And I lay there, hazily watching a dark red spot of my own blood shaping itself into a butterfly, glistening and soaking into the soiled gray world of the canvas.

When the voice drawled TEN I was lifted up and dragged to a chair. I sat dazed. My eye pained and swelled with each throb of my pounding heart and I wondered if now I would be allowed to speak. I was wringing wet, my mouth still bleeding. We were grouped along the wall now. The other boys ignored me as they congratulated Tatlock and speculated as to how much they would be paid. One boy whimpered over his smashed hand. Looking up front, I saw attendants in white jackets rolling the portable ring away and placing a small square rug in the vacant space surrounded by chairs. Perhaps, I thought, I will stand on the rug to deliver my speech.

Then the M.C. called to us, "Come on up here boys and get your money."

We ran forward to where the men laughed and talked in their chairs, waiting. Everyone seemed friendly now.

"There it is on the rug," the man said. I saw the rug covered with coins of all dimensions and a few crumpled bills. But what excited me, scattered here and there, were the gold pieces.

"Boys, it's all yours," the man said. "You get all you grab."

"That's right, Sambo," a blond man said, winking at me confidentially.

I trembled with excitement, forgetting my pain. I would get the gold and the bills, I thought. I would use both hands. I would throw my body against the boys nearest me to block them from the gold.

"Get down around the rug now," the man commanded, "and don't anyone touch it until I give the signal."

"This ought to be good," I heard.

As told, we got around the square rug on our knees. Slowly the man raised his freckled hand as we followed it upward with our eyes.

I heard, "These niggers look like they're about to pray!"

Then, "Ready," the man said. "Go!"

I lunged for a yellow coin lying on the blue design of the carpet, touching it and sending a surprised shriek to join those rising around me. I tried frantically to remove my hand but could not let go. A hot, violent force tore through my body, shaking me like a wet rat. The rug was electrified. The hair bristled up on my head as I shook myself free. My muscles jumped, my

216

nerves jangled, writhed. But I saw that this was not stopping the other boys. Laughing in fear and embarrassment, some were holding back and scooping up the coins knocked off by the painful contortions of the others. The men roared above us as we struggled.

"Pick it up, goddamnit, pick it up!" someone called like a bass-voiced parrot. "Go on, get it!"

I crawled rapidly around the floor, picking up the coins, trying to avoid the coppers and to get greenbacks and the gold. Ignoring the shock by laughing, as I brushed the coins off quickly, I discovered that I could contain the electricity—a contradiction, but it works. Then the men began to push us onto the rug. Laughing embarrassedly, we struggled out of their hands and kept after the coins. We were all wet and slippery and hard to hold. Suddenly I saw a boy lifted into the air, glistening with sweat like a circus seal, and dropped, his wet back landing flush upon the charged rug, heard him yell and saw him literally dance upon his back, his elbows beating a frenzied tattoo upon the floor, his muscles twitching like the flesh of a horse stung [b]y many flies. When he finally rolled off, his face was gray and no one stopped him when he ran from the floor amid booming laughter.

"Get the money," the M.C. called. "That's good hard American cash!"

And we snatched and grabbed, snatched and grabbed. I was careful not to come too close to the rug now, and when I felt the hot whiskey breath descend upon me like a cloud of foul air I reached out and grabbed the leg of a chair. It was occupied and I held on desperately.

"Leggo, nigger! Leggo!"

The huge face wavered down to mine as he tried to push me free. But my body was slippery and he was too drunk. It was Mr. Colcord, who owned a chain of movie houses and "entertainment palaces." Each time he grabbed me I slipped out of his hands. It became a real struggle. I feared the rug more than I did the drunk, so I held on, surprising myself for a moment by trying to topple *him* upon the rug. It was such an enormous idea that I found myself actually carrying it out. I tried not to be obvious, yet when I grabbed his leg, trying to tumble him out of the chair, he raised up roaring with laughter, and, looking at me with soberness dead in the eye, kicked me viciously in the chest. The chair leg flew out of my hand and I felt myself going and rolled. It was as though I had rolled through a bed of hot coals. It seemed a whole century would pass before I would roll free, a century in which I was seared through the deepest levels of my body to the

217

fearful breath within me and the breath seared and heated to the point of explosion. It'll all be over in a flash, I thought as I rolled clear. It'll all be over in a flash.

But not yet, the men on the other side were waiting, red faces swollen as though from apoplexy as they bent forward in their chairs. Seeing their fingers coming toward me I rolled away as a fumbled football rolls off the receiver's fingertips, back into the coals. That time I luckily sent the rug sliding out of place and heard the coins ringing against the floor and the boys scuffling to pick them up and the M.C. calling, "All right, boys, that's all. Go get dressed and get your money."

I was limp as a dish rag. My back felt as though it had been beaten with wires.

When we had dressed the M.C. came in and gave us each five dollars, except Tatlock, who got ten for being last in the ring. Then he told us to leave. I was not to get a chance to deliver my speech, I thought. I was going out into the dim alley in despair when I was stopped and told to go back. I returned to the ballroom, where the men were pushing back their chairs and gathering in groups to talk.

The M.C. knocked on a table for quiet. "Gentlemen," he said, "we almost forgot an important part of the program. A most serious part, gentlemen. This boy was brought here to deliver a speech which he made at his graduation yesterday . . ."

"Bravo!"

"I'm told that he is the smartest boy we've got out there in Greenwood. I'm told that he knows more big words than a pocket-sized dictionary."

Much applause and laughter.

"So now, gentlemen, I want you to give him your attention."

There was still laughter as I faced them, my mouth dry, my eye throbbing. I began slowly, but evidently my throat was tense, because they began shouting, "Louder! Louder!"

"We of the younger generation extol the wisdom of that great leader and educator," I shouted, "who first spoke these flaming words of wisdom: 'A ship lost at sea for many days suddenly sighted a friendly vessel. From the mast of the unfortunate vessel was seen a signal: "Water, water; we die of thirst!" The answer from the friendly vessel came back: "Cast down your bucket where you are." The captain of the distressed vessel, at last heeding the injunction, cast down his bucket, and it came up full of fresh sparkling

218

water from the mouth of the Amazon River.' And like him I say, and in his words, 'To those of my race who depend upon bettering their condition in a foreign land, or who underestimate the importance of cultivating friendly relations with the Southern white man, who is his next-door neighbor, I would say: "Cast down your bucket where you are"—cast it down in making friends in every manly way of the people of all races by whom we are surrounded . . .' "

I spoke automatically and with such fervor that I did not realize that the men were still talking and laughing until my dry mouth, filling up with blood from the cut, almost strangled me. I coughed, wanting to stop and go to one of the tall brass, sand-filled spittoons to relieve myself, but a few of the men, especially the superintendent, were listening and I was afraid. So I gulped it down, blood, saliva and all, and continued. (What powers of endurance I had during those days! What enthusiasm! What a belief in the rightness of things!) I spoke even louder in spite of the pain. But still they talked and still they laughed, as though deaf with cotton in dirty ears. So I spoke with greater emotional emphasis. I closed my ears and swallowed blood until I was nauseated. The speech seemed a hundred times as long as before, but I could not leave out a single word. All had to be said, each memorized nuance considered, rendered. Nor was that all. Whenever I uttered a word of three or more syllables a group of voices would yell for me to repeat it. I used the phrase "social responsibility" and they yelled:

"What that word you say, boy?"

"Social responsibility," I said.

"What?"

"Social . . ."

"Louder."

". . . responsibility."

"More!"

"Respon—"

"Repeat!"

"—sibility."

The room filled with the uproar of laughter until, no doubt, distracted by having to gulp down my blood, I made a mistake and yelled a phrase I had often seen denounced in newspaper editorials, heard debated in private.

"Social . . ."

219

"What?" they yelled.

". . . equality—"

The laughter hung smokelike in the sudden stillness. I opened my eyes, puzzled. Sounds of displeasure filled the room. The M.C. rushed forward. They shouted hostile phrases at me. But I did not understand.

A small dry mustached man in the front row blared out, "Say that slowly, son!"

"What sir?"

"What you just said!"

"Social responsibility, sir," I said.

"You weren't being smart, were you, boy?" he said, not unkindly.

"No, sir!"

"You sure that about 'equality' was a mistake?"

"Oh, yes, sir," I said. "I was swallowing blood."

"Well, you had better speak more slowly so we can understand. We mean to do right by you, but you've got to know your place at all times. All right, now, go on with your speech."

I was afraid. I wanted to leave but I wanted also to speak and I was afraid they'd snatch me down.

"Thank you, sir," I said, beginning where I had left off, and having them ignore me as before.

Yet when I finished there was a thunderous applause. I was surprised to see the superintendent come forth with a package wrapped in white tissue paper, and, gesturing for quiet, address the men.

"Gentlemen, you see that I did not overpraise this boy. He makes a good speech and some day he'll lead his people in the proper paths. And I don't have to tell you that that is important in these days and times. This is a good, smart boy, and so to encourage him in the right direction, in the name of the Board of Education I wish to present him a prize in the form of this . . ."

He paused, removing the tissue paper and revealing a gleaming calfskin brief case.

". . . in the form of this first-class article from Shad Whitmore's shop."

"Boy," he said, addressing me, "take this prize and keep it well. Consider it a badge of office. Prize it. Keep developing as you are and some day it will be filled with important papers that will help shape the destiny of your people."

220

I was so moved that I could hardly express my thanks. A rope of bloody saliva forming a shape like an undiscovered continent drooled upon the leather and I wiped it quickly away. I felt an importance that I had never dreamed.

"Open it and see what's inside," I was told.

My fingers a-tremble, I complied, smelling the fresh leather and finding an official-looking document inside. It was a scholarship to the state college for Negroes. My eyes filled with tears and I ran awkwardly off the floor.

I was overjoyed; I did not even mind when I discovered that the gold pieces I had scrambled for were brass pocket tokens advertising a certain make of automobile.

When I reached home everyone was excited. Next day the neighbors came to congratulate me. I even felt safe from grandfather, whose deathbed curse usually spoiled my triumphs. I stood beneath his photograph with my brief case in hand and smiled triumphantly into his stolid black peasant's face. It was a face that fascinated me. The eyes seemed to follow everywhere I went.

That night I dreamed I was at a circus with him and that he refused to laugh at the clowns no matter what they did. Then later he told me to open my brief case and read what was inside and I did, finding an official envelope stamped with the state seal; and inside the envelope I found another and another, endlessly, and I thought I would fall of weariness. "Them's years," he said. "Now open that one." And I did and in it I found an engraved document containing a short message in letters of gold. "Read it," my grandfather said. "Out loud."

"To Whom It May Concern," I intoned. "Keep This Nigger-Boy Running."

I awoke with the old man's laughter ringing in my ears.

(It was a dream I was to remember and dream again for many years after. But at that time I had no insight into its meaning. First I had to attend college.)

CHAPTER FOUR FROM *I Know Why the Caged Bird Sings*

MAYA ANGELOU

What sets one Southern town apart from another, or from a Northern town or hamlet, or city high-rise? The answer must be the experience shared between the unknowing majority (it) and the knowing minority (you). All of childhood's unanswered questions must finally be passed back to the town and answered there. Heroes and bogey men, values and dislikes, are first encountered and labeled in that early environment. In later years they change faces, places and maybe races, tactics, intensities and goals, but beneath those penetrable masks they wear forever the stocking-capped faces of childhood.

Mr. McElroy, who lived in the big rambling house next to the Store, was very tall and broad, and although the years had eaten away the flesh from his shoulders, they had not, at the time of my knowing him, gotten to his high stomach, or his hands or feet.

He was the only Negro I knew, except for the school principal and the visiting teachers, who wore matching pants and jackets. When I learned that men's clothes were sold like that and called suits, I remember thinking that somebody had been very bright, for it made men look less manly, less threatening and a little more like women.

Mr. McElroy never laughed, and seldom smiled, and to his credit was the fact that he liked to talk to Uncle Willie. He never went to church, which Bailey and I thought also proved he was a very courageous person. How great it would be to show up like that, to be able to stare religion down, especially living next door to a woman like Momma.

I watched him with the excitement of expecting him to do anything at any time. I never tired of this, or became disappointed or disenchanted with him, although from the perch of age, I see him now as a very simple and uninteresting man who sold patent medicine and tonics to the less sophisticated people in towns (villages) surrounding the metropolis of Stamps.

222

There seemed to be an understanding between Mr. McElroy and Grandmother. This was obvious to us because he never chased us off his land. In summer's late sunshine I often sat under the chinaberry tree in his yard, surrounded by the bitter aroma of its fruit and lulled by the drone of flies that fed on the berries. He sat in a slotted swing on his porch, rocking in his brown three-piece, his wide Panama nodding in time with the whir of insects.

One greeting a day was all that could be expected from Mr. McElroy. After his "Good morning, child," or "Good afternoon, child," he never said a word, even if I met him again on the road in front of his house or down by the well, or ran into him behind the house escaping in a game of hide-and-seek.

He remained a mystery in my childhood. A man who owned his land and the big many-windowed house with a porch that clung to its sides all around the house. An independent Black man. A near anachronism in Stamps.

Bailey was the greatest person in my world. And the fact that he was my brother, my only brother, and I had no sisters to share him with, was such good fortune that it made me want to live a Christian life just to show God that I was grateful. Where I was big, elbowy and grating, he was small, graceful and smooth. When I was described by our playmates as being shit color, he was lauded for his velvet-black skin. His hair fell down in black curls, and my head was covered with black steel wool. And yet he loved me.

When our elders said unkind things about my features (my family was handsome to a point of pain for me), Bailey would wink at me from across the room, and I knew that it was a matter of time before he would take revenge. He would allow the old ladies to finish wondering how on earth I came about, then he would ask, in a voice like cooling bacon grease, "Oh Mizeriz Coleman, how is your son? I saw him the other day, and he looked sick enough to die."

Aghast, the ladies would ask, "Die? From what? He ain't sick."

And in a voice oilier than the one before, he'd answer with a straight face, "From the Uglies."

I would hold my laugh, bite my tongue, grit my teeth and very seriously erase even the touch of a smile from my face. Later, behind the house by the black-walnut tree, we'd laugh and laugh and howl.

Bailey could count on very few punishments for his consistently outra-geous behavior, for he was the pride of the Henderson/Johnson family.

His movements, as he was later to describe those of an acquaintance, were activated with oiled precision. He was also able to find more hours in the day than I thought existed. He finished chores, homework, read more books than I and played the group games on the side of the hill with the best of them. He could even pray out loud in church, and was apt at stealing pickles from the barrel that sat under the fruit counter and Uncle Willie's nose.

Once when the Store was full of lunchtime customers, he dipped the strainer, which we also used to sift weevils from meal and flour, into the barrel and fished for two fat pickles. He caught them and hooked the strainer onto the side of the barrel where they dripped until he was ready for them. When the last school bell rang, he picked the nearly dry pickles out of the strainer, jammed them into his pockets and threw the strainer behind the oranges. We ran out of the Store. It was summer and his pants were short, so the pickle juice made clean streams down his ashy legs, and he jumped with his pockets full of loot and his eyes laughing a "How about that?" He smelled like a vinegar barrel or a sour angel.

After our early chores were done, while Uncle Willie or Momma minded the Store, we were free to play the children's games as long as we stayed within yelling distance. Playing hide-and-seek, his voice was easily identified, singing, "Last night, night before, twenty-four robbers at my door. Who all is hid? Ask me to let them in, hit 'em in the head with a rolling pin. Who all is hid?" In follow the leader, naturally he was the one who created the most daring and interesting things to do. And when he was on the tail of the pop the whip, he would twirl off the end like a top, spin-ning, falling, laughing, finally stopping just before my heart beat its last, and then he was back in the game, still laughing.

Of all the needs (there are none imaginary) a lonely child has, the one that must be satisfied, if there is going to be hope and a hope of wholeness, is the unshaking need for an unshakable God. My pretty Black brother was my Kingdom Come.

In Stamps the custom was to can everything that could possibly be preserved. During the killing season, after the first frost, all neighbors helped each other to slaughter hogs and even the quiet, big-eyed cows if they had stopped giving milk.

224

The missionary ladies of the Christian Methodist Episcopal Church helped Momma prepare the pork for sausage. They squeezed their fat arms elbow deep in the ground meat, mixed it with gray nose-opening sage, pepper and salt, and made tasty little samples for all obedient children who brought wood for the slick black stove. The men chopped off the larger pieces of meat and laid them in the smoke-house to begin the curing process. They opened the knuckle of the hams with their deadly-looking knives, took out a certain round harmless bone ("it could make the meat go bad") and rubbed salt, coarse brown salt that looked like fine gravel, into the flesh, and the blood popped to the surface.

Throughout the year, until the next frost, we took our meals from the smokehouse, the little garden that lay cousin-close to the Store and from the shelves of canned foods. There were choices on the shelves that could set a hungry child's mouth to watering. Green beans, snapped always the right length, collards, cabbage, juicy red tomato preserves that came into their own on steaming buttered biscuits, and sausage, beets, berries and every fruit grown in Arkansas.

But at least twice yearly Momma would feel that as children we should have fresh meat included in our diets. We were then given money—pennies, nickels, and dimes entrusted to Bailey—and sent to town to buy liver. Since the whites had refrigerators, their butchers bought the meat from commercial slaughterhouses in Texarkana and sold it to the wealthy even in the peak of summer.

Crossing the Black area of Stamps which in childhood's narrow measure seemed a whole world, we were obliged by custom to stop and speak to every person we met, and Bailey felt constrained to spend a few minutes playing with each friend. There was a joy in going to town with money in our pockets (Bailey's pockets were as good as my own) and time on our hands. But the pleasure fled when we reached the white part of town. After we left Mr. Willie Williams' Do Drop Inn, the last stop before whitefolksville, we had to cross the pond and adventure the railroad tracks. We were explorers walking without weapons into man-eating animals' territory.

In Stamps the segregation was so complete that most Black children didn't really, absolutely know what whites looked like. Other than that they were different, to be dreaded, and in that dread was included the hostility of the powerless against the powerful, the poor against the rich, the worker against the worked for and the ragged against the well dressed.

I remember never believing that whites were really real.

Many women who worked in their kitchens traded at our Store, and when they carried their finished laundry back to town they often set the big baskets down on our front porch to pull a singular piece from the starched collection and show either how graceful was their ironing hand or how rich and opulent was the property of their employers.

I looked at the items that weren't on display. I knew, for instance, that white men wore shorts, as Uncle Willie did, and that they had an opening for taking out their "things" and peeing, and that white women's breasts weren't built into their dresses, as some people said, because I saw their brassieres in the baskets. But I couldn't force myself to think of them as people. People were Mrs. LaGrone, Mrs. Hendricks, Momma, Reverend Sneed, Lillie B, and Louise and Rex. Whitefolks couldn't be people because their feet were too small, their skin too white and see-through, and they didn't walk on the balls of their feet the way people did—they walked on their heels like horses.

People were those who lived on my side of town. I didn't like them all, or, in fact, any of them very much, but they were people. These others, the strange pale creatures that lived in their alien un-life, weren't considered folks. They were whitefolks.

The West

Throughout American history the frontier has continually changed. At first it was western New York State whose settlements sprang up with the building of the Erie Canal. Then the Ohio Canal pushed the frontier farther west, toward the Mississippi—and here the river became the gateway to yet another frontier, the West. The most famous Mississippi frontier town in American literature is Hannibal, Missouri, the boyhood home of Mark Twain and the setting of his book, *Life on the Mississippi*. Two selections, "The Boy's Ambition" and "My Boyhood's Home" follow—satiric, affectionate reminiscences of his own childhood.

Beyond the Mississippi River stretched the Great Plains. The western prairie towns were the province of writers like Hamlin Garland, whose story "A Day's Pleasure" paints a bleak picture of the loneliness of frontier life—especially for the wives and families of homesteaders. But for the men life was different. The frontier meant excitement and adventure. It also meant the possibility of striking it rich—for beyond the plains was the mountain country of the gold rush: Utah, Nevada, Colorado, Montana, and California—and here the mining settlements, the "boom towns" of the gold rush era sprang up. Bret Harte depicts one such mining town in "The Luck of Roaring Camp": the population "numbered about a hundred men. One or two of these were actual fugitives from justice, some were criminal, and all were reckless." William Stafford's poems, "Quiet Town" and "The Letter," provide a striking contrast to the rough-and-tumble frontier experience. Here we catch a glimpse of the frontier once it has been tamed—but Stafford's images of it betray a bitter irony and ambivalence.

Julian, California

California was the "last" frontier of the continental United States. It still to this day retains for many the romance that characterized its early beginnings. Two very different pictures of it are printed here. In "Johnny Bear" John Steinbeck weaves a taut and suspenseful tale about small-town scandal and its aftermath. William Saroyan's "Raisins" is a modern-day parable—at first glance it is a simple story of small-town industry and initiative; and on another level it is a delightful statement of what it means to be first, an American; second, a Californian; and third, a small-towner.

The Boys' Ambition*

MARK TWAIN

When I was a boy, there was but one permanent ambition among my comrades in our village on the west bank of the Mississippi River. That was, to be a steamboatman. We had transient ambitions of other sorts, but they were only transient.

When a circus came and went, it left us all burning to become clowns; the first Negro minstrel show that came to our section left us all suffering to try that kind of life; now and then we had a hope that if we lived and were good, God would permit us to be pirates. These ambitions faded out, each in its turn; but the ambition to be a steamboatman always remained.

Once a day a cheap, gaudy packet arrived upward from St. Louis, and another downward from Keokuk. Before these events, the day was glorious with expectancy; after them, the day was a dead and empty thing. Not only the boys, but the whole village, felt this. After all these years I can picture that old time to myself now, just as it was then: the white town drowsing in the sunshine of a summer's morning; the streets empty, or pretty nearly so; one or two clerks sitting in front of the Water Street stores, with their splint-bottomed chairs tilted back against the wall, chins on breasts, hats slouched over their faces, asleep—with shingle shavings enough around to show what broke them down; a sow and a litter of pigs loafing along the sidewalk, doing a good business in watermelon rinds and seeds; two or three lonely little freight piles scattered about the "levee"; a pile of "skids" on the slope of the stone-paved wharf, and the fragrant town drunkard asleep in the shadow of them; two or three wood flats at the head of the wharf, but nobody to listen to the peaceful lapping of the wavelets against them; the great Mississippi, the majestic, the magnificent Mississippi, rolling its mile-wide tide along, shining in the sun; the dense forest away on the other side; the "point" above the town, and the "point" below, bounding

*Chapter IV from *Life on the Mississippi*.

231

the river-glimpse and turning it into a sort of sea, and withal a very still and brilliant and lonely one. Presently a film of dark smoke appears above one of those remote "points"; instantly a Negro drayman, famous for his quick eye and prodigious voice, lifts up the cry, "S-t-e-a-m-boat a-comin'!" and the scene changes! The town drunkard stirs, the clerks wake up, a furious clatter of drays follows, every house and store pours out a human contribution, and all in a twinkling the dead town is alive and moving. Drays, carts, men, boys, all go hurrying from many quarters to a common center, the wharf. Assembled there, the people fasten their eyes upon the coming boat as upon a wonder they are seeing for the first time. And the boat *is* rather a handsome sight, too. She is long and sharp and trim and pretty; she has two tall, fancy-topped chimneys, with a gilded device of some kind swung between them; a fanciful pilothouse, all glass and "gingerbread," perched on top of the "texas" deck behind them; the paddle-boxes are gorgeous with a picture or with gilded rays above the boat's name; the boiler deck, the hurricane deck, and the texas deck are fenced and ornamented with clean white railings; there is a flag gallantly flying from the jack-staff; the furnace doors are open and the fires glaring bravely; the upper decks are black with passengers; the captain stands by the big bell, calm, imposing, the envy of all; great volumes of the blackest smoke are rolling and tumbling out of the chimneys—a husbanded grandeur created with a bit of pitch pine just before arriving at a town; the crew are grouped on the forecastle; the broad stage is run far out over the port bow, and an envied deck hand stands picturesquely on the end of it with a coil of rope in his hand; the pent steam is screaming through the gauge cocks; the captain lifts his hand, a bell rings, the wheels stop; then they turn back, churning the water to foam, and the steamer is at rest. Then such a scramble as there is to get aboard, and to get ashore, and to take in freight and to discharge freight, all at one and the same time; and such a yelling and cursing as the mates facilitate it all with! Ten minutes later the steamer is under way again, with no flag on the jack-staff and no black smoke issuing from the chimneys. After ten more minutes the town is dead again, and the town drunkard asleep by the skids once more.

My father was a justice of the peace, and I supposed he possessed the power of life and death over all men and could hang anybody that offended him. This was distinction enough for me as a general thing; but the desire to be a steamboatman kept intruding, nevertheless. I first wanted to be a cabin

Belle of Louisville

boy, so that I could come out with a white apron on and shake a tablecloth over the side, where all my old comrades could see me; later I thought I would rather be the deck hand who stood on the end of the stage plank with the coil of rope in his hand, because he was particularly conspicuous. But these were only daydreams,—they were too heavenly to be contemplated as real possibilities. By and by one of our boys went away. He was not heard of for a long time. At last he turned up as apprentice engineer or "striker" on a steamboat. This thing shook the bottom out of all my Sunday-school teachings. That boy had been notoriously worldly, and I just the reverse; yet he was exalted to this eminence, and I left in obscurity and misery. There was nothing generous about this fellow in his greatness. He would always manage to have a rusty bolt to scrub while his boat tarried at our town, and he would sit on the inside guard and scrub it, where we could all see him and envy him and loathe him. And whenever his boat was laid up he would come home and swell around the town in his blackest and greasiest clothes, so that nobody could help remembering that he was a steamboatman; and he used all sorts of steamboat technicalities in his talk, as if he were so used to them that he forgot common people could not understand them. He would speak of the "labboard" side of a horse in an easy, natural way that would make one wish he was dead. And he was always talking about "St. Looy" like an old citizen; he would refer casually to occasions when he "was coming down Fourth Street," or when he was "passing by the Planter's House," or when there was a fire and he took a turn on the brakes of "the old Big Missouri"; and then he would go on and lie about how many towns the size of ours were burned down there that day. Two or three of the boys had long been persons of consideration among us because they had been to St. Louis once and had a vague general knowledge of its wonders, but the day of their glory was over now. They lapsed into a humble silence, and learned to disappear when the ruthless "cub" engineer approached. This fellow had money, too, and hair oil. Also an ignorant silver watch and a showy brass watch chain. He wore a leather belt and used no suspenders. If ever a youth was cordially admired and hated by his comrades, this one was. No girl could withstand his charms. He "cut out" every boy in the village. When his boat blew up at last, it diffused a tranquil contentment among us such as we had not known for months. But when he came home the next week, alive, renowned, and appeared in church all battered up and bandaged, a shining hero, stared at and wondered over by everybody, it seemed to us that the partiality of Providence for an undeserving reptile had reached a point where it was open to criticism.

This creature's career could produce but one result, and it speedily followed. Boy after boy managed to get on the river. The minister's son became an engineer. The doctor's and the postmaster's sons became "mud clerks"; the wholesale liquor dealer's son became a barkeeper on a boat; four sons of the chief merchant, and two sons of the county judge, became pilots. Pilot was the grandest position of all. The pilot, even in those days of trivial wages, had a princely salary—from a hundred and fifty to two hundred and fifty dollars a month, and no board to pay. Two months of his wages would pay a preacher's salary for a year. Now some of us were left disconsolate. We could not get on the river—at least our parents would not let us.

So by and by I ran away. I said I never would come home again till I was a pilot and could come in glory. But somehow I could not manage it. I went meekly aboard a few of the boats that lay packed together like sardines at the long St. Louis wharf, and very humbly inquired for the pilots, but got only a cold shoulder and short words from mates and clerks. I had to make the best of this sort of treatment for the time being, but I had comforting daydreams of a future when I should be a great and honored pilot, with plenty of money, and could kill some of these mates and clerks and pay for them.

My Boyhood's Home *

MARK TWAIN

We took passage in one of the fast boats of the St. Louis and St. Paul Packet Company, and started up the river.

When I, as a boy, first saw the mouth of the Missouri River, it was twenty-two or twenty-three miles above St. Louis, according to the estimate of pilots; the wear and tear of the banks has moved it down eight miles since then; and the pilots say that within five years the river will cut through and move the mouth down five miles more, which will bring it within ten miles of St. Louis.

About nightfall we passed the large and flourishing town of Alton, Illinois; and before daylight next morning the town of Louisiana, Missouri, a sleepy village in my day, but a brisk railway center now; however, all the towns out there are railway centers now. I could not clearly recognize the place. This seemed odd to me, for when I retired from the rebel army in '61 I retired upon Louisiana in good order; at least in good enough order for a person who had not yet learned how to retreat according to the rules of war, and had to trust to native genius. It seemed to me that for a first attempt at a retreat it was not badly done. I had done no advancing in all that campaign that was at all equal to it.

There was a railway bridge across the river here well sprinkled with glowing lights, and a very beautiful sight it was.

At seven in the morning we reached Hannibal, Missouri, where my boyhood was spent. I had had a glimpse of it fifteen years ago, and another glimpse six years earlier, but both were so brief that they hardly counted. The only notion of the town that remained in my mind was the memory of it as I had known it when I first quitted it twenty-nine years ago. That picture of it was still as clear and vivid to me as a photograph. I stepped ashore with the feeling of one who returns out of a dead-and-gone generation. I had a

---

* Chapter LIII from *Life on the Mississippi*.

sort of realizing sense of what the Bastille prisoners must have felt when they used to come out and look upon Paris after years of captivity, and note how curiously the familiar and the strange were mixed together before them. I saw the new houses—saw them plainly enough—but they did not affect the older picture in my mind, for through their solid bricks and mortar I saw the vanished houses, which had formerly stood there, with perfect distinctness.

It was Sunday morning, and everybody was abed yet. So I passed through the vacant streets, still seeing the town as it was, and not as it is, and recognizing and metaphorically shaking hands with a hundred familiar objects which no longer exist; and finally climbed Holiday's Hill to get a comprehensive view. The whole town lay spread out below me then, and I could mark and fix every locality, every detail. Naturally, I was a good deal moved. I said, "Many of the people I once knew in this tranquil refuge of my childhood are now in heaven; some, I trust, are in the other place."

The things about me and before me made me feel like a boy again—convinced me that I was a boy again, and that I had simply been dreaming an unusually long dream; but my reflections spoiled all that; for they forced me to say, "I see fifty old houses down yonder, into each of which I could enter and find either a man or a woman who was a baby or unborn when I noticed those houses last, or a grandmother who was a plump young bride at that time."

From this vantage ground the extensive view up and down the river, and wide over the wooded expanses of Illinois, is very beautiful—one of the most beautiful on the Mississippi, I think: which is a hazardous remark to make, for the eight hundred miles of river between St. Louis and St. Paul afford an unbroken succession of lovely pictures. It may be that my affection for the one in question biases my judgment in its favor; I cannot say as to that. No matter, it was satisfyingly beautiful to me, and it had this advantage over all the other friends whom I was about to greet again: it had suffered no change; it was as young and fresh and comely and gracious as ever it had been; whereas, the faces of the others would be old, and scarred with the campaigns of life, and marked with their griefs and defeats, and would give me no upliftings of spirit.

An old gentleman, out on an early morning walk, came along, and we discussed the weather, and then drifted into other matters. I could not remember his face. He said he had been living here twenty-eight years. So

237

he had come after my time, and I had never seen him before. I asked him various questions; first about a mate of mine in Sunday school—what became of him?

"He graduated with honor in an Eastern college, wandered off into the world somewhere, succeeded at nothing, passed out of knowledge and memory years ago, and is supposed to have gone to the dogs."

"He was bright, and promised well when he was a boy."

"Yes, but the thing that happened is what became of it all."

I asked after another lad, altogether the brightest in our village school when I was a boy.

"He, too, was graduated with honors, from an Eastern college; but life whipped him in every battle, straight along and he died in one of the Territories, years ago, a defeated man."

I asked after another of the bright boys.

"He is a success, always has been, always will be, I think."

I inquired after a young fellow who came to the town to study for one of the professions when I was a boy.

"He went at something else before he got through—went from medicine to law, or from law to medicine—then to some other new thing; went away for a year, came back with a young wife; fell to drinking, then to gambling behind the door; finally took his wife and two young children to her father's, and went off to Mexico; went from bad to worse, and finally died there, without a cent to buy a shroud, and without a friend to attend the funeral."

"Pity, for he was the best-natured, and most cheery and hopeful young fellow that ever was."

I named another boy.

"Oh, he is all right. Lives here yet; has a wife and children, and is prospering."

Same verdict concerning other boys.

I named three schoolgirls.

"The first two live here, are married and have children; the other is long ago dead—never married."

I named, with emotion, one of my early sweethearts.

"She is all right. Been married three times; buried two husbands, divorced from the third, and I hear she is getting ready to marry an old fellow out in Colorado somewhere. She's got children scattered around here and there, most everywheres."

238

The answer to several other inquiries was brief and simple—

"Killed in the war."

I named another boy.

"Well, now, his case *is* curious! There wasn't a human being in this town but knew that that boy was a perfect chucklehead; perfect dummy; just a stupid ass, as you may say. Everybody knew it, and everybody said it. Well, if that very boy isn't the first lawyer in the State of Missouri today, I'm a Democrat!"

"Is that so?"

"It's actually so. I'm telling you the truth."

"How do you account for it?"

"Account for it? There ain't any accounting for it, except that if you send a damned fool to St. Louis, and you don't tell them he's a damned fool, *they'll* never find it out. There's one thing sure—if I had a damned fool I should know what to do with him: ship him to St. Louis—it's the noblest market in the world for that kind of property. Well, when you come to look at it all around, and chew at it and think it over, *don't* it just bang anything you ever heard of?"

"Well, yes, it does seem to. But don't you think maybe it was the Hannibal people who were mistaken about the boy, and not the St. Louis people?"

"Oh, nonsense! The people here have known him from the very cradle—they knew him a hundred times better than the St. Louis idiots *could* have known him. No, if you have got any damned fools that you want to realize on, take my advice—send them to St. Louis."

I mentioned a great number of people whom I had formerly known. Some were dead, some were gone away, some had prospered, some had come to naught; but as regarded a dozen or so of the lot, the answer was comforting:

"Prosperous—live here yet—town littered with their children."

I asked about Miss——.

"Died in the insane asylum three or four years ago—never was out of it from the time she went in; and was always suffering, too; never got a shred of her mind back."

If he spoke the truth, here was a heavy tragedy, indeed. Thirty-six years in a madhouse, that some young fools might have some fun! I was a small boy, at the time; and I saw those giddy young ladies come tiptoeing into the room where Miss——sat reading at midnight by a lamp. The girl at the head of the file wore a shroud and a doughface; she crept behind the victim, touched here on the shoulder, and she looked up and screamed, and then fell into convulsions. She did not recover from the fright, but went mad. In these days it seems incredible that people believed in ghosts so short a time ago. But they did.

After asking after such folk as I could call to mind, finally inquired about *myself*:

"Oh, he succeeded well enough—another case of damned fool. If they'd sent him to St. Louis, he'd have succeeded sooner."

It was with much satisfaction that I recognized the wisdom of having told this candid gentleman, in the beginning, that my name was Smith.

A Day's Pleasure

HAMLIN GARLAND

When Markham came in from shovelling his last wagon-load of corn into the crib he found that his wife had put the children to bed, and was kneading a batch of dough with the dogged action of a tired and sullen woman.

He slipped his soggy boots off his feet, and having laid a piece of wood on top of the stove, put his heels on it comfortably. His chair squeaked as he leaned back on its hinder legs, but he paid no attention; he was used to it, exactly as he was used to his wife's lameness and ceaseless toil.

"That closes up my corn," he said after a silence. "I guess I'll go to town to-morrow to git my horses shod."

"I guess I'll git ready and go along," said his wife, in a sorry attempt to be firm and confident of tone.

"What do you want to go to town fer?" he grumbled.

"What does anybody want to go to town fer?" she burst out, facing him. "I ain't been out o' this house fer six months, while you go an' go!"

"Oh, it ain't six months. You went down that day I got the mower."

"When was that? The tenth of July, and you know it."

"Well, mebbe 'twas. I didn't think it was so long ago. I ain't no objection to your goin', only I'm goin' to take a load of wheat."

"Well, jest leave off a sack, an' that'll balance me an' the baby," she said spiritedly.

"All right," he replied good-naturedly, seeing she was roused. "Only that wheat ought to be put up to-night if you're goin'. You won't have any time to hold sacks for me in the morning with them young ones to get off to school."

"Well, let's go do it then," she said, sullenly resolute.

"I hate to go out agin; but I s'pose we'd better."

He yawned dismally and began pulling his boots on again, stamping his swollen feet into them with grunts of pain. She put on his coat and one of

241

the boy's caps, and they went out to the granary. The night was cold and clear.

"Don't look so much like snow as it did last night," said Sam. "It may turn warm."

Laying out the sacks in the light of the lantern, they sorted out those which were whole, and Sam climbed into the bin with a tin pail in his hand, and the work began.

He was a sturdy fellow, and he worked desperately fast; the shining tin pail dived deep into the cold wheat and dragged heavily on the woman's tired hands as it came to the mouth of the sack, and she trembled with fatigue, but held on and dragged the sacks away when filled, and brought others, till at last Sam climbed out, puffing and wheezing, to tie them up.

"I guess I'll load 'em in the morning," he said. "You needn't wait fer me. I'll tie 'em up alone."

"Oh, I don't mind," she replied, feeling a little touched by his unexpectedly easy acquiescence to her request. When they went back to the house the moon had risen.

It had scarcely set when they were wakened by the crowing roosters. The man rolled stiffly out of bed and began rattling at the stove in the dark, cold kitchen.

His wife arose lamer and stiffer than usual, and began twisting her thin hair into a knot.

Sam did not stop to wash, but went out to the barn. The woman, however, hastily soused her face into the hard limestone water at the sink, and put the kettle on. Then she called the children. She knew it was early, and they would need several callings. She pushed breakfast forward, running over in her mind the things she must have: two spools of thread, six yards of cotton flannel, a can of coffee, and mittens for Kitty. These she must have—there were oceans of things she needed.

The children soon came scudding down out of the darkness of the upstairs to dress tumultuously at the kitchen stove. They humped and shivered, holding up their bare feet from the cold floor, like chickens in new fallen snow. They were irritable, and snarled and snapped and struck like cats and dogs. Mrs. Markham stood it for a while with mere commands to "hush up," but at last her patience gave out, and she charged down on the struggling mob and cuffed them right and left.

They ate their breakfast by lamplight, and when Sam went back to his work around the barnyard it was scarcely dawn. The children, left alone with their mother, began to tease her to let them go to town also.

"No, sir—nobody goes but baby. Your father's goin' to take a load of wheat."

She was weak with the worry of it all when she had sent the older children away to school and the kitchen work was finished. She went into the cold bedroom off the little sitting room and put on her best dress. It had never been a good fit, and now she was getting so thin it hung in wrinkled folds everywhere about the shoulders and waist. She lay down on the bed a moment to ease that dull pain in her back. She had a moment's distaste for going out at all. The thought of sleep was more alluring. Then the thought of the long, long day, and the sickening sameness of her life, swept over her again, and she rose and prepared the baby for the journey.

It was but little after sunrise when Sam drove out into the road and started for Belleplain. His wife sat perched upon the wheat-sacks behind him, holding the baby in her lap, a cotton quilt under her, and a cotton horse-blanket over her knees.

Sam was disposed to be very good-natured, and he talked back at her occasionally, though she could only understand him when he turned his face toward her. The baby stared out at the passing fence-posts, and wiggled his hands out of his mittens at every opportunity. He was merry at least.

It grew warmer as they went on, and a strong south wind arose. The dust settled upon the woman's shawl and hat. Her hair loosened and blew unkemptly about her face. The road which led across the high, level prairie was quite smooth and dry, but still it jolted her, and the pain in her back increased. She had nothing to lean against, and the weight of the child grew greater, till she was forced to place him on the sacks beside her, though she could not loose her hold for a moment.

The town drew in sight—a cluster of small frame houses and stores on the dry prairie beside a railway station. They were no trees yet which could be called shade trees. The pitilessly severe light of the sun flooded everything. A few teams were hitched about, and in the lee of the stores a few men could be seen seated comfortably, their broad hat-rims flopping up and down, their faces brown as leather.

Markham put his wife out at one of the grocery-stores, and drove off down toward the elevators to sell his wheat.

The grocer greeted Mrs. Markham in a perfunctorily kind manner, and offered her a chair, which she took gratefully. She sat for a quarter of an hour almost without moving, leaning against the back of the high chair. At last the child began to get restless and troublesome, and she spent half an hour helping him amuse himself around the nail-kegs.

At length she rose and went out on the walk, carrying the baby. She went into the dry-goods store and took a seat on one of the little revolving stools. A woman was buying some woollen goods for a dress. It was worth twenty-seven cents a yard, the clerk said, but he would knock off two cents if she took ten yards. It looked warm, and Mrs. Markham wished she could afford it for Mary.

A pretty young girl came in and laughed and chatted with the clerk, and bought a pair of gloves. She was the daughter of the grocer. Her happiness made the wife and mother sad. When Sam came back she asked him for some money.

"What you want to do with it?" he asked.

"I want to spend it," she said.

She was not to be trifled with, so he gave her a dollar.

"I need a dollar more."

"Well, I've got to go take up that note at the bank."

"Well, the children's got to have some new underclo'es," she said.

He handed her a two-dollar bill and then went out to pay his note.

She bought her cotton flannel and mittens and thread, and then sat leaning against the counter. It was noon, and she was hungry. She went out to the wagon, got the lunch she had brought, and took it into the grocery to eat it—where she could get a drink of water.

The grocer gave the baby a stick of candy and handed the mother an apple.

"It'll kind o' go down with your doughnuts," he said.

After eating her lunch she got up and went out. She felt ashamed to sit there any longer. She entered another dry-goods store, but when the clerk came toward her saying, "Anything to-day, Mrs.——?" she answered, "No, I guess not," and turned away with foolish face.

She walked up and down the street, desolately homeless. She did not know what to do with herself. She knew no one except the grocer. She grew bitter as she saw a couple of ladies pass, holding their demi-trains in the latest city fashion. Another woman went by pushing a baby carriage, in which sat a child just about as big as her own. It was bouncing itself up and down

Roswell, New Mexico, 1908

on the long slender springs, and laughing and shouting. Its clean round face glowed from its pretty fringed hood. She looked down at the dusty clothes and grimy face of her own little one, and walked on savagely.

She went into the drug store where the soda fountain was, but it made her thirsty to sit there and she went out on the street again. She heard Sam laugh, and saw him in a group of men over by the blacksmith shop. He was having a good time and had forgotten her.

Her back ached so intolerably that she concluded to go in and rest once more in the grocer's chair. The baby was growing cross and fretful. She bought five cents' worth of candy to take home to the children, and gave baby a little piece to keep him quiet. She wished Sam would come. It must be getting late. The grocer said it was not much after one. Time seemed terribly long. She felt that she ought to do something while she was in town. She ran over her purchases—yes, that was all she had planned to buy. She fell to figuring on the things she needed. It was terrible. It ran away up into twenty or thirty dollars at the least. Sam, as well as she, needed underwear for the cold winter, but they would have to wear the old ones, even if they were thin and ragged. She would not need a dress, she thought bitterly, because she never went anywhere. She rose and went out on the street once more, and wandered up and down, looking at everything in the hope of enjoying something.

A man from Boon Creek backed a load of apples up to the sidewalk, and as he stood waiting for the grocer he noticed Mrs. Markham and the baby, and gave the baby an apple. This was a pleasure. He had such a hearty way about him. He on his part saw an ordinary farmer's wife with dusty dress, unkempt hair, and tired face. He did not know exactly why she appealed to him, but he tried to cheer her up.

The grocer was familiar with these bedraggled and weary wives. He was accustomed to see them sit for hours in his big wooden chair, and nurse tired and fretful children. Their forlorn, aimless, pathetic wandering up and down the street was a daily occurrence, and had never possessed any special meaning to him.

II

In a cottage around the corner from the grocery store two men and a woman were finishing a dainty luncheon. The woman was dressed in cool, white garments, and she seemed to make the day one of perfect comfort.

The home of the Honorable Mr. Hall was by no means the costliest in the town, but his wife made it the most attractive. He was one of the leading lawyers of the county, and a man of culture and progressive views. He was entertaining a friend who had lectured the night before in the Congregational church.

They were by no means in serious discussion. The talk was rather frivolous. Hall had the ability to caricature men with a few gestures and attitudes, and was giving to his Eastern friend some descriptions of the old-fashioned Western lawyers he had met in his practice. He was very amusing, and his guest laughed heartily for a time.

But suddenly Hall became aware that Otis was not listening. Then he perceived that he was peering out of the window at some one, and that on his face a look of bitter sadness was falling.

Hall stopped. "What do you see, Otis?"

Otis replied, "I see a forlorn, weary woman."

Mrs. Hall rose and went to the window. Mrs. Markham was walking by the house, her baby in her arms. Savage anger and weeping were in her eyes and on her lips, and there was hopeless tragedy in her shambling walk and weak back.

In the silence Otis went on: "I saw the poor, dejected creature twice this morning. I couldn't forget her."

"Who is she?" asked Mrs. Hall, very softly.

"Her name is Markham; she's Sam Markham's wife," said Hall.

The young wife led the way into the sitting room, and the men took seats and lit their cigars. Hall was meditating a diversion when Otis resumed suddenly:

"That woman came to town to-day to get a change, to have a little play-spell, and she's wandering around like a starved and weary cat. I wonder if there is a woman in this town with sympathy enough and courage enough to go out and help that woman? The saloon-keepers, the politicians, and the grocers make it pleasant for the man—so pleasant that he forgets his wife. But the wife is left without a word."

Mrs. Hall's work dropped, and on her pretty face was a look of pain. The man's harsh words had wounded her—and wakened her. She took up her hat and hurried out on the walk. The men looked at each other, and then the husband said:

"It's going to be a little sultry for the men around these diggings. Suppose we go out for a walk."

Delia felt a hand on her arm as she stood at the corner.

"You look tired, Mrs. Markham; won't you come in a little while? I'm Mrs. Hall."

Mrs. Markham turned with a scowl on her face and a biting word on her tongue, but something in the sweet, round little face of the other woman silenced her, and her brow smoothed out.

"Thank you kindly, but it's most time to go home. I'm looking fer Mr. Markham now."

"Oh, come in a little while, the baby is cross and tired out; please do."

Mrs. Markham yielded to the friendly voice, and together the two women reached the gate just as two men hurriedly turned the other corner.

"Let me relieve you," said Mrs. Hall.

The mother hesitated: "He's so dusty."

"Oh, that won't matter. Oh, what a big fellow he is! I haven't any of my own," said Mrs. Hall, and a look passed like an electric spark between the two women, and Delia was her willing guest from that moment.

They went into the little sitting room, so dainty and lovely to the farmer's wife, and as she sank into an easy-chair she was faint and drowsy with the pleasure of it. She submitted to being brushed. She gave the baby into the hands of the Swedish girl, who washed its face and hands and sang it to sleep, while its mother sipped some tea. Through it all she lay back in her easy-chair, not speaking a word, while the ache passed out of her back, and her hot, swollen head ceased to throb.

But she saw everything—the piano, the pictures, the curtains, the wall-paper, the little tea-stand. They were almost as grateful to her as the food and fragrant tea. Such housekeeping as this she had never seen. Her mother had worn her kitchen floor thin as brown paper in keeping a speckless house, and she had been in houses that were larger and costlier, but something of the charm of her hostess was in the arrangement of vases, chairs, or pictures. It was tasteful.

Mrs. Hall did not ask about her affairs. She talked to her about the sturdy little baby, and about the things upon which Delia's eyes dwelt. If she seemed interested in a vase she was told what it was and where it was made. She was shown all the pictures and books. Mrs. Hall seemed to read her visitor's mind. She kept as far from the farm and her guest's affairs as possible, and at last she opened the piano and sang to her—not slow-moving hymns, but catchy love-songs full of sentiment, and then played some simple melodies, knowing that Mrs. Markham's eyes were studying her hands, her rings, and the flash of her fingers on the keys—seeing more than she heard—and through it all Mrs. Hall conveyed the impression that she, too, was having a good time.

The rattle of the wagon outside roused them both. Sam was at the gate for her. Mrs. Markham rose hastily. "Oh, it's almost sundown!" she gasped in astonishment as she looked out of the window.

"Oh, that won't kill anybody," replied her hostess. "Don't hurry. Carrie, take the baby out to the wagon for Mrs. Markham while I help her with her things."

"Oh, I've had such a good time," Mrs. Markham said as they went down the little walk.

"So have I," replied Mrs. Hall. She took the baby a moment as her guest climbed in. "Oh, you big, fat fellow!" she cried as she gave him a squeeze. "You must bring your wife in oftener, Mr. Markham," she said, as she handed the baby up.

Sam was staring with amazement.

"Thank you, I will," he finally managed to say.

"Good-night," said Mrs. Markham.

"Good-night, dear," called Mrs. Hall, and the wagon began to rattle off.

The tenderness and sympathy in her voice brought the tears to Delia's eyes—not hot or bitter tears, but tears that cooled her eyes and cleared her mind.

The wind had gone down, and the red sunlight fell mistily over the world of corn and stubble. The crickets were still chirping and the feeding cattle were drifting toward the farmyards. The day had been made beautiful by human sympathy.

The Luck of Roaring Camp

BRET HARTE

There was commotion in Roaring Camp. It could not have been a fight, for in 1850 that was not novel enough to have called together the entire settlement. The ditches and claims were not only deserted, but "Tuttle's grocery" had contributed its gamblers, who, it will be remembered, calmly continued their game the day that Franch Pete and Kanaka Joe shot each other to death over the bar in the front room. The whole camp was collected before a rude cabin on the outer edge of the clearing. Conversation was carried on in a low tone, but the name of a woman was frequently repeated. It was a name familiar enough in the camp,—"Cherokee Sal."

Perhaps the less said of her the better. She was a coarse and, it is to be feared, a very sinful woman. But at that time she was the only woman in Roaring Camp, and was just then lying in sore extremity, when she most needed the ministration of her own sex. Dissolute, abandoned, and irreclaimable, she was yet suffering a martyrdom hard enough to bear even when veiled by sympathizing womanhood, but now terrible in her loneliness. The primal curse had come to her in that original isolation which must have made the punishment of the first transgression so dreadful. It was, perhaps, part of the expiation of her sin that, at a moment when she most lacked her sex's intuitive tenderness and care, she met only the half-contemptuous faces of her masculine associates. Yet a few of the spectators were, I think, touched by her sufferings. Sandy Tipton thought it was "rough on Sal," and, in the contemplation of her condition, for a moment rose superior to the fact that he had an ace and two bowers in his sleeve.

It will be seen also that the situation was novel. Deaths were by no means uncommon in Roaring Camp, but a birth was a new thing. People had been dismissed from the camp effectively, finally, and with no possibility of return; but this was the first time that anybody had been introduced *ab initio*. Hence the excitement.

250

"You go in there, Stumpy," said a prominent citizen known as "Kentuck," addressing one of the loungers. "Go in there, and see what you kin do. You've had experience in them things."

Perhaps there was a fitness in the selection. Stumpy, in other climes, had been the putative head of two families; in fact, it was owing to some legal informality in these proceedings that Roaring Camp—a city of refuge—was indebted to his company. The crowd approved the choice, and Stumpy was wise enough to bow to the majority. The door closed on the extempore surgeon and midwife, and Roaring Camp sat down outside, smoked its pipe, and awaited the issue.

The assemblage numbered about a hundred men. One or two of these were actual fugitives from justice, some were criminal, and all were reckless. Physically they exhibited no indication of their past lives and character. The greatest scamp had a Raphael face, with a profusion of blonde hair; Oakhurst, a gambler, had the melancholy air and intellectual abstraction of a Hamlet; the coolest and most courageous man was scarcely over five feet in height, with a soft voice and an embarrassed, timid manner. The term "roughs" applied to them was a distinction rather than a definition. Perhaps in the minor details of fingers, toes, ears, etc., the camp may have been deficient, but these slight omissions did not detract from their aggregate force. The strongest man had but three fingers on his right hand; the best shot had but one eye.

Such was the physical aspect of the men that were dispersed around the cabin. The camp lay in a triangular valley between two hills and a river. The only outlet was a steep trail over the summit of a hill that faced the cabin, now illuminated by the rising moon. The suffering woman might have seen it from the rude bunk whereon she lay,—seen it winding like a silver thread until it was lost in the stars above.

A fire of withered pine boughs added sociability to the gathering. By degrees the natural levity of Roaring Camp returned. Bets were freely offered and taken regarding the result. Three to five that "Sal would get through with it"; even that the child would survive; side bets as to the sex and complexion of the coming stranger. In the midst of an excited discussion an exclamation came from those nearest the door, and the camp stopped to listen. Above the swaying and moaning of the pines, the swift rush of the river, and the crackling of the fire rose a sharp, querulous cry,—a cry unlike anything heard before in the camp. The pines stopped moaning, the river ceased to rush, and the fire to crackle. It seemed as if Nature had stopped to listen too.

The camp rose to its feet as one man! It was proposed to explode a barrel of gunpowder; but in consideration of the situation of the mother, better counsels prevailed, and only a few revolvers were discharged; for whether owing to the rude surgery of the camp, or some other reason, Cherokee Sal was sinking fast. Within an hour she had climbed, as it were, that rugged road that led to the stars, and so passed out of Roaring Camp, its sin and shame, forever. I do not think that the announcement disturbed them much, except in speculation as to the fate of the child. "Can he live now?" was asked of Stumpy. The answer was doubtful. The only other being of Cherokee Sal's sex and maternal condition in the settlement was an ass. There was some conjecture as to fitness, but the experiment was tried. It was less problematical than the ancient treatment of Romulus and Remus, and apparently as successful.

When these details were completed, which exhausted another hour, the door was opened, and the anxious crowd of men, who had already formed themselves into a queue, entered in single file. Beside the low bunk or shelf, on which the figure of the mother was starkly outlined below the blankets, stood a pine table. On this a candle-box was placed, and within it, swathed in staring red flannel, lay the last arrival at Roaring Camp. Beside the candle-box was placed a hat. Its use was soon indicated. "Gentlemen," said Stumpy, with a singular mixture of authority and *ex officio* complacency,—"gentlemen will please pass in at the front door, round the table, and out at the back door. Them as wishes to contribute anything toward the orphan will find a hat handy." The first man entered with his hat on; he uncovered, however, as he looked about him, and so unconsciously set an example to the next. In such communities good and bad actions are catching. As the procession filed in comments were audible,—criticisms addressed perhaps rather to Stumpy in the character of showman: "Is that him?" "Mighty small specimen"; "Hasn't more'n got the color"; "Ain't bigger nor a derringer." The contributions were as characteristic: A silver tobacco box; a doubloon; a navy revolver, silver mounted; a gold specimen; a very beautifully embroidered lady's handkerchief (from Oakhurst the gambler); a diamond breastpin; a diamond ring (suggested by the pin, with the remark from the giver that he "saw that pin and went two diamonds better"); a slung-shot; a Bible (contributor not detected); a golden spur; a silver teaspoon (the initials, I regret to say, were not the giver's); a pair of surgeon's shears; a lancet; a Bank of England note for £5; and about $200 in loose gold and silver coin. During these proceedings Stumpy maintained a silence as impassive as the dead on his left, a gravity as inscrutable as that of the newly born on his right. Only one incident occurred to break the monotony of the curious procession. As Kentuck bent over the candle-box half curiously, the child turned, and, in a spasm of pain, caught at his groping finger, and held it fast for a moment. Kentuck looked foolish and embarrassed. Something like a blush tried to assert itself in his weather-beaten cheek. "The d—d little cuss!" he said, as he extricated his finger, with perhaps more tenderness and care than he might have been deemed capable of showing. He held that finger a little apart from its fellows as he went out, and examined it curiously. The examination provoked the same original remark in regard to the child. In fact, he seemed to enjoy repeating it. "He rastled with my finger," he remarked to Tipton, holding up the member, "the d—d little cuss!"

It was four o'clock before the camp sought repose. A light burnt in the cabin where the watchers sat, for Stumpy did not go to bed that night. Nor did Kentuck. He drank quite freely, and related with great gusto his experience, invariably ending with his characteristic condemnation of the newcomer. It seemed to relieve him of any unjust implication of sentiment, and Kentuck had the weaknesses of the nobler sex. When everybody else had gone to bed he walked down to the river and whistled reflectingly. Then he walked up the gulch past the cabin, still whistling with demonstrative unconcern. At a large redwood-tree he paused and retraced his steps, and again passed the cabin. Halfway down to the river's bank he again paused, and then returned and knocked at the door. It was opened by Stumpy. "How goes it?" said Kentuck, looking past Stumpy toward the candle-box. "All serene!" replied Stumpy. "Anything up?" "Nothing." There was a pause—an embarrassing one—Stumpy still holding the door. Then Kentuck had recourse to his finger, which he held up to Stumpy. "Rastled with it,—the d—d little cuss," he said, and retired.

The next day Cherokee Sal had such rude sepulture as Roaring Camp afforded. After her body had been committed to the hillside, there was a formal meeting of the camp to discuss what should be done with her infant. A resolution to adopt it was unanimous and enthusiastic. But an animated discussion in regard to the manner and feasibility of providing for its wants at once sprang up. It was remarkable that the argument partook of none of those fierce personalities with which discussions were usually conducted at Roaring Camp. Tipton proposed that they should send the child to Red Dog,—a distance of forty miles,—where female attention could be procured. But the unlucky suggestion met with fierce and unanimous opposition. It was evident that no plan which entailed parting from their new acquisition would for a moment be entertained. "Besides," said Tom Ryder, "them fellows at Red Dog would swap it, and ring in somebody else on us." A disbelief in the honesty of other camps prevailed at Roaring Camp, as in other places.

The introduction of a female nurse in the camp also met with objection. It was argued that no decent woman could be prevailed to accept Roaring Camp as her home, and the speaker urged that "they didn't want any more of the other kind." This unkind allusion to the defunct mother, harsh as it may seem, was the first spasm of propriety,—the first symptom of the camp's regeneration. Stumpy advanced nothing. Perhaps he felt a certain delicacy in interfering with the selection of a possible successor in office. But when questioned, he averred stoutly that he and "Jinny"—the mammal before alluded to—could manage to rear the child. There was something original, independent, and heroic about the plan that pleased the camp. Stumpy was retained. Certain articles were sent for to Sacramento. "Mind," said the treasurer, as he pressed a bag of gold-dust into the expressman's hand, "the best that can be got,—lace, you know, and filigree-work and frills,—d—n the cost!"

Strange to say, the child thrived. Perhaps the invigorating climate of the mountain camp was compensation for material deficiencies. Nature took the foundling to her broader breast. In that rare atmosphere of the Sierra foothills,—that air pungent with balsamic odor, that ethereal cordial at once bracing and exhilarating,—he may have found food and nourishment, or a subtle chemistry that transmuted ass's milk to lime and phosphorus. Stumpy inclined to the belief that it was the latter and good nursing. "Me and that ass," he would say, "has been father and mother to him! Don't you," he would add, apostrophizing the helpless bundle before him, "never go back on us."

By the time he was a month old the necessity of giving him a name became apparent. He had generally been known as "The Kid," "Stumpy's Boy," "The Coyote" (an allusion to his vocal powers), and even by Kentuck's

254

endearing diminutive of "The d—d little cuss." But these were felt to be vague and unsatisfactory, and were at last dismissed under another influence. Gamblers and adventurers are generally superstitious, and Oakhurst one day declared that the baby had brought "the luck" to Roaring Camp. It was certain that of late they had been successful. "Luck" was the name agreed upon, with the prefix of Tommy for greater convenience. No allusion was made to the mother, and the father was unknown. "It's better," said the philosophical Oakhurst, "to take a fresh deal all round. Call him Luck, and start him fair." A day was accordingly set apart for the christening. What was meant by this ceremony the reader may imagine who has already gathered some idea of the reckless irreverence of Roaring Camp. The master of ceremonies was one "Boston," a noted wag, and the occasion seemed to promise the greatest facetiousness. This ingenious satirist had spent two days in preparing a burlesque of the Church service, with pointed local allusions. The choir was properly trained, and Sandy Tipton was to stand godfather. But after the procession had marched to the grove with music and banners, and the child had been deposited before a mock altar, Stumpy stepped before the expectant crowd. "It ain't my style to spoil fun, boys," said the little man, stoutly eying the faces around him, "but it strikes me that this thing ain't exactly on the squar. It's playing it pretty low down on this yer baby to ring in fun on him that he ain't goin' to understand. And ef there's goin' to be any godfathers round, I'd like to see who's got any better rights than me." A silence followed Stumpy's speech. To the credit of all humorists be it said that the first man to acknowledge its justice was the satirist thus stopped of his fun. "But," said Stumpy, quickly following up his advantage, "we're here for a christening, and we'll have it. I proclaim you Thomas Luck, according to the laws of the United States and the State of California, so help me God," It was the first time that the name of the Deity had been otherwise uttered than profanely in the camp. The form of christening was perhaps even more ludicrous than the satirist had conceived; but strangely enough, nobody saw it and nobody laughed. "Tommy" was christened as seriously as he would have been under a Christian roof, and cried and was comforted in as orthodox fashion.

And so the work of regeneration began in Roaring Camp. Almost imperceptibly a change came over the settlement. The cabin assigned to "Tommy Luck"—or "The Luck," as he was more frequently called—first showed signs of improvement. It was kept scrupulously clean and whitewashed.

Then it was boarded, clothed, and papered. The rosewood cradle, packed eighty miles by mule, had, in Stumpy's way of putting it, "sorter killed the rest of the furniture." So the rehabilitation of the cabin became a necessity. The men who were in the habit of lounging in at Stumpy's to see "how 'The Luck' got on" seemed to appreciate the change, and in self-defense the rival establishment of "Tuttle's grocery" bestirred itself and imported a carpet and mirrors. The reflections of the latter on the appearance of Roaring Camp tended to produce stricter habits of personal cleanliness. Again Stumpy imposed a kind of quarantine upon those who aspired to the honor and privilege of holding The Luck. It was a cruel mortification to Kentuck— who, in the carelessness of a large nature and the habits of frontier life, had begun to regard all garments as a second cuticle, which, like a snake's, only sloughed off through decay—to be debarred this privilege from certain prudential reasons. Yet such was the subtle influence of innovation that he thereafter appeared regularly every afternoon in a clean shirt and face still shining from his ablutions. Nor were moral and social sanitary laws neglected. "Tommy," who was supposed to spend his whole existence in a persistent attempt to repose, must not be disturbed by noise. The shouting and yelling, which had gained the camp its infelicitous title, were not permitted within hearing distance of Stumpy's. The men conversed in whispers or smoked with Indian gravity. Profanity was tacitly given up in these sacred precincts, and throughout the camp a popular form of expletive, known as "D—n the luck!" and "Curse the luck!" was abandoned, as having a new personal bearing. Vocal music was not interdicted, being supposed to have a soothing, tranquilizing quality; and one song, sung by "Man-o'-War Jack," an English sailor from Her Majesty's Australian colonies, was quite popular as a lullaby. It was a lugubrious recital of the exploits of "The Arethusa, Seventy-four," in a muffled minor, ending with a prolonged dying fall at the burden of each verse, "On b-oo-o-ard of the Arethusa." It was a fine sight to see Jack holding The Luck, rocking from side to side as if with the motion of a ship, and crooning forth this naval ditty. Either through the peculiar rocking of Jack or the length of his song,—it contained ninety stanzas, and was continued with conscientious deliberation to the bitter end,— the lullaby generally had the desired effect. At such times the men would lie at full length under the trees in the soft summer twilight, smoking their pipes and drinking in the melodious utterances. An indistinct idea that this was pastoral happiness pervaded the camp. "This 'ere kind o' think," said the Cockney Simmons, meditatively reclining on his elbow, "is 'evingly." It reminded him of Greenwich.

On the long summer days The Luck was usually carried to the gulch from whence the golden store of Roaring Camp was taken. There, on a blanket spread over pine boughs, he would lie while the men were working in the ditches below. Latterly there was a rude attempt to decorate this bower with flowers and sweet-smelling shrubs, and generally some one would bring him a cluster of wild honeysuckles, azaleas, or the painted blossoms of Las Mariposas. The men had suddenly awakened to the fact that there were beauty and significance in these trifles, which they had so long trodden carelessly beneath their feet. A flake of glittering mica, a fragment of variegated quartz, a bright pebble from the bed of the creek, became beautiful to eyes thus cleared and strengthened, and were invariably put aside for the The Luck. It was wonderful how many treasures the woods and hillsides yielded that "would do for Tommy." Surrounded by playthings such as never child out of fairyland had before, it is to be hoped that Tommy was content. He appeared to be serenely happy, albeit there was an infantine gravity about him, a contemplative light in his round gray eyes, that sometimes worried Stumpy. He was always tractable and quiet, and it is recorded that once, having crept beyond his "corral," —a hedge of tessellated pine boughs, which surrounded his bed,—he dropped over the bank on his head in the soft earth, and remained with his mottled legs in the air in that position for at least five minutes with unflinching gravity. He was extricated without a murmur. I hesitate to record the many other instances of his sagacity, which rest, unfortunately, upon the statements of prejudiced friends. Some of them were not without a tinge of superstition. "I crep' up the bank just now," said Kentuck one day, in a breathless state of excitement, "and dern my skin if he wasn't a-talking to a jaybird as was a-sittin' on his lap. There they was, just as free and sociable as anything you please, a-jawin' at each other just like two cherrybums." Howbeit, whether creeping over the pine boughs or lying lazily on his back blinking at the leaves above him, to him the birds sang, the squirrels chattered, and the flowers bloomed. Nature was his nurse and playfellow. For him she would let slip between the leaves golden shafts of sunlight that fell just within his grasp; she would send wandering breezes to visit him with the balm of bay and resinous gum; to him the tall redwoods nodded familiarly and sleepily, the bumblebees buzzed, and the rooks cawed a slumbrous accompaniment.

Such was the golden summer of Roaring Camp. They were "flush times," and the luck was with them. The claims had yielded enormously. The camp was jealous of its privileges and looked suspiciously on strangers. No encouragement was given to immigration, and, to make their seclusion more perfect, the land on either side of the mountain wall that surrounded the camp they duly preëmpted. This, and a reputation for singular proficiency with the revolver, kept the reserve of Roaring Camp inviolate. The expressman—their only connecting link with the surrounding world—sometimes told wonderful stories of the camp. He would say, "They've a street up there in 'Roaring' that would lay over any street in Red Dog. They've got vines and flowers round their houses, and they wash themselves twice a day. But they're mighty rough on strangers, and they worship an Ingin baby."

With the prosperity of the camp came a desire for further improvement. It was proposed to build a hotel in the following spring, and to invite one or two decent families to reside there for the sake of The Luck, who might perhaps profit by female companionship. The sacrifice that this concession to the sex cost these men, who were fiercely skeptical in regard to its general virtue and usefulness, can only be accounted for by their affection for Tommy. A few still held out. But the resolve could not be carried into effect for three months, and the minority meekly yielded in the hope that something might turn up to prevent it. And it did.

The winter of 1851 will long be remembered in the foothills. The snow lay deep on the Sierras, and every mountain creek became a river, and every river a lake. Each gorge and gulch was transformed into a tumultuous watercourse that descended the hillsides, tearing down giant trees and scattering its drift and débris along the plain. Red Dog had been twice under water, and Roaring Camp had been forewarned. "Water put the gold into them gulches," said Stumpy. "It's been here once and will be here again!" And that night the North Fork suddenly leaped over its banks and swept up the triangular valley of Roaring Camp.

In the confusion of rushing water, crashing trees, and crackling timber, and the darkness which seemed to flow with the water and blot out the fair valley, but little could be done to collect the scattered camp. When the morning broke, the cabin of Stumpy, nearest the river-bank, was gone. Higher up the gulch they found the body of its unlucky owner; but the pride, the hope, the joy, The Luck, of Roaring Camp had disappeared.

They were returning with sad hearts when a shout from the bank recalled them.

It was a relief-boat from down the river. They had picked up, they said, a man and an infant, nearly exhausted, about two miles below. Did anybody know them, and did they belong here?

It needed but a glance to show them Kentuck lying there, cruelly crushed and bruised, but still holding The Luck of Roaring Camp in his arms. As they bent over the strangely assorted pair, they saw that the child was cold and pulseless. "He is dead," said one. Kentuck opened his eyes. "Dead?" he repeated feebly. "Yes, my man, and you are dying too." A smile lit the eyes of the expiring Kentuck. "Dying!" he repeated; "he's a-taking me with him. Tell the boys I've got The Luck with me now"; and the strong man, clinging to the frail babe as a drowning man is said to cling to a straw, drifted away into the shadowy river that flows forever to the unknown sea.

Quiet Town

WILLIAM STAFFORD

Here in our cloud we talk
baking powder. Our yeast feet
make tracks that fill up with fog.
Tongue like a sponge, we describe
the air that we eat—how it has its own
lungs, inhales many a stranger.

Our stories have executives who flash
ornamental knives. Their children use them
afternoons to toast marshmallows.
Technicians in suicide plan courses
in high school for as long as it takes.

For our gestures, feathers are emphatic
enough; a snowflake smashes through
revealed rock. Our town balances,
and we have a railroad. Pitiful bandits
who storm the bank are led away,
their dreamy guns kicked into the gutter
by kids coming out of the movie.

No one is allowed to cross our lake at night.
Every Christmas we forget by selective remembering.
Overhead planes mutter our fear
and are dangerous, are bombs exploding
a long time, carrying bombs elsewhere to explode.

A Letter

WILLIAM STAFFORD

Dear Governor:
      Rather than advise you this time or complain
I will report on one of our little towns
where I stopped last week at evening.
This town has no needs. Not one person stirred
by the three lights on Main Street. It lay
so mild and lost that I wanted you to know
how some part of your trust appears, too far
or too dim to demand or be afraid.
Now I let it all go back into its mist from
the silent river. Maybe no one will
report it to you may more.
      You could think of that place annually
on this date, for reassurance—a place where we
have done no wrong. For these days to find out
what to forgive one must listen and watch:
even our friends draft us like vampires, and it is
the non-localized hurts that do the damage.
We have to forgive carefully those demands
for little helps, those unhappy acquaintances.
We must manage the ultimate necessary withdrawal
somehow, sometimes let the atoms swirl by.
      So, this time, please keep on being the way
you are, and think of that town. A locust tree
put its fronds, by the way, quietly into the
streetlight; repeated breaths of river wind
came up-canyon. Let that—the nothing, the no one,
the calm night——often recur to you.

Sincerely,
A Friend

Raisins

WILLIAM SAROYAN

A man could walk four or five miles in any direction from the heart of our city and see our streets dwindle to land and weeds. In many places the land would be vineyard and orchard land, but in most places it would be desert land and the weeds would be the strong dry weeds of deserts, and in this land there would be the living things that had had their being in the quietness of deserts for centuries. There would be snakes and horned toads, prairie dogs and jack-rabbits, and in the sky above this land would be buzzards and hawks, and the hot sun. And everywhere in our desert would be the marks of wagons that had made lonely roads, so that we knew men were living in this dry country.

Two miles from the heart of our city a man could come to the desert and feel the loneliness of a desolate area, of a place lost in the earth, far from the solace of human thought, and it was a tremendous thing to know that we had men in our valley who were slowly filling this desert with the moments of their lives, their minds, their quiet talk, and their energy. Standing at the edge of our city, a man could feel that we had made this place of streets and dwellings in the stillness and loneliness of the desert, and that we had done a brave thing. We had come to this dry area that was without history, and we had paused in it and built our houses and we were slowly creating the legend of our labour. We were digging for water and we were leading streams through the dry land. We were planting and ploughing and standing in the midst of the garden we were making.

Our trees were not yet tall enough to make much shade, and we had planted a number of kinds of trees we ought not to have planted because they were of weak stuff and would never live a century, but we had made a pretty good beginning. Our cemeteries were few and the graves in them were few. We had buried no great men because we hadn't had time to produce any great men, we had been too busy trying to get water into the desert, and the shadow of no great mind was over our city. But we had a

262

playground called Cosmos Playground. We had public schools named after Emerson and Hawthorne and Lowell and Longfellow and Edison. Two great railways had their lines running through our city and trains were always coming to us from the great cities of America and somehow we could not feel that we were wholly lost. We had two newspapers and a Civic Auditorium and a public library one-third full of books. We had the Parlour Lecture Club. We had every sort of church except a Christian Science church. Every house in our city had a Bible in it, and a lot of houses had as many as four Bibles in them.

Or a man could feel that we had made this city in the desert and that it was a fake thing and that our lives were empty lives, and that we were the contemporaries of jack-rabbits. Or a man could have one viewpoint in the morning and another in the evening. At any rate, the dome of our courthouse was high and it was shaped as a dome should be shaped, but it was ugly and it looked spurious because a dome had nothing to do with our desert and our vineyards and it had very little to do with what we were trying to do in the desert, and it was largely a cheap imitation of something out of Rome or out of Greece. We had a mayor but he wasn't a great man and he didn't look like a mayor. He looked like a farmer and he *was* a farmer, but he was elected mayor. We had no really great men in our city, but the whole bunch of us put together amounted to something that was very nearly great, and our mayor was not above carrying on a conversation with a Slavonian farmer from Fowler who could speak very little English, and our mayor was not a proud man and he sometimes got drunk with his friends, and he liked to tell folks how to dig for water or how to prune muscat vines in order to get a good crop, and on the whole he was an admirable man. And of course we had to have a mayor, and of course *somebody* had to be mayor.

Nevertheless, there was something small and almost pathetic about our enterprise. It wasn't on a vast scale and it wasn't even on a medium-sized scale. There was nothing slick about anything we were doing. Our enterprise was neither scientific nor inhuman, as the enterprise of a growing city ought to be. Nobody knew the meaning of the word efficiency, and the most insipid word ever used by our mayor in public orations was *progress*, but by *progress* he meant, and our people understood him to mean, the paving of the walk in front of the City Hall, and the purchase by our city of a Ford automobile for the mayor. Our biggest merchant was a small man

263

named Kimball, who liked to loaf around in his immense department store, with a sharpened pencil on his left ear, and he liked to wait on his customers personally, even though he had over two dozen alert clerks working for him. I am sure they were alert during the winter, and if they sometimes dozed during the long summer afternoons, it was because our whole city slept during those afternoons and there was nothing else to do. And this sort of thing was the rule all over our city, and it gave our city an amateur appearance, as if we were only experimenting and weren't quite sure if we had more of a right to be in the desert than the jack-rabbits and the horned toads, and as if we didn't really believe we had started something that was going to be very big and that would eventually make a tremendous change in the history of the world.

But in time a genius appeared among us and he said that we would change the history of the world, and he said that we would do it with raisins. He said that we would change the eating habits of man, at any rate.

Nobody thought he was crazy because he wore spectacles and looked important. He appeared to be what our people liked to call *an educated man*, and any man who had had an education, any man who had gone through a university and read books, must be an important man. He had statistics and the statistical method of proving a point. He proved mathematically that he would be able to do everything he said he was going to do. What our valley needed, he said, was a system whereby the raisin would be established as a necessary part of the national diet, and he said that he had evolved this system and that it was available for our valley. He made eloquent speeches in our Civic Auditorium and in the public halls of the small towns around our city, and he said after we got America accustomed to eating raisins day in and day out, we would begin to teach Europe and Asia and maybe Australia to eat raisins. He said that if we could get the Chinese, for example, to eat our raisins, our valley would become the richest valley in the whole world. China, he said, was swarming with Chinese. He shouted the exact number of Chinese in China, and it was a stupendous figure, and all the farmers in the Civic Auditorium didn't know whether to applaud or object. He said that if we could get every living Chinaman to place only one raisin, only one, mind you, in every pot of rice he cooked, why, then, we could dispose of all our raisins at a good price and everybody in our valley would have money in the bank, and would be able to purchase all the indispensable conveniences of modern life, bath-tubs, carpet-sweepers, house electricity, and automobiles.

Rice, he said. That's all they eat. But we can teach them to drop one raisin in every pot of rice they cook.

Raisins had a good taste, he said. People liked to eat raisins. People were so fond of eating raisins they would be glad to pay money for them. The trouble was that people had gotten out of the habit of eating raisins. It was because grocers all over the country hadn't been carrying raisins for years, or if they had been carrying them, the raisins hadn't been packed in attractive packages.

All we needed, he said, was a raisin association with an executive department and a central packing and distributing plant. He would do the rest. He would have an attractive package designed, and he would create a patented trade-name for our raisins, and he would place full-page advertisements in the *Saturday Evening Post* and other national periodicals, and he would organize a great sales force, and, in short, he would do everything. If our farmers would join this raisin association of his, he would do everything, and our city would grow to be one of the liveliest cities in California, and our valley would grow to be one of the richest agricultural centres of the world. He used big words like *co-operation, mass production, modern efficiency, modern psychology, modern advertising,* and *modern distribution,* and all the farmers who couldn't understand what he was talking about felt that he was very wise and that they must join the raisin association and help make raisins famous.

He was an orator, this man, and he was a statistician, and he was a genius. I forget his name, and our whole valley has forgotten his name, but in his day he made something of a stir, and for a while it looked as if he had had the right idea.

The editor of the *Morning Republican* studied this man's proposal and found it sound, and the editor of the *Evening Herald* said that it was a good thing, and our mayor was in favour of it, and there was excitement all over our valley. Farmers from all over our valley came to town in surreys and buggies, and they gathered in small and large groups in front of our public buildings, and they talked about this idea of making the raisin famous.

It *sounded* all right.

The basic purpose of the raisin association was to gather together all the raisins of our valley, and after creating a demand for them through national advertising, to offer them for sale at a price that would pay for all the

266

operating expenses of the association and leave a small margin for the farmers themselves. Well, the association was established and it was called the Sun-Maid Raisin Association, and a six-storey Sun-Maid Raisin Building was erected in our city, and an enormous packing and distributing plant was erected, and it contained the finest of modern machinery, and these machines cleaned the raisins and took the stems from them, and the whole plant was a picture of order and efficiency.

Every Thursday in those days I went down to Knapp's on Broadway and got a dozen copies of the *Saturday Evening Post,* and in those days the magazine was very thick and a dozen of them weighed sometimes as much as twenty-five pounds, and I used to carry them in a sack slung over my shoulder, and by the time I had walked a block my shoulder would be sore. I do not know why I ever wanted to bother about selling the *Saturday Evening Post,* but I suppose it was partly because I knew Benjamin Franklin had founded it years ago in Philadelphia, and partly because I liked to take a copy of the magazine home and look at the advertisements of automobiles and Fisk tyres and flash lights and Jello and Cream of Wheat. I think for a while I even got in the habit of reading the stories of George Agnew Chamberlain. One Thursday evening I had a copy of the *Saturday Evening Post* spread before me on our living-room table, and I was turning the pages and looking at the things that were being made and advertised in our country, and on one page I read the words, *Have you had your iron to-day?* And it was a full-page advertisement of our Raisin Association. And the advertisement explained in impeccable English that raisins contained iron and that wise people were eating a five-cent package of our raisins every afternoon. It banished fatigue, the advertisement said. And at the bottom of the page was the name of our Association, its street address, and the name of our city, and it was true, we were not lost in the wilderness, because the name of our city was printed in the *Saturday Evening Post.*

And these advertisements began to appear regularly in the *Saturday Evening Post,* and it was marvellous that our little city was coming to be a place with a name and that it was coming to mean a place for people who were actually living. People were hearing about us. It was very expensive to have a full-page advertisement in the *Post,* but people were being taught to eat raisins, and that was the important thing.

And for a while they actually did eat raisins. Instead of spending a nickel for a bottle of Coco-Cola or for a bar of candy, people were buying small packages of raisins. And the price of raisins began to move upward, and after several years, when all of America was enjoying great prosperity, the price of raisins became so high that a man with only ten acres of vineyard was considered a man of considerable means, and as a matter of fact he was. Some farmers who had only ten acres were buying brand-new automobiles and driving them around in our city.

And everybody in our city was proud of our Raisin Association, and everything looked pretty fine, and values were way up, and a man had to pay a lot of money for a little bit of desert. Then something happened. It wasn't the fault of our Raisin Association. It just happened. People stopped eating raisins. Maybe it was because there was no longer as much prosperity as there had been, or maybe it was because people had simply become tired of eating raisins. There are other things that people can buy for a nickel and eat, bread and milk and meat and other things. At any rate, people stopped eating raisins. Our advertisements kept appearing in the *Saturday Evening Post* and we kept asking the people of America if they had had their iron, but it wasn't doing any good. We had more raisins in our Sun-Maid warehouse than we could ever sell, even to the Chinese, even if they were to drop *three* raisins in every pot of rice they cooked. And the price of raisins began to drop, and the great executives of the Association began to worry, and they began to try to think up new ways to use raisins. They hired chemists and they invented a raisin syrup. It was supposed to be at least as good as maple syrup, but it wasn't. Not by a long shot. It didn't taste like syrup at all. It simply had a syrupy texture, that's all. But the executives of our Association were desperate men and they wanted to dispose of our surplus raisins and they were ready to fool themselves, if necessary, into believing that our valley would grow prosperous through the manufacture and distribution of raisin syrup, and for a while they did believe this. But people who were buying the syrup didn't believe it. And the price of raisins kept on going down, and it got so low that it looked as if we had made a mistake in the first place by pausing in this desolate place and building our city, and it looked as if we *were* the contemporaries of jack-rabbits.

Then we found out that it was the same all over the country. That prices were low everywhere, and that no matter how efficient we were, or how cleverly we wrote our advertisements, or how attractive we made our packages of raisins we couldn't hope for anything higher than the price we were getting, and our great six-story building looked very sad, and all the old ex-

citement died away, and our great packing house became a useless or-
nament in the landscape, and all its mighty machinery became junk, and we
knew that a great American idea had gone down to death. We hadn't
changed the taste of man. Bread was still preferable to raisins. And we
hadn't taught the Chinese to drop a raisin in their pots of cooking rice. They
were satisfied to have the rice without the raisin. And so we began to eat
our raisins ourselves. It was really amazing how we learned to eat raisins.
We had talked so much about them that we had forgotten that they could
actually be eaten. And we learned to cook raisins. And they were good
stewed and they had a fine taste with bread, and all over our valley we were
eating raisins for food because we couldn't sell them. People couldn't buy
raisins because they were a luxury, and we had to eat raisins because they
were a luxury.

Johnny Bear

JOHN STEINBECK

The village of Loma is built, as its name implies, on a low round hill that rises like an island out of the flat mouth of the Salinas Valley in central California. To the north and east of the town a black tule swamp stretches for miles, but to the south the marsh has been drained. Rich vegetable land has been the result of the draining, land so black with wealth that the lettuce and cauliflowers grow to giants.

The owners of the swamp to the north of the village began to covet the black land. They banded together and formed a reclamation district. I work for the company which took the contract to put a ditch through. The floating clam-shell digger arrived, was put together and started eating a ditch of open water through the swamp.

I tried living in the floating bunkhouse with the crew for a while, but the mosquitoes that hung in banks over the dredger and the heavy pestilential mist that sneaked out of the swamp every night and slid near to the ground drove me into the village of Loma, where I took a furnished room, the most dismal I have ever seen, in the house of Mrs. Ratz. I might have looked farther, but the idea of having my mail come in care of Mrs. Ratz decided me. After all, I only slept in the bare cold room. I ate my meals in the galley of the floating bunkhouse.

There aren't more than two hundred people in Loma. The Methodist church has the highest place on the hill; its spire is visible for miles. Two groceries, a hardware store, an ancient Masonic Hall and the Buffalo Bar comprise the public buildings. On the side of the hills are the small wooden houses of the population, and on the rich southern flats are the houses of the landowners, small yards usually enclosed by high walls of clipped cypress to keep out the driving afternoon winds.

There was nothing to do in Loma in the evening except to go to the saloon, an old board building with swinging doors and a wooden sidewalk awning. Neither prohibition nor repeal had changed its business, its clientele, or the quality of its whisky. In the course of an evening every male inhabitant of Loma over fifteen years old came at least once to the Buffalo Bar, had a drink, talked a while and went home.

Fat Carl, the owner and bartender, greeted every newcomer with a phlegmatic sullenness which nevertheless inspired familiarity and affection. His face was sour, his tone downright unfriendly, and yet—I don't know how he did it. I know I felt gratified and warm when Fat Carl knew me well enough to turn his sour pig face to me and say with some impatience, "Well, what's it going to be?" He always asked that although he served only whisky, and only one kind of whisky. I have seen him flatly refuse to squeeze some lemon juice into it for a stranger. Fat Carl didn't like fumadiddles. He wore a big towel tied about his middle and he polished the glasses on it as he moved about. The floor was bare wood sprinkled with sawdust, the bar an old store counter, the chairs were hard and straight; the only decorations were the posters and cards and pictures stuck to the wall by candidates for county elections, salesmen and auctioneers. Some of these were many years old. The card of Sheriff Rittal still begged for re-election although Rittal had been dead for seven years.

The Buffalo Bar sounds, even to me, like a terrible place, but when you walked down the night street, over the wooden sidewalks, when the long streamers of swamp fog, like waving, dirty bunting, flapped in your face, when finally you pushed open the swinging doors of Fat Carl's and saw men sitting around talking and drinking, and Fat Carl coming along toward you, it seemed pretty nice. You couldn't get away from it.

There would be a game of the mildest kind of poker going on. Timothy Ratz, the husband of my landlady, would be playing solitaire, cheating pretty badly because he took a drink only when he got it out. I've seen him get it out five times in a row. When he won he piled the cards neatly, stood up and walked with great dignity to the bar. Fat Carl, with a glass half filled before he arrived, asked, "What'll it be?"

"Whisky," said Timothy gravely.

In the long room, men from the farms and the town sat in the straight hard chairs or stood against the old counter. A soft, monotonous rattle of conversation went on except at times of elections or big prize fights, when there might be orations or loud opinions.

I hated to go out into the damp night, and to hear far off in the swamp

271

the chuttering of the Diesel engine on the dredger and the clang of the bucket, and then to go to my own dismal room at Mrs. Ratz'.

Soon after my arrival in Loma I scraped an acquaintance with Mae Romero, a pretty half-Mexican girl. Sometimes in the evenings I walked with her down the south side of the hill, until the nasty fog drove us back into town. After I escorted her home I dropped in at the bar for a while.

I was sitting in the bar one night talking to Alex Hartnell, who owned a nice little farm. We were talking about black bass fishing, when the front doors opened and swung closed. A hush fell on the men in the room. Alex nudged me and said, "It's Johnny Bear." I looked around.

His name described him better than I can. He looked like a great, stupid, smiling bear. His black matted head bobbed forward and his long arms hung out as though he should have been on all fours and was only standing upright as a trick. His legs were short and bowed, ending with strange, square feet. He was dressed in dark blue denim, but his feet were bare; they didn't seem to be crippled or deformed in any way, but they were square, just as wide as they were long. He stood in the doorway, swinging his arms jerkily the way half-wits do. On his face there was a foolish happy smile. He moved forward and for all his bulk and clumsiness, he seemed to creep. He didn't move like a man, but like some prowling night animal. At the bar he stopped, his little bright eyes went about from face to face expectantly, and he asked, "Whisky?"

Loma was not a treating town. A man might buy a drink for another if he were pretty sure the other would immediately buy one for him. I was surprised when one of the quiet men laid a coin on the counter. Fat Carl filled the glass. The monster took it and gulped the whisky.

"What the devil——" I began. But Alex nudged me and said, "Sh."

There began a curious pantomime. Johnny Bear moved to the door and then he came creeping back. The foolish smile never left his face. In the middle of the room he crouched down on his stomach. A voice came from his throat, a voice that seemed familiar to me.

"But you are too beautiful to live in a dirty little town like this."

The voice rose to a soft throaty tone, with just a trace of accent in the words. "You just tell me that."

I'm sure I nearly fainted. The blood pounded in my ears. I flushed. It was my voice coming out of the throat of Johnny Bear, my words, my intonation. And then it was the voice of Mae Romero—exact. If I had not seen

the crouching man on the floor I would have called to her. The dialogue
went on. Such things sound silly when someone else says them. Johnny
Bear went right on, or rather I should say I went right on. He said things
and made sounds. Gradually the faces of the men turned from Johnny Bear,
turned toward me, and they grinned at me. I could do nothing. I knew that
if I tried to stop him I would have a fight on my hands, and so the scene
went on, to a finish. When it was over I was cravenly glad Mae Romero had
no brothers. What obvious, forced, ridiculous words had come from Johnny
Bear. Finally he stood up, still smiling the foolish smile, and he asked again,
"Whisky?"

I think the men in the bar were sorry for me. They looked away from
me and talked elaborately to one another. Johnny Bear went to the back of
the room, crawled under a round card table, curled up like a dog and went
to sleep.

Alex Hartnell was regarding me with compassion. "First time you ever
heard him?"

"Yes, what in hell is he?"

Alex ignored my question for a moment. "If you're worrying about
Mae's reputation, don't. Johnny Bear has followed Mae before."

"But how did he hear us? I didn't see him."

"No one sees or hears Johnny Bear when he's on business. He can move
like no movement at all. Know what our young men do when they go out
with girls? They take a dog along. Dogs are afraid of Johnny and they can
smell him coming."

"But good God! Those voices——"

Alex nodded. "I know. Some of us wrote up to the university about
Johnny, and a young man came down. He took a look and then he told us
about Blind Tom. Ever hear of Blind Tom?"

"You mean the Negro piano player? Yes, I've heard of him."

"Well, Blind Tom was a half-wit. He could hardly talk, but he could imitate anything he heard on the piano, long pieces. They tried him with fine
musicians and he reproduced not only the music but every little personal
emphasis. To catch him they made little mistakes, and he played the mistakes. He photographed the playing in the tiniest detail. The man says
Johnny Bear is the same, only he can photograph words and voices. He
tested Johnny with a long passage in Greek and Johnny did it exactly. He
doesn't know the words he's saying, but just says them. He hasn't brains

enough to make anything up, so you know that what he says is what he heard."

"But why does he do it? Why is he interested in listening if he doesn't understand?"

Alex rolled a cigarette and lighted it. "He isn't, but he loves whisky. He knows if he listens in windows and comes here and repeats what he hears, someone will give him whisky. He tries to palm off Mrs. Ratz' conversation in the store, or Jerry Noland arguing with his mother, but he can't get whisky for such things."

I said, "It's funny somebody hasn't shot him while he was peeking in windows."

Alex picked at his cigarette. "Lots of people have tried, but you just don't see Johnny Bear, and you don't catch him. You keep your windows closed, and even then you talk in a whisper if you don't want to be repeated. You were lucky it was dark tonight. If he had seen you, he might have gone through the action too. You should see Johnny Bear screw up his face to look like a young girl. It's pretty awful."

I looked toward the sprawled figure under the table. Johnny Bear's back was turned to the room. The light fell on his black matted hair. I saw a big fly land on his head, and then I swear I saw the whole scalp shiver the way the skin of a horse shivers under flies. The fly landed again and the moving scalp shook it off. I shuddered too, all over.

Conversation in the room had settled to the bored monotone again. Fat Carl had been polishing a glass on his apron towel for the last ten minutes. A little group of men near me was discussing fighting dogs and fighting cocks, and they switched gradually to bullfighting.

Alex, beside me, said, "Come have a drink."

We walked to the counter. Fat Carl put out two glasses. "What'll it be?"

Neither of us answered. Carl poured out the brown whisky. He looked sullenly at me and one of his thick, meaty eyelids winked at me solemnly. I don't know why, but I felt flattered. Carl's head twitched back toward the card table. "Got you, didn't he?"

I winked back at him. "Take a dog next time." I imitated his clipped sentences. We drank our whisky and went back to our chairs. Timothy Ratz won a game of solitaire and piled his cards and moved up on the bar.

I looked back at the table under which Johnny Bear lay. He had rolled over on his stomach. His foolish, smiling face looked out at the room. His

274

head moved and he peered all about, like an animal about to leave its den. And then he came sliding out and stood up. There was a paradox about his movement. He looked twisted and shapeless, and yet he moved with complete lack of effort.

Johnny Bear crept up the room toward the bar, smiling about at the men he passed. In front of the bar his insistent question arose. "Whisky? Whisky?" It was like a bird call. I don't know what kind of bird, but I've heard it—two notes on a rising scale, asking a question over and over, "Whisky? Whisky?"

The conversation in the room stopped, but no one came forward to lay money on the counter. Johnny smiled plaintively. "Whisky?"

Then he tried to cozen them. Out of his throat an angry woman's voice issued. "I tell you it was all bone. Twenty cents a pound, and half bone." And then a man, "Yes, ma'am. I didn't know it. I'll give you some sausage to make it up."

Johnny Bear looked around expectantly. "Whisky?" Still none of the men offered to come forward. Johnny crept to the front of the room and crouched. I whispered, "What's he doing?"

Alex said, "Sh. Looking through a window. Listen!"

A woman's voice came, a cold, sure voice, the words clipped. "I can't quite understand it. Are you some kind of monster? I wouldn't have believed it if I hadn't seen you."

Another woman's voice answered her, a voice low and hoarse with misery. "Maybe I am a monster. I can't help it. I can't help it."

"You *must* help it," the cold voice broke in. "Why you'd be better dead."

I heard a soft sobbing coming from the thick smiling lips of Johnny Bear. The sobbing of a woman in hopelessness. I looked around at Alex. He was sitting stiffly, his eyes wide open and unblinking. I opened my mouth to whisper a question, but he waved me silent. I glanced about the room. All the men were stiff and listening. The sobbing stopped. "Haven't you ever felt that way, Emalin?"

Alex caught his breath sharply at the name. The cold voice announced, "Certainly not."

"Never in the night? Not ever—ever in your life?"

"If I had," the cold voice said, "if ever I had, I would cut that part of me away. Now stop your whining, Amy. I won't stand for it. If you don't get

275

control of your nerves I'll see about having some medical treatment for you. Now go to your prayers."

Johnny Bear smiled on. "Whisky?"

Two men advanced without a word and put down coins. Fat Carl filled two glasses and, when Johnny Bear tossed off one after the other, Carl filled one again. Everyone knew by that how moved he was. There were no drinks on the house at the Buffalo Bar. Johnny Bear smiled about the room and then he went out with that creeping gait of his. The doors folded together after him, slowly and without a sound.

Conversation did not spring up again. Everyone in the room seemed to have a problem to settle in his own mind. One by one they drifted out and the back-swing of the doors brought in little puffs of tule fog. Alex got up and walked out and I followed him.

The night was nasty with the evil-smelling fog. It seemed to cling to the buildings and to reach out with free arms into the air. I doubled my pace and caught up with Alex. "What was it?" I demanded. "What was it all about?"

For a moment I thought he wouldn't answer. But then he stopped and turned to me. "Oh, damn it. Listen! Every town has its aristocrats, its family above reproach. Emalin and Amy Hawkins are our aristocrats, maiden ladies, kind people. Their father was a congressman. I don't like this. Johnny Bear shouldn't do it. Why! they feed him. Those men shouldn't give him whisky. He'll haunt that house now. . . . Now he knows he can get whisky for it."

I asked, "Are they relatives of yours?"

"No, but they're—why, they aren't like other people. They have the farm next to mine. Some Chinese farm it on shares. You see, it's hard to explain. The Hawkins women, they're symbols. They're what we tell our kids when we want to—well, to describe good people."

"Well," I protested, "nothing Johnny Bear said would hurt them, would it?"

"I don't know. I don't know what it means. I mean, I kind of know. Oh! Go on to bed. I didn't bring the Ford. I'm going to walk out home." He turned and hurried into that slow squirming mist.

I walked along to Mrs. Ratz' boardinghouse. I could hear the chuttering of the Diesel engine off in the swamp and the clang of the big steel mouth that ate its way through the ground. It was Saturday night. The dredger

276

would stop at seven Sunday morning and rest until midnight Sunday. I could tell by the sound that everything was all right. I climbed the narrow stairs to my room. Once in bed I left the light burning for a while and stared at the pale insipid flowers on the wallpaper. I thought of those two voices speaking out of Johnny Bear's mouth. They were authentic voices, not reproductions. Remembering the tones, I could see the women who had spoken, the chill-voiced Emalin, and the loose, misery-broken face of Amy. I wondered what caused the misery. Was it just the lonely suffering of a middle-aged woman? It hardly seemed so to me, for there was too much fear in the voice. I went to sleep with the light on and had to get up later and turn it off.

About eight the next morning I walked down across the swamp to the dredger. The crew was busy bending some new wire to the drums and coiling the worn cable for removal. I looked over the job and at about eleven o'clock walked back to Loma. In front of Mrs. Ratz' boardinghouse Alex Hartnell sat in a model-T Ford touring car. He called to me, "I was just going to the dredger to get you. I knocked off a couple of chickens this morning. Thought you might like to come out and help with them."

I accepted joyfully. Our cook was a good cook, a big pasty man; but lately I had found a dislike for him arising in me. He smoked Cuban cigarettes in a bamboo holder. I didn't like the way his fingers twitched in the morning. His hands were clean—floury like a miller's hands. I never knew before why they called them moth millers, those little flying bugs. Anyway I climbed into the Ford beside Alex and we drove down the hill to the rich land of the southwest. The sun shown brilliantly on the black earth. When I was little, a Catholic boy told me that the sun always shone on Sunday, if only for a moment, because it was God's day. I always meant to keep track to see if it were true. We rattled down to the level plain.

Alex shouted, "Remember about the Hawkinses?"

"Of course I remember."

He pointed ahead. "That's the house."

Little of the house could be seen, for a high thick hedge of cypress surrounded it. There must be a small garden inside the square too. Only the roof and the tops of the windows showed over the hedge. I could see that the house was painted tan, trimmed with dark brown, a combination favored for railroad stations and schools in California. There were two wicket gates in the front and side of the hedge. The barn was outside the green

277

barrier to the rear of the house. The hedge was clipped square. It looked incredibly thick and strong.

"The hedge keeps the wind out," Alex shouted above the roar of the Ford.

"It doesn't keep Johnny Bear out," I said.

A shadow crossed his face. He waved at a whitewashed square building standing out in the field. "That's where the Chink sharecroppers live. Good workers. I wish I had some like them."

At that moment from behind the corner of the hedge a horse and buggy appeared and turned into the road. The grey horse was old but well groomed, the buggy shiny and the harness polished. There was a big silver H on the outside of each blinder. It seemed to me that the check-rein was too short for such an old horse.

Alex cried, "There they are now, on their way to church."

We took off our hats and bowed to the women as they went by, and they nodded formally to us. I had a good look at them. It was a shock to me. They looked almost exactly as I thought they would. Johnny Bear was more monstrous even than I had known, if by the tone of voice he could describe the features of his people. I didn't have to ask which was Emalin and which was Amy. The clear straight eyes, the sharp sure chin, the mouth cut with the precision of a diamond, the stiff, curveless figure, that was Emalin. Amy was very like her, but so unlike. Her edges were soft. Her eyes were warm, her mouth full. There was a swell to her breast, and yet she did look like Emalin. But whereas Emalin's mouth was straight by nature, Amy *held* her mouth straight. Emalin must have been fifty or fifty-five and Amy about ten years younger. I had only a moment to look at them, and I never saw them again. It seems strange that I don't know anyone in the world better than those two women.

Alex was shouting, "You see what I meant about aristocrats?"

I nodded. It was easy to see. A community would feel kind of—safe, having women like that about. A place like Loma with its fogs, with its great swamp like a hideous sin, needed, really needed, the Hawkins women. A few years there might do things to a man's mind if those women weren't there to balance matters.

It was a good dinner. Alex's sister fried the chicken in butter and did everything else right. I grew more suspicious and uncharitable toward our cook. We sat around in the dining room and drank really good brandy.

I said, "I can't see why you ever go into the Buffalo. That whisky is———"

"I know," said Alex. "But the Buffalo is the mind of Loma. It's our newspaper, our theater and our club."

This was so true that when Alex started the Ford and prepared to take me back I knew, and he knew, we would go for an hour or two to the Buffalo Bar.

We were nearly into town. The feeble lights of the car splashed about on the road. Another car rattled toward us. Alex swung across the road and stopped. "It's the doctor, Doctor Holmes," he explained. The oncoming car pulled up because it couldn't get around us. Alex called, "Say, Doc, I was going to ask you to take a look at my sister. She's got a swelling on her throat."

Doctor Holmes called back, "All right, Alex, I'll take a look. Pull out, will you? I'm in a hurry."

Alex was deliberate. "Who's sick, Doc?"

"Why, Miss Amy had a little spell. Miss Emalin phoned in and asked me to hurry. Get out of the way, will you?"

Alex squawked his car back and let the doctor by. We drove on. I was about to remark that the night was clear when, looking ahead, I saw the rags of fog creeping around the hill from the swamp side and climbing like slow snakes on the top of Loma. The Ford shuddered to a stop in front of the Buffalo. We went in.

Fat Carl moved toward us, wiping a glass on his apron. He reached under the bar for the nearby bottle. "What'll it be?"

"Whisky."

For a moment a faint smile seemed to flit over the fat sullen face. The room was full. My dredger crew was there, all except the cook. He was probably on the scow, smoking his Cuban cigarettes in a bamboo holder. He didn't drink. That was enough to make me suspicious of him. Two deck hands and an engineer and three levermen were there. The levermen were arguing about a cutting. The old lumber adage certainly held for them: "Women in the woods and logging in the honky-tonk."

That was the quietest bar I ever saw. There weren't any fights, not much singing and no tricks. Somehow the sullen baleful eyes of Fat Carl made drinking a quiet, efficient business rather than a noisy game. Timothy Ratz was playing solitaire at one of the round tables. Alex and I drank our whisky. No chairs were available, so we just stayed leaning against the bar,

279

talking about sports and markets and adventures we had had or pretended we had—just a casual barroom conversation. Now and then we bought another drink. I guess we hung around for a couple of hours. Alex had already said he was going home, and I felt like it. The dredger crew trooped out, for they had to start to work at midnight.

The doors unfolded silently, and Johnny Bear crept into the room, swinging his long arms, nodding his big hairy head and smiling foolishly about. His square feet were like cats' feet.

"Whisky?" he chirruped. No one encouraged him. He got out his wares. He was down on his stomach the way he had been when he got me. Sing-song nasal words came out, Chinese I thought. And then it seemed to me that the same words were repeated in another voice, slower and not nasally. Johnny Bear raised his shaggy head and asked, "Whisky?" He got to his feet with effortless ease. I was interested. I wanted to see him perform. I slid a quarter along the bar. Johnny gulped his drink. A moment later I wished I hadn't. I was afraid to look at Alex; for Johnny Bear crept to the middle of the room and took that window pose of his.

The chill voice of Emalin said, "She's in here, doctor." I closed my eyes against the looks of Johnny Bear, and the moment I did he went out. It was Emalin Hawkins who had spoken.

I had heard the doctor's voice in the road, and it was his veritable voice that replied, "Ah—you said a fainting fit?"

"Yes, doctor."

There was a little pause, and then the doctor's voice again, very softly, "Why did she do it, Emalin?"

"Why did she do what?" There was almost a threat in the question.

"I'm your doctor, Emalin. I was your father's doctor. You've got to tell me things. Don't you think I've seen that kind of a mark on the neck before? How long was she hanging before you got her down?"

There was a longer pause then. The chill left the woman's voice. It was soft, almost a whisper. "Two or three minutes. Will she be all right, doctor?"

"Oh, yes, she'll come around. She's not badly hurt. Why did she do it?"

The answering voice was even colder than it had been at first. It was frozen. "I don't know, sir."

"You mean you won't tell me?"

"I mean what I say."

280

Then the doctor's voice went on giving directions for treatment, rest, milk and a little whisky. "Above all, be gentle." he said. "Above everything, be gentle with her."

Emalin's voice trembled a little. "You would never—tell, doctor?"

"I'm your doctor," he said softly. "Of course I won't tell. I'll send down some sedatives tonight."

"Whisky?" My eyes jerked open. There was the horrible Johnny Bear smiling around the room.

The men were silent, ashamed. Fat Carl looked at the floor. I turned apologetically to Alex, for I was really responsible. "I didn't know he'd do that," I said. "I'm sorry."

I walked out the door and went to the dismal room at Mrs. Ratz'. I opened the window and looked out into that coiling, pulsing fog. Far off in the marsh I heard the Diesel engine start slowly and warm up. And after a while I heard the clang of the big bucket as it went to work on the ditch.

The next morning one of those series of accidents so common in construction landed on us. One of the new wires parted on the in-swing and dropped the bucket on one of the pontoons, sinking it and the works in eight feet of ditch water. When we sunk a dead man and got a line out to it to pull us from the water, the line parted and clipped the legs neatly off one of the deck hands. We bound the stumps and rushed him to Salinas. And then little accidents happened. A leverman developed blood poisoning from a wire scratch. The cook finally justified my opinion by trying to sell a little can of marijuana to the engineer. Altogether there wasn't much peace in the outfit. It was two weeks before we were going again with a new pontoon, a new deck hand and a new cook.

The new cook was a sly, dark, little long-nosed man, with a gift for subtle flattery.

My contact with the social life of Loma had gone to pot, but when the bucket was clanging into the mud again and the big old Diesel was chuttering away in the swamp I walked out to Alex Hartnell's farm one night. Passing the Hawkins place, I peered in through one of the little wicket gates in the cypress hedge. The house was dark, more than dark because a low light glowed in one window. There was a gentle wind that night, blowing balls of fog like tumbleweeds along the ground. I walked in the clear a moment, and then was swallowed in a thick mist, and then was in the clear again. In the starlight I could see those big silver fog balls moving like elementals across the fields. I thought I heard a soft moaning in the Hawkins yard behind the hedge, and once when I came suddenly out of the fog I saw a dark figure hurrying along in the field, and I knew from the dragging footsteps that it was one of the Chinese field hands walking in sandals. The Chinese eat a great many things that have to be caught at night.

Alex came to the door when I knocked. He seemed glad to see me. His sister was away. I sat down by his stove and he brought out a bottle of that nice brandy. "I heard you were having some trouble," he said.

I explained the difficulty. "It seems to come in series. The men have it figured out that accidents come in groups of three, five, seven and nine."

Alex nodded. "I kind of feel that way myself."

"How are the Hawkins sisters?" I asked. "I thought I heard someone crying as I went by."

Alex seemed reluctant to talk about them, and at the same time eager to talk about them. "I stopped over about a week ago. Miss Amy isn't feeling very well. I didn't see her. I only saw Miss Emalin." Then Alex broke out, "There's something hanging over those people, something——"

"You almost seem to be related to them," I said.

"Well, their father and my father were friends. We called the girls Aunt Amy and Aunt Emalin. They can't do anything bad. It wouldn't be good for any of us if the Hawkins sisters weren't the Hawkins sisters."

"The community conscience?" I asked.

"The safe thing," he cried. "The place where a kid can get gingerbread. The place where a girl can get reassurance. They're proud, but they believe in things we hope are true. And they live as though—well, as though honesty really is the best policy and charity really is its own reward. We need them."

"I see."

"But Miss Emalin is fighting something terrible and—I don't think she's going to win."

"What do you mean?"

"I don't know what I mean. But I've thought I should shoot Johnny Bear and throw him in the swamp. I've really thought about doing it."

"It's not his fault," I argued. "He's just a kind of recording and reproducing device, only you use a glass of whisky instead of a nickel."

We talked of some other things then, and after a while I walked back to Loma. It seemed to me that that fog was clinging to the cypress hedge of the Hawkins house, and it seemed to me that a lot of the fog balls were clustered about it and others were slowly moving in. I smiled as I walked along at the way a man's thought can rearrange nature to fit his thoughts. There was no light in the house as I went by.

A nice steady routine settled on my work. The big bucket cut out the ditch ahead of it. The crew felt the trouble was over too, and that helped, and the new cook flattered the men so successfully that they would have eaten fried cement. The personality of a cook has a lot more to do with the happiness of a dredger crew than his cooking has.

In the evening of the second day after my visit to Alex I walked down the wooden sidewalk trailing a streamer of fog behind me and went into the Buffalo Bar. Fat Carl moved toward me polishing the whisky glass. I cried, "Whisky," before he had a chance to ask what it would be. I took my glass and went to one of the straight chairs. Alex was not there. Timothy Ratz was playing solitaire and having a phenomenal run of luck. He got it out four times in a row and had a drink each time. More and more men arrived. I don't know what we would have done without the Buffalo Bar.

At about ten o'clock the news came. Thinking about such things afterwards, you never can remember quite what transpired. Someone comes in; a whisper starts; suddenly everyone knows what has happened, knows details. Miss Amy had committed suicide. Who brought in the story? I don't know. She had hanged herself. There wasn't much talk in the barroom about it. I could see the men were trying to get straight on it. It was a thing that didn't fit into their schemes. They stood in groups, talking softly.

The swinging doors opened slowly and Johnny Bear crept in, his great hairy head rolling, and that idiot smile on his face. His square feet slid quietly over the floor. He looked about and chirruped, "Whisky? Whisky for Johnny?"

Now those men really wanted to know. They were ashamed of wanting to know, but their whole mental system required the knowledge. Fat Carl poured out a drink. Timothy Ratz put down his cards and stood up. Johnny Bear gulped the whisky. I closed my eyes.

The doctor's tone was harsh. "Where is she, Emalin?"

I've never heard a voice like that one that answered, cold control, layer and layer of control, but cold penetrated by the most awful heartbreak. It was a monotonous tone, emotionless, and yet the heartbreak got into the vibrations. "She's in here, doctor."

"H-m-m." A long pause. "She was hanging a long time."

"I don't know how long, doctor."

"Why did she do it, Emalin?"

The monotone again. "I don't—know, doctor."

A longer pause, and then, "H-m-m. Emalin, did you know she was going to have a baby?"

The chill voice cracked and a sigh came through. "Yes, doctor," very softly.

"If that was why you didn't find her for so long—— No, Emalin, I didn't mean that, poor dear."

The control was back in Emalin's voice. "Can you make out the certificate without mentioning——"

"Of course I can, sure I can. And I'll speak to the undertaker, too. You needn't worry."

"Thank you, doctor."

"I'll go and telephone now. I won't leave you here alone. Come into the other room, Emalin. I'm going to fix you a sedative. . . ."

"Whisky? Whisky for Johnny?" I saw the smile and the rolling hairy head. Fat Carl poured out another glass. Johnny Bear drank it and then crept to the back of the room and crawled under a table and went to sleep.

No one spoke. The men moved up to the bar and laid down their coins silently. They looked bewildered, for a system had fallen. A few minutes later Alex came into the silent room. He walked quickly over to me. "You've heard?" he asked softly.

"Yes."

"I've been afraid," he cried. "I told you a couple of nights ago. I've been afraid."

I said, "Did you know she was pregnant?"

Alex stiffened. He looked around the room and then back at me. "Johnny Bear?" he asked.

I nodded.

Alex ran his palm over his eyes. "I don't believe it." I was about to answer when I heard a little scuffle and looked to the back of the room. Johnny Bear crawled like a badger out of his hole and stood up and crept toward the bar.

"Whisky?" He smiled expectantly at Fat Carl.

Then Alex stepped out and addressed the room. "Now you guys listen!

284

This has gone far enough. I don't want any more of it." If he had expected opposition he was disappointed. I saw the men nodding to one another.

"Whisky for Johnny?"

Alex turned on the idiot. "You ought to be ashamed. Miss Amy gave you food, and she gave you all the clothes you ever had."

Johnny smiled at him. "Whisky?"

He got out his tricks. I heard the sing-song nasal language that sounded like Chinese. Alex looked relieved.

And then the other voice, slow, hesitant, repeating the words without the nasal quality.

Alex sprang so quickly that I didn't see him move. His fist splatted into Johnny Bear's smiling mouth. "I told you there was enough of it," he shouted.

Johnny Bear recovered his balance. His lips were split and bleeding, but the smile was still there. He moved slowly and without effort. His arms enfolded Alex as the tentacles of an anemone enfold a crab. Alex bent backward. Then I jumped and grabbed one of the arms and wrenched at it, and could not tear it loose. Fat Carl came rolling over the counter with a bung-starter in his hand. And he beat the matted head until the arms relaxed and Johnny Bear crumpled. I caught Alex and helped him to a chair. "Are you hurt?"

He tried to get his breath. "My back's wrenched, I guess," he said. "I'll be all right."

"Got your Ford outside? I'll drive you home."

Neither of us looked at the Hawkins place as we went by. I didn't lift my eyes off the road. I got Alex to his own dark house and helped him to bed and poured a hot brandy into him. He hadn't spoken all the way home. But after he was propped in the bed he demanded, "You don't think anyone noticed, do you? I caught him in time, didn't I?"

"What are you talking about? I don't know yet why you hit him."

"Well, listen," he said. "I'll have to stay close for a little while with this back. If you hear anyone say anything, you stop it, won't you? Don't let them say it."

"I don't know what you're talking about."

He looked into my eyes for a moment. "I guess I can trust you," he said. "That second voice—that was Miss Amy."

About the Authors

James Agee (1909–1955) was born in Knoxville, Tennessee, and raised in the Cumberland Mountain region; his feeling for this area and its people provided inspiration for his writing. He graduated from Harvard in 1932. In 1936 he lived with several Alabama sharecropper families, and his moving description of their lives was published as *Let Us Now Praise Famous Men* (1941). A highly acclaimed film critic and screen writer, his novel, *A Death in the Family*, was posthumously awarded a Pulitzer Prize.

Maya Angelou (1928–) was born in St. Louis, Missouri and grew up in Stamps, Arkansas. After some college work in San Francisco, she became successful as a professional actress, singer, dancer, song-writer, poetess, teacher, editor, film scriptwriter, and director. She is a champion of the Civil Rights movement. She speaks French, Spanish, Italian, Arabic, West African Fant, as well as English. Angelou lives in Berkeley, California and is best known for her autobiography, *I Know Why the Caged Bird Sings.*

Sherwood Anderson (1876–1941) was born in Camden, Ohio and grew up in the town of Clyde. His education was irregular. He worked as a paint manufacturing executive in Elyria, Ohio, but dissatisfied with this life, he went to Chicago where he became associated with a group of writers who were part of the Midwest literary group. He received little attention from his first two novels before acquiring fame in 1919 with the publication of *Winesburg, Ohio.* This loosely connected group of stories is concerned with youth in revolt against respectability and the conventions of society. It is a realistic, psychological portrayal of frustrated small-town inhabitants who are thwarted by provincialism and crushed by industrialism. The simplicity of Anderson's style has influenced the writing of Hemingway, Wolfe, Saroyan, and Steinbeck.

Arna Bontemps (1902–1973) was a poet, novelist, author of short stories and juvenile literature, critic, anthologist, playwright, librarian, and educator. He played a prominent role in the support of the NAACP, and in the development of black American literature. In his later years he was associated with the Harlem Renaissance. He was born in Alexandria, Louisiana, and educated at Pacific Union

286

College. He returned to live in the South after publication of his first novel. In the sixties he taught at the University of Illinois, Chicago Circle.

Willa Cather (1873–1947) was born in Virginia but spent most of her youth in Nebraska. A graduate of the state university at Lincoln, she worked as a teacher of Latin and English in Pittsburgh, and then came to New York as managing editor for *McClure's Magazine.*

Most of her work takes place on the Nebraska frontier, and one of her recurring themes is that of the artist's confrontation with rural, "non-artistic" life. It was a theme about which she had great personal knowledge. Among her many books are *O Pioneers!, My Antonia, Song of the Lark, Death Comes for the Archbishop,* and *Shadow on the Rocks.* Two of her most famous short story collections are *The Troll Garden* and *Obscure Destinies.*

Ralph Ellison (1914–) was born in Oklahoma City and studied music at Tuskegee Institute. He has contributed short stories and essays to various publications and has lectured at many universities. His only novel, *Invisible Man,* received the National Book Award in 1953. Ellison has also written reviews, short stories, articles, and literary criticism.

William Faulkner (1897–1962), descendant of an old and well-known Mississippi family, was born in New Albany, Mississippi, but his family moved to the town of Oxford in 1902 and this town became the "Jefferson" of his novels.

Not eager for a formal education, Faulkner attended the University of Mississippi for a little more than a year, where he was admitted as a "special" student— he had dropped out of high school at the end of the tenth grade. He then served briefly with the Royal Canadian Air Force in World War I and did odd jobs in and around Oxford while he tried to establish himself as an author. Next he spent some time in New Orleans, where Sherwood Anderson gave him perhaps the best advice he would ever receive: "You're a country boy; all you know is that little patch up there in Mississippi where you started from. But that's all right too." Thus Faulkner returned to Oxford and lived his life in his home town where he could be close to his material.

Among his many works are *The Sound and the Fury* (1929), *As I Lay Dying* (1930), and *Light in August.* He was awarded the Nobel Prize in Literature in 1949.

Dorothy Canfield Fisher (1879–1958) was born in Lawrence, Kansas. After her marriage in 1907 she settled in the Green Mountains of Vermont and thus became a New Englander, with a strong attachment for the people and the area. During her long and active life she taught at seven colleges; served on the selection

287

committee of the Book-of-the-Month Club and on the Vermont State Board of Education; wrote essays, textbooks, novels, and short stories; and reared two children. Among her most widely read novels are *The Squirrel Cage*, *Her Son's Wife*, and *The Deepening Stream*. Seventeen of her short stories are collected in *Four Square*.

Mary E. Wilkins Freeman (1852–1930) was born in Randolph, Massachusetts, where she spent much of her life until she married in 1902. Her tales are chiefly of New England rural life. She gives intimate psychological portrayals of her characters who are often plain simple folk, unable to develop and prosper due to the harsh New England environment. Although most famous for her short stories, she is also the author of four plays and a novel.

Hamlin Garland (1860–1940) was born in western Wisconsin on the edge of the frontier. Garland and his family moved west and homesteaded in the Dakota territory. He knew intimately the rough life of the western settler, and his works have been called "the chief forerunners of American realism." Rejected by Harvard, he was self-educated in the Boston Public Library. In 1884 he became first a student then a teacher at the Boston School of Oratory. In 1887 he returned from the West to visit his relatives; he saw in their harsh and bleak existence material for stories that would be a realistic look at frontier lives and a cry for social justice. His works are invaluable accounts of his era. Among the most popular are *Main-Traveled Roads* and *A Son of the Middle Border*.

Donald Hall (1928–   ) was born in New Haven, Connecticut and studied at Harvard and Oxford Universities. He has taught both at Harvard and at the University of Michigan and is now living in New Hampshire. New England is the setting for much of his poetry. He is the recipient of many awards, the National Book Award among them.

Bret Harte (1836–1902) was an editor, poet, short-story writer, novelist, dramatist, and diplomatic consul. He left school early, read widely, and published his first poem in 1947. Born in Albany, New York, he moved to San Francisco in 1854, where he mined for gold, taught, and finally entered the field of journalism. He helped make San Francisco the literary capital of the West, and was a mentor there for writers such as Mark Twain. He had a tremendous influence on later Western literature and film. He first wrote humorous sketches, then verse, and finally gained worldwide fame through his short stories.

Shirley Jackson (1919–1965) was born in San Francisco and she and her husband, the critic Stanley Edgar Hyman, lived in Vermont. New England is the setting for much of her work. Four of her novels are nonfiction chronicles, humorously portraying her life as a housewife and mother of four children. Her short stories and other novels show this same realism, but there is also a strong element of the fantastic and bizarre which occurs disturbingly against the background of ordinary life. Among her most popular novels are *The Haunting of Hill House* and *We Have Always Lived in the Castle;* her short story, "The Lottery," is one of the most unsettling in recent American Literature.

Sinclair Lewis (1885–1951) was an awkward, insecure adolescent who characterized himself as a dreamer with few friends. He spent his first year at Oberlin before attending Yale. He was a romanticist as well as a realist and satirist. In 1920 he wrote *Main Street,* his first well-known novel, and became the first American to win the Nobel Prize for Literature. The book is about the sterility of life in Gopher Prairie, a fictional town based on his home town of Sauk Center, Minnesota. This novel once and for all debunked the sentimental myth of the "happy village" which had dominated the literature of rural life since the nineteenth century. Other famous novels include *Babbit,* a stinging indictment of modern industrialism, and *Arrowsmith, Elmer Gantry,* and *Dodsworth.*

Vachel Lindsay (1870–1931) was similar to both Ralph Waldo Emerson and Walt Whitman in that he served as both a voice and a critic of democracy. Born in Springfield, Illinois, he attended Hiram College in Ohio and art schools in Chicago and New York, writing poems to express the meanings of his curious drawings. From his artistic mother he inherited a love of beauty, from his evangelist grandfather a crusading temperament. He was influenced by the writings of Poe and Whitman, as well as by gospel hymns, revivalist sermons, the addresses of Lincoln, Salvation Army music, and Negro jazz.

Edgar Lee Masters (1868–1950) was born in Kansas. He grew up in a small town in southern Illinois, and became a lawyer to please his father who was also a lawyer. Having taught himself English literature, Latin and Greek, he yearned to write and began publishing as early as 1898. Although he wrote over fifty volumes of poetry and fiction, his reputation rests on *Spoon River Anthology,* a book of some two hundred epitaphs, which in tone and subject matter strongly influenced the literature of the following decade. The village of Spoon River was a combination of the Illinois towns of Petersburg and Lewiston.

H. L. Mencken (1880–1956), newspaperman, editor, and writer, was born in Baltimore and attended Baltimore Polytechnic. He became famous in the early years of the twentieth century for his brilliant and unsparing use of satire—he was a relentless critic of American life and ways. In a long literary life, his most successful publication was his book *The American Language,* first published in 1919. In a series of six books written between 1919–1927 he vented his *Prejudices;* "The Libido for the Ugly," a scathing attack on the American small town, is an excerpt from one of these. His acerbic wit secured him a richly-deserved reputation as a brilliant satirist and social critic, and as a mentor for other distinguished writers, Theodore Dreiser and Sinclair Lewis among them.

Joyce Carol Oates (1938–   ) was born in Lockport, New York. She received her B.A. from Syracuse University in 1960 and her M.A. in 1961. She is presently professor of English at the University of Windsor, Ontario, Canada. An O. Henry Prize Story Award Winner, she is the author of several volumes of short stories as well as novels and plays.

Edward Arlington Robinson (1869–1935) grew up in Gardiner, Maine, the "Tilbury Town" of his poetry, and studied at Harvard. Although supported in his writing at one point by President Theodore Roosevelt, and a three-time winner of the coveted Pulitzer Prize, his life was not a happy one, for he fell victim to financial insecurity, depression, and loneliness.

His literary technique is founded in a realism often bordering on naturalism. His characters are generally the malcontents and failures of the world: the alcoholics, the defeatists, the weary. His poems are collected in several volumes: *The Children of the Night* (his most famous), *The Torrent and the Night, The Town Down the River,* and *Man Against The Sky.* He is also the author of several plays.

William Saroyan (1908–   ) was born in Fresno, California. He spent his early years in an orphanage until his widowed mother was able to support her numerous children. He attended Fresno Junior High School until he was twelve, then left school to become a telegraph messenger. After that he held many jobs but he never stayed on one job very long, and finally after disappearing from work completely, he was blacklisted by the employment bureau.

He was always an avid reader and he began writing when he was sixteen, even though editors rejected his first stories. He persevered and finally gained recognition with "The Daring Young Men on the Flying Trapeze" in 1933. He is of Armenian descent, and his stories are often about the ethnic communities of the small towns of central California. His style is tender yet breezy, often mixing comedy and sentimentality. *The Human Comedy* (1942) and *My Name is Aram* (1940), both largely autobiographical, are favorites with high school students.

290

William Stafford (1914–   ) was born in Hutchinson, Kansas. He has worked in sugar-beet fields, in an oil refinery, and in the United States Forest Service. He received his B.A. and M.A. degrees from the University of Kansas, and his Ph.D. from the University of Iowa. Among his many volumes of poetry are *West of Your City, Traveling through the Dark, The Rescued Years,* and *Stories that Could be True.* Stafford has taught at universities in Kansas, Iowa, California, Indiana and Oregon, and was Consultant in Poetry to the Library of Congress in 1970–71.

John Steinbeck (1902–1968) was born in Salinas, California, and some of his best scenes are set in this area where he spent most of his life. After attending Stanford University and majoring in marine biology, he then traveled the Panama Canal in a freight boat, worked in a trout hatchery, on fruit ranches, as a surveyor, an apprentice painter, a chemist—and always as a writer. Awarded the Pulitzer Prize for *The Grapes of Wrath* (1939) and the Nobel Prize for Literature in 1962, his writing displays a deep understanding of manual laborers, of "half-wits, the unfinished children of nature," and of the common, simple man.

Jesse Stuart (1907–   ) was born in W-Hollow, deep in the hill country of Kentucky, where he still lives. No one else in the family had a high school education; indeed, his father was illiterate and his mother had only attended school through the second grade. However, Stuart had a strong desire to be a writer and so he worked hard in various menial jobs to finance his schooling.

While teaching and farming in his native region he has published poetry, novels, and short stories. His characters, based on his own family, neighbors and friends, show a genuine simplicity coupled with wit and native wisdom.

Mark Twain (Samuel Langhorne Clemens, 1835–1910) spent his youth in Hannibal, Missouri. Throughout his life he was to look back on childhood as "the only time of life worth living over again, the only period whose memories are wholly pathetic—pathetic because we see now that we were in heaven then and there was no one able to make us know it though no doubt many a kindly poor devil tried to." He was a soldier, miner, newspaperman, riverboat pilot, lecturer, and one of the greatest writers of all time. One of America's best-loved humorists, he was the author of short stories, essays, and novels, the most exalted of which is *The Adventures of Huckleberry Finn.*

John Updike (1932–   ) was born in Pennsylvania and graduated from Harvard. He now lives in Massachusetts. The New England scene is important in many of his stories, particularly those that examine the lives of Massachusetts "summer"

291

people. Among his novels are *Rabbit Run, The Centaur,* and *Marry Me;* his short story collections include *The Same Door, Pidgeon Feathers,* and *Museums and Women.*

William A. White (1868–1944), a writer and a newspaperman, worked for the *Kansas City Star* and then bought the *Emporia Gazette.* He made both himself and the paper famous with a scathing editorial entitled *What's the Matter with Kansas?.* From the viewpoint of a small-town midwestern Republican he interpreted the changes in America during his lifetime, and became an eloquent spokesman for midwestern attitudes and ideas.

Thomas Wolfe (1900–1938) was born in Asheville, North Carolina. His father was a stonecutter who liked to recite Shakespeare to him, and his mother operated a boarding house. Wolfe later incorporated much of his early experience into his writing. Although a college education was not financially easy for him, he graduated from the University of North Carolina and then received an M.A. from Harvard, where he studied playwriting. From 1924 to 1930 he taught English intermittently at New York University while also traveling to Europe where he could write without interruption.

Look Homeward, Angel, his first novel, was published in 1929. The novel, largely autobiographical, was generally well received except in Asheville, where the citizens were insulted by what they considered to be unfriendly revelations of their lives. Following *Look Homeward, Angel* he wrote prolifically, usually using his own background as a setting, until his early death from pneumonia and a brain infection. His other masterpieces include *Of Time and the River, The Web and the Rock,* and *You Can't Go Home Again*—the last two were published posthumously.

(continued from page iv)

EDGAR ARLINGTON ROBINSON, "Richard Cory." Reprinted by permission of Charles Scribner's Sons. "Flammonde." Reprinted with permission of Macmillan Publishing Co., Inc. from *Collected Poems* by Edwin Arlington Robinson. Copyright 1916 by Edwin Arlington Robinson, renewed 1944 by Ruth Nivision.

SHIRLEY JACKSON, "Strangers in Town". Copyright ©, 1959 by Shirley Jackson. Reprinted by permission of Brandt & Brandt Literary Agency, Inc.

JOHN UPDIKE, "A&P." Copyright © 1962 by John Updike. Reprinted from *Pigeon Feathers and Other Stories,* by John Updike, by permission of Alfred A. Knopf, Inc. Originally appeared in *The New Yorker.*

DONALD HALL, "Kicking the Leaves." From *Kicking The Leaves.* Copyright © 1975 by Donald Hall. By permission of Harper & Row, Publishers, Inc.

EDGAR LEE MASTERS, "Minerva Jones," " 'Indignation' Jones," "Doctor Meyers," and " 'Butch' Weldy." From *Spoon River Anthology,* 1931, Macmillan Publishing Co., Inc. Reprinted by permission of Ellen C. Masters.

SINCLAIR LEWIS, from *Main Street* by Sinclair Lewis, copyright, 1920, by Harcourt Brace Jovanovich, Inc.; copyright, 1948, by Sinclair Lewis. Reprinted by permission of the publisher.

H. L. MENCKEN, "The Libido for the Ugly." Copyright 1927 by Alfred A. Knopf, Inc. and renewed 1955 by H. L. Mencken. Reprinted from *A. Mencken Crestomathy,* by H. L. Mencken, by permission of Alfred A. Knopf, Inc.

SHERWOOD ANDERSON, "The American Small Town." From *Home Town.* Reprinted by permission of Harold Ober Associates Incorporated. Copyright 1940 by Sherwood Anderson. Copyright renewed 1968 by Eleanor Copenhaver Anderson. "The Age." From *Sherwood Anderson's Memoirs: A Critical Edition,* edited by Ray Lewis White. © 1942, 1969 The University of North Carolina Press. By permission of the publisher.

WILLIAM ALLEN WHITE, "Mary White." From *Forty Years on Main Street* compiled by Russell H. Fitzgibbon. Copyright 1937 by William Allen White. Copyright © 1965 by Holt, Rinehart and Winston. Reprinted by permission of Holt, Rinehart and Winston, Publishers.

VACHEL LINDSAY, "The Illinois Village." Reprinted with permission of Macmillan Publishing Co., Inc. from *Collected Poems* of Vachel Lindsay.

JOYCE CAROL OATES, "Normal Love." Reprinted from *Marriages and Infidelities* by Joyce Carol Oates, by permission of the publisher, The Vanguard Press, Inc. Copyright, ©, 1968, 1969, 1970, 1971, 1972 by Joyce Carol Oates.

WILLIAM FAULKNER, "That Evening Sun." Copyright 1931 and renewed 1959 by William Faulkner. Reprinted from *Collected Stories of William Faulkner,* by permission of Random House, Inc.

THOMAS WOLFE, "The Lost Boy, Part I." From *The Hills Beyond* by Thomas Wolfe. Copyright 1937 by Maxwell Perkins as Executor; renewed 1965 by Paul Gitlin as Administrative CTA. By permission of Harper & Row, Publishers, Inc.

JESSE STUART, "Sunday Afternoon Hanging." From *Plowshare In Heaven* by Jesse Stuart. Copyright © 1955 by McGraw-Hill Inc. Used with permission of McGraw-Hill Book Company.

JAMES AGEE, "Knoxville: Summer 1915." From *A Death in the Family* by James Agee, copyright © 1957 by The James Agee Trust. Used by permission of Grosset & Dunlap, Inc.

ARNA BONTEMPS, "Saturday Night." Reprinted by permission of Dodd, Mead & Company,

Acknowledgments

Inc. from *The Old South* by Arna Bontemps. Copyright © 1973 by Alberta Bontemps, Executrix.

RALPH ELLISON, from *Invisible Man.* Copyright 1947 by Ralph Ellison. Reprinted from *Invisible Man,* by Ralph Ellison by permission of Random House, Inc.

MAYA ANGELOU, from *I Know Why the Caged Bird Sings,* by Maya Angelou. Copyright © 1969 by Maya Angelous. Reprinted by permission of Random House, Inc.

HAMLIN GARLAND, "A Day's Pleasure." From *Main Travelled Roads* by Hamlin Garland. Reprinted by permission of New American Library, Inc.

WILLIAM STAFFORD, "Quiet Town," and "A Letter." From *Stories That Could Be True: New and Collected Poems* (1977) by William Stafford. Copyright © 1967 by William Stafford. By permission of Harper & Row, Publishers, Inc.

WILLIAM SAROYAN, "Raisins." Reprinted by permission of author.

JOHN STEINBECK, "Johnny Bear." From *The Long Valley* by John Steinbeck. Copyright © renewed 1965 by John Steinbeck. All rights reserved. Reprinted by permission of Viking Penguin, Inc.

PICTURE CREDITS

Page 2: American School, early 19th Century. (Photograph by courtesy of The National Gallery of Art, Washington, D.C. Gift of Edgar William & Bernice Chrysler Garbisch, 1955)

Page 6: Town Church and Meeting House. (Heath Paley/The Picture Cube)

Page 18: Rocking chair and window. (Photograph by Mike Mazzaschi. Stock, Boston)

Page 52: Ladies Showing off their Quilt. (Photograph by Michael D. Sullivan)

Page 68: Northwest Side Chicago, Illinois. (Read D. Brugger/The Picture Cube)

Page 72: Cemetery. (Photograph by Judy Olausen, Webb Photos)

Page 110: Edward Hopper, *Early Sunday Morning.* (Collection of Whitney Museum of American Art, New York. Photograph by Geoffrey Clements)

Page 123: Vermont Church. (Photograph by Stuart Cohen. Stock, Boston)

Page 155: Wooden houses. (Photograph by Michael D. Sullivan)

Page 172: General Store Interior. Moundville Alabama, Summer 1936. (Photograph by Walker Evans, FSA Collection, Library of Congress)

Page 205: Cafeteria interior. (Photograph by Larry Roepke. Webb Photos)

Page 209: Main Street, Greensboro, Alabama, Summer 1936. (Photograph by Walker Evans. FSA Collection, Library of Congress)

Page 228: Julian, California. (© Yvonne Freund)

Page 233: Belle of Louisville (Courtesy of Environmental Protection Agency)

Page 245: Roswell, New Mexico. (Photograph by Edith Upton Flory)

Page 265: Cinderella Raisins Factory, Selma, 1977. (Photograph by John Schultheiss)

Index

Index

296